SOCIAL WRITINGS OF THE 1930s:1

POETRY

SOCIAL POETRY
OF THE 1930s

A Selection

Edited by Jack Salzman
and Leo Zanderer

BURT FRANKLIN & CO., INC.

Library of Congress Cataloging in Publication Data

Main entry under title:
Social poetry of the 1930s.
  (Social writings of the 1930s: Poetry)

  Bibliography: p. 333
  1. American poetry—20th century. 2. Social
problems—Poetry. 3. Labor and laboring classes—
Poetry. I. Salzman, Jack. II. Zanderer, Leo.
III. Series.

PS595.S75S6   811'.5'208   78-1617
ISBN 0-89102-046-2

Contents

Foreword

The purpose of this anthology is to provide, for the first time, a representative selection of American social poetry of the 1930s. Although numerous anthologies that deal with specific areas and periods in American literature have been published in recent years, the poetry produced by the literary left during the 1930s remains largely unavailable. Moreover, as Allen Guttman noted in his essay on "The Brief Embattled Course of Proletarian Poetry," while the standard *Literary History of the United States* (by Robert Spiller and others) includes a brief discussion of Fanny Fern and Kimball Flaccus, it completely ignores poets Joy Davidman and Edwin Rolfe. This, in fact, is true of most of the poets represented here. And it is not only in the *LHUS* that these writers have been ignored; with startlingly few exceptions, they have been excluded from most of the contemporary studies of American literary history. It is no wonder that Guttman concludes that "reassessment is necessary." But reassessment will not be possible until the writings of the literary left become readily available, and it is to this end that we offer the following selection of social poems of the 1930s.

Because our main desire has been to represent, as fully as possible, the works of the major social poets of the Depression decade, this collection has been arranged alphabetically by poet. But a thematic organization might have served as well, for it is clear as one goes through the volume that, at least for a while, the poets included here shared many of the same concerns. Whether their political position was akin to Mike Gold and Isidor Schneider's total commitment to communism and the Soviet Union or to the more sceptical and iconoclastic views of Kenneth Fearing and Horace Gregory, their poetry is permeated with the sense of America's failure and the need to build a new world. Social injustice, the Depression, the Spanish Civil War, Joe Hill, the Scottsboro boys: these were the subjects on which the social poems of the thirties centered, whether it was a poem by Alfred Hayes in *Partisan Review*, James Neugass in *The New Republic*, H. H. Lewis in *New Masses*, or Norman Macleod in *Front*. There was a world to win, and, for many, poetry was a force in the class struggle.

Not all the social poems of the 1930s, of course, came from poets who were identified with the Left. Some of the very best social poems of the decade were written by Stephen Vincent Benét, Robinson Jeffers, Archibald MacLeish, Edna St. Vincent Millay, and Delmore Schwartz. But the work of these poets is well known; their social poems are easily accessible, and little purpose would have been served by representing them in this anthology. There are several poets, however, whose inclusion was desired, and had there been none of the practical considerations with which all anthologists have to contend— could this volume have been all-inclusive—we would have reprinted poems by Maxwell Bodenheim, A. B. Magil, Jim Waters, and Don West. And had permission been forthcoming, which it was not, we would have included Langston Hughes' "Good Morning Revolution," "Ballad of Lenin," "For Tom Mooney," "Park Bench," "Roar China," "The Quick and the Dead," and "Let America Be America Again."

Of the twenty-four poets represented in this collection, perhaps two—Joseph Freeman and Michael Gold—might have been omitted. Most of their social poems were written in the twenties and thus, strictly speaking, do not belong here. But their influence on the younger left-wing poets was formidable, and their inclusion therefore seems essential. No claim is made about the quality of their verse or that of any of the other poets in this volume. A few—Fearing, Gregory, Patchen, and Rukeyser, for example—need no defense; their art almost always transcended the limits of social proselytizing. Many of the lesser known poets, moreover, were considerably more sophisticated than the term "proletarian poet" (that ambiguous label so often misapplied to the poets of the thirties) tends to imply. Horace Gregory and Muriel Rukeyser, for example, were not the only social poets of the time whose works were inspired and informed by those "decadent" reactionaries Ezra Pound and T. S. Eliot. Such poems as Herman Spector's "Urbanite Delapidate," Sol Funaroff's "What the Thunder Said," and Ettore Rella's "The Bone and the Baby" clearly show the influence of Pound and Eliot. Even Hart Crane, one of the most "obscure" and apolitical of poets, had a marked impact on several left-wing poets, as the poems of Ben Maddow and Alfred Hayes well demonstrate.

No doubt many of the poems in this collection have considerably more historical and cultural importance than literary excellence. Yet, for all the sloganizing frequently found in place of poetry, many fine poems were written by the poets on the Left, and we have attempted to include not only their most representative poems but their finest ones as well. This, we hope, will facilitate the much-needed process of reassessment.

Acknowledgments

We would like to thank Horace Gregory, Alfred Hayes, Joseph Kalar, Norman Macleod, Ben Maddow, Ettore Rella, Muriel Rukeyser, and Isidor Schneider for permission to publish from their works. Mary Rolfe and Charmion von Wiggand (Mrs. Jospeh Freeman) graciously allowed us to reprint poems by their late husbands, and Kenneth Durant gave us permission to publish the poems by Genevieve Taggard. Our thanks are also due to the following publishers and literary agencies: the Evelyn Singer Agency for permission to reprint the poems by Michael Gold; Indiana University Press for permission to reprint from *New and Selected Poems* by Kenneth Fearing, copyright © 1956 by Kenneth Fearing; New Directions for permission to reprint from Kenneth Patchen, *Collected Poems*, copyright 1936 by Kenneth Patchen, copyright 1939 by New Directions Publishing Corporation; Paul R. Reynolds, Inc. for permission to reprint from *I Have Seen Black Hands* and *Between the World and Me* by Richard Wright, copyright © 1935 by the *Partisan Review;* Yale University Press for permission to reprint from Joy Davidman's *Letter to a Comrade;* and New Directions for permission to reprint from *Collected Poems of John Wheelwright*, Alwin H. Rosenfeld, ed., copyright © 1971 by Louise Wheelwright Damon.

Social Poetry of the 1930s

Stanley Burnshaw

I, JIM ROGERS
(Mass Recitation for Speaker and Chorus)

I, Jim Rogers, saw her
And I can believe my eyes
And you had better believe me
Instead of the sugary lies
You read in the papers. I saw her
Slip into our waiting-room
Among us thin blank men
And women waiting our turn.
But none of us looked like her
With her starved-in face, dazed eyes,
And the way she clung to the thing
Her arms pressed against her bosom.

Somebody told her at noon:
Come back tomorrow! Too busy!
Too many here already!

And she walked out, clutching the thing
(In these days of marking time,
While the whole tense land marks time),
And crept in again the next morning.
(None of us knew she had trudged
Two times three cold miles;
And I can't explain how she did it . . .
But I guess her desperate question
Made enough of fire to fuel
The parcel of flesh and bones
And breath that stood for her body).
She needed to know why the thing
Warmed by the rags in her arms

1

Wouldn't answer her any more,
Wouldn't make sound or movement.

She uncovered a pale limp baby.
The man who looked at it gasped—
Its arms as thin as my finger,
The filmy blue eyes staring. . . .

"It's dead," he told her. She looked,
Glared, and fell to the floor.
Some gathered up her body,
Others entered a record:

One infant, American, starved.
Address—? They'd wait to ask.
They waited, asked; she answered:
"What do you mean, she's dead?
I'll never let you thieves
Bury my child alive.
Show her to me!" That evening
She escaped to god-knows-where—
But I've been trying to learn
In these days of marking time,
While the whole tense land marks time;
And I've heard enough already
To hold some people guilty.
All through Charles Street I trailed her,
Where she'd lived the last half-year
In a dank, windowless room
Feeding the year-old baby
Her husband had planted in her
On a frantic anniversary:
One year his Jersey mill
Had closed down its lists of men . . .
(In these days of marking time,
While the whole tense land marks time).
One morning he walked to South Ferry,
Begged a nickel from someone
And jumped aboard. The ferry
Whistled five minutes later,
Screamed out: *Man overboard!* . . .

But I guess it didn't surprise her:
There's something in being twenty.
She rolled up her things, and somehow
Made a new home, and somehow
Gave birth to child . . . then, of all things,
Landed a job—as a wrapper
Of toys, stockings, and whatnot
In a Fourteenth-street store basement . . .
(In these days of marking time
While the whole tense land marks time).

Every day: 8 till 8 . . .
Not much time for a mother
To bring up the young of a nation
And make them fit for living. . . .

But she would never complain:
'Twas they complained about her:
Too weak, too slow, wastes time.
"You'll be so much happier, Miss,
In a job that won't drain all your strength!
Good-day, and the Firm's best wishes!"

And that's how she came to Charles Street:
Too proud to beg, too weak
In blood or mind to rebel
Alone against this fierce world
That fell down over her head
And now has caved in her heart
And maybe blacked out her mind—

Somewhere on streets of this town,
In these days of marking time,
Alone and maybe thinking
To follow her man in the sea,
But maybe to live instead,
She's walking now. And if I
Knew where to point my voice to
I'd yell out: Where are you? Answer!
Don't run away!—Wait, answer!
Whom are you hiding from?
The miserly dog who fired you?
Listen: you're not alone!

You're never alone any more:
All of your brother-millions
(Now marking time) will stand by you
Once they have learned your tale!

—If any of you who've listened,
See some evening walking
A frail caved-in white figure
That looks as if one time
It flowed with warm woman-blood,
See her ghosting the street
With a film of pain on her eyes,
Tell her that I, Jim Rogers,
Hold out whatever I own
A scrap of food, four walls—
Not much to give but enough
For rest and for arming the bones—

And a hard swift fist for defence
Against the dogs of the world
Ready to tear her down. . . .
Tell her I offer this
In these days of marking time,
Till our numberless scattered millions
In mill and farm and sweatshop
Straining with arms for rebellion,
Tie up our forces together
To salvage this earth from despair
And make it fit for the living.

NEW YOUNGFELLOW
(Draft of a Park-Bench Incident)

A shabby man on a bench
Turning his head toward a young man slunk nearby:

Well, son, has the New Deal dealt you a job?
No, of course. But why such a grunt at me?
None of my business?—I'm not so sure
                                        (thinking:
        like it or not, all the jobless are brothers
        once you dig beneath the skin of the pose)

Laid off just a week? My congratulations!
Now you can see the world you've been sheltered from
Stuck in some office soundproofed against the curses
Of millions of men turned out to starve
                              (and he thought:
    today your tour of the world begins; tomorrow
    let's hope you'll know its sting
    of fierce sweet mutiny driving your heart and bones)

Who am I to be grinning to queerly? What am I
Putting on airs? The fact is: since they fired me
I've tried retaliating by quietly sending
Them all to hell . . . Don't be
Surprised! It's really simple.
My eyes gave out one day; they deserted me
One morning after twenty-two years of straining
Writing ledgers and ads for a downtown broker . . .
Sight just quietly died
                         (he thought: *it was strangely*
    peaceful to be suddenly freed from the piercing
    thrust of rebellious muscles sending their signal
    of warning in never-ceasing circuits of pain
    banding my head—as if my head or another's
    caught in the breadwinning brainstorm alone could dare
    to follow the warning of two eyes burning out—
    a warning that breathes a trail of united meanings
    and ends by showing reason a path to truth)

No, I'm not stone blind.
I use this cane only to keep from falling
Down open manholes or streets with guts torn open;
One eye still can tell the day from the night;
Twilight begins the dark for me. I'm able
To pick my path before dark covers the city
So I can make the lodging-house by night.

But if you wonder how I survive I'll tell you,
Though you'll probably shiver with fine disgust,—
But that won't be your fault: you're just beginning.
You see, I beg—yes BEG. Why shouldn't I?
Is it because of some guilt-crime I committed
That no man's willing to write me on a payroll?
        (and he thought: *blame my eyes that gave up striving?*
    against electric pitiless glare, and writing

selling-slogans to pillage defenseless, tracing
bitterly perfect numbers in hard white ledgers,
illuminating latter-day business-bibles!)
Paid for my self-mutilation with a "Goodbye,
Regrets, and heartfelt wishes," and let's not forget
The "gratitude" for my "faithful services"
                              (*swine*
     stupid enough to be frightened by bigger swine
     above them—equally witless, heartless, bloodless)
Every big city-tower
Is a stony nest for the buzzards to swarm in, leap from,
And snatch up another defenseless human morsel
To stuff in their glutted maws . . .

No, I'm not just bitter . . . And there's no use
Sparing you son. You were probably stuffed full of slime
Of the church and Y.M.C.A. and other "ideals"
That poison the blood of our young. But it's turning strangely,
Someone read me a piece last week about boys
At colleges. . . . I tell you
Hearing the way those youngbloods set about lashing
Into one of their oily-tongued teachers—it was enough
To make me jump from my chair and throw back my head
In a dizzy bitter laugh—
I yelled out, "God, God, hear me,
You slimy, gluttonish fraud who poisoned the world
With 'the poor you have always with you,' wake up, wake up,
Beware their rising blood—they'll drown out your halos,
Soak up every last glimmer and float a truth,
Strong and clean and guiltless, to fill the sick void
In the lives of men who once believed in your grace" . . .

Object to blasphemy? Sorry, I always think
Most grown men feel as I do; but I guess
I'm far too hopeful. Result of a frantic faith
In the ultimate wit of men. But I think I'd better
Not jar you with a short tale about last night . . .

I can tell it to someone else, but it's yours if you want it.
It's brief
     (*as all tales told*
     by the blind must be, since at least
     half of living floats on the eyes; one can't ask

too much from the suddenly sharper senses that nature
sends to cajole her maimed)
Don't mind if I muse or ramble
(it's so much simpler
by tongue than on feet turned loose
without reference-charts of color and substances
to prove a walker his feet are printing the ground)

Well, yesterday brought me nothing. I begged from eight
Till half-past nine . . . Then in a desperation
I'm sometimes foolish enough to give in to, feet
Brought me to Broadway under the neon glares
And giddy noises . . . I picked my way to Times Square
(where I know it's long past dusk even though eyes
adjusted to my particular clockwork of darkness
under electric glare can converse with shadows
moving and talking enough for my head triumphant
to tell the sidewalk, lamp-post, or whatever else
happens to listen: I'm not blind, I can see!)

That's where I went last night—under a canopy
Outside a theatre. And with aid of words
Picked out of talk from passersby, I knew
A fine long car had driven up, and two priests
Stepped out. Straightway I moved
Into their path and said: "Will you help a blindman
With enough to lodge him tonight, please?" They both stopped,
And looked. Then one rasped: "Why don't you go instead
To the lodging-house! Why must you beg!" In a second
I rushed up at him and roared so loud that a crowd
Stopped and gasped: "Why don't you take off your collar
And do a day's work once in your life instead
Of feeding on others!" . . .

He didn't try to answer
But he must have squirmed; and hurriedly sent a hand
Down a trouser pocket, for soon he had pulled out a dollar
And flung it between my fingers.
And I did nothing—nothing.
Just laughed, though I hadn't planned to, because my heart
Was thumping so fast I thought it would whirl me over
In a heap on the sidewalk
(strange how I've always found

serious laughter's my one escape—
action enough to cover
the heart's pounding frenzy, and truth enough to feed
my mind with assurance the spirit isn't quite dead)

What, you must leave? So soon, and I just beginning
To feel at home with words? But maybe I'll see you
Again, unless my petition
Is granted. . . . Oh, it's nothing much.
I merely thought I'd like to ship off to Russia
And find out the way they live and if it's true
No man like me is forced to starve or beg there.
    (and his blood turn sour because he was born with eyes
    that could not fight assaults of pitiless light)

Of course I had to give them my family tree.
Fair enough, they said. Father and mother
American all the way back to the first New England.
And two old uncles killed in the revolution—
No, not the first; the second, in '65.

"Children," you asked? Have I a son?—
                (he'd be armed
    and ready to go to war
    in our third, last revolution . . . if I had one)
This father-need may explain
Why I turned to you and tied you with all my talking.
That's what I do to each promising new youngfellow
I can lay words on
        (having no son of my own
    like a weak magnet I tread the fields of the young,
    hoping sometime one of you will move toward me,
    hoping this one will be steadied by fierce sweet blood).

DILEMMA OF A DEAD MAN
ABOUT TO WAKE UP

September: the noon hour: a thriving prince
Walking with three of his men
Across a field soaked in gold by sunclouds
Following a rain.

They talked of new steel girders and the motion
Slim wheels use to slice and pattern bars,
When gradually the prince's voice quieted
And the four walkers made no sound but tramped
The grasses draped in rain.

Then the prince suddenly bellowed, "Some day!"
While the others nodded yes he blurted,
"I used to get the best fun out of walking
In the woods after rain—you know
A real fresh smell comes out of the grass—It's great
To walk in the woods that way."
A silence.
As the walkers awaited more words from the prince
Whose sudden soft confession stunned them; now
His face burned in crimson . . .
His sternness then was only a mask? But no:
Quick to cover his shame he answered with news
About "some job that came this morning. Brand-new
Lines of towers for New Hampshire—
Half a million clear!"

The troop marched in the lunch-room; soon returning
By the same path. Now each hanging raindrop
Offered their blood a fragment of the sky—
But they were troubled passing this acre where
Their prince had bared his heart.
The landscape glistened but each walker knew
Praise of the earth or sky
Was meant for other tongues than theirs; wherefore
Behind the armor of no words they plodded,
Prince and his men, over the path and back
To the rooms guarded by walls: this was their earth.

Outside—so far away—the sun had drowned
The world in gold; in the fields
Rainsoaked trees and grasses trilled with wind
And children far away played in the hedges.

The dynamos whir in the sheds of steel.
The powerhouse of steel distributes pain—
And you outside in your hidden segment of mind
Plate this land with a crust of images
Till it emerges a gorgeous hideous monster

Giddy with strength, reeling, tumbling, crashing
Through avenues of now—half-beast, half-god—
And never see nor care to look in the face
Beneath the image-plate; nor grant the eyes
Truth that shows this thing a glib, smooth case
Of wheels and gears of calibrated dullness
Humming a brassy croon through metal lips
Fixed in a ghastly grin that drools black oil,
Grease, and drops of blood . . . silent, smooth,
Slick unviolent robot whose pure voice
Tells no word of its daily murdering hands
Slowly, quietly creeping into the brain,
The heart, the eyes, the flesh of men who feed
The flame for dynamos—
And glut the powerhouse till its wires swell,
Its engines howl, its bottom scream with food
To send through copper tubes the cabled essence—
The final genius of mankind-triumphant . . .

The dynamos whir in the sheds of steel.
The powerhouse of steel distributes pain.

MR. TUBBE'S MORNING SERVICE
(Homage to T. S. Eliot)

The priceless Mr. Waldo Tubbe
And all his little Tubbes now dare
Approach the world they long to snub,
Well insulated with despair.

The junior Tubbes accost their sire:
"Haven't the masses gone too far,
Trying to soil *us* with the mire
Of vulgar, droll U.S.S.R.?"

Their ancient sage prepares to speak
In holy numbers presto-pronto:
Fused Hindu-Latin-Chinese-Greek,
The special Tubbey esperanto.

Whereon each pupil makes a wish.
And Bishop Tubbe prepares to drool
A priceless strain of gibberish
Concocted in the learned school.

While all the little Tubbes let pass
Secretions of orgasmic glee.
Tubbe father empties out a glass
Of quintessential poesy

Compounded by rare formulae
Of liquid siftings, while Laforgue's
And ghosts of other live men die
Once more in the scholastic morgues. . . .

But not to make small Tubbeys prate,
Hound, or horn him with discontent,
But wait—while father concentrate
In holy philosophic bent;

For he will find them magic toys—
This wizard of the cult, Despair—
Blinders for all his tender boys,
Protective from what's in the air.

While each one sobs in holy pains
Sweet inner masochisms storm,
And Waldo's philosophic strains
Of adolescence keep them warm.

A COIL OF GLASS (I)

Somewhere there is a coil of glass within
Whose range the fire of stars
Thousands of light-years gone gives back the gleam
Once shed from earth—
Lost light of crumpled hours.

He who finds this glass
Reclaims at will whatever sleeps in time.
Nothing that was need ever fade so long

As air floods the redoubts of space and worlds
Roll on their pivots:
All the dead years sleep
On the faces of quiet stars.

Whoever owns this glass may one day turn
The lenses toward the face
Of the farthest star and bring at last a sight
For which men grieved through lightless
Centuries: first moment
A seed of dust unloosed the multiple flowers
Bound in its atom strength, and locked the shapes
In one vast whole of interbalanced need,
And broke forever the vile or sacred sound
Of earth before men quarreled with the ground.

A COIL OF GLASS (II)

A book might be the lens of pure hard tears,
The coil of glass that sights whatever sleeps
In time—gone light of earth holding the crumpled hours.
Focus the glass at will: look at the man—
Adam, Arthur, Christ. Look at the woman—
Lilith, Iseult, Helen. Light up the brain
Of the priests and kings, the file
Of heroes set on the seeded steps of time.
Then watch these idols crash on the floor of your mind.

Mythless your heart breaks
On the edges of days revived. Nothing can heal
The wound until you learn the lens, until you know
Builders of myth were men whose hungering minds,
Cutting through shells of sense, needed to image
The fact they hoped to see.

Focus the glass at will: it may show how men
First rose up, lost in the jungle's day
And found themselves in the dim fraternities of blood-and-mind,
Only to lose themselves again in a darker
Fiercer jungle, where wind

Is scissored by screams from a lightless ground,
Where feet trample on bleeding skulls—

Our world—our father's world. . . . Our night is broken
In a coil of glass.
Look through the pure hard tears.
What do you see?
Whose hands are pushing up through the darkness? Whose eyes
Carry a flame of signs that tell how the earth's
Long fierce darkness shall be plumed with suns?

BREAD

This that I give you now,
This bread that your mouth receives,
Never knows that its essence
Slept in the hanging leaves

Of a waving wheatfield thriving
With the sun's light, soil, and the rain,
A season ago, before knives
And wheels took life from the grain

That leaf might be flour—and the flour
Bread for the breathers' need . . .
Nor cared that some night one breather
Might watch how each remnant seed

Invades the blood, to become
Your tissue of flesh, and molests
Your body's secrets, swift-changing
To arms and the mounds of your breasts,

To thigh, hand, hair, to voices,
Your heart and your woman's mind . . .
For whatever the bread, do not grieve now
That soon a flash of the wind

May hurry away what remains
Of this quiet valiance of grass:

It entered your body, it fed you
So that you too can pass

From valiance to quiet, from thriving
To silenced flesh, and to ground:
Such is our meager cycle
That turns but a single round

For the deathless flesh of the earth,
For the signless husks of men dead,
For the folded oceans and mountains,
For birds, and fields, and for bread.

ANCHORAGE IN TIME (I)

On pavements wet with the misty wind of spring
We walk while our bodies burn
For places where hands of trees draw sleep from a brook
And the air is damp with fern . . .

If waters image cloud, a man can see
A heaven underneath, but if he change
To look up at the sky, let him remember
His anchorage to earth. Whoever stares
May see suddenly over blue pools of sky
Moving foam of cloud: at once his mind
Will fever for truth, for his anchorage in time,
Balancing earth and heaven in his eyes . . .
Then wakes from staring and puts back the sea
And sun in place, yet never again certain
Which eyes to trust, saying in voiceless words:

What is a man, who strides against the light:
A coat of flesh drawn on the bracing bones?
And the furled earth beneath his feet: a skin
Of sand muffling the burning ribs of stone?
Or is his blood an impulse of all breath:
Flesh fused with bone in one vast atomy
With sand and stone—with earth, whose ground and fire
Speaks for all breath? Which eyes to trust, which eyes? . . .

Let those who search look to their anchorage
In time, before they balance earth and heaven.

ANCHORAGE IN TIME (II)

The vast stone trunk of mountain lifts above
The ground no more nor less than its rocky knees
Have sunk in tight brown earth, while everywhere
Water is steadily grinding down the hills;
Water will pour the powder into the sea
Until the day the suns no longer boil
The air or scorch the grass,
Blowing from the pale disc of yellow stone
Not flame enough to melt the frozen wave
Blinding the rock and sea—
Hot earth become ice-star.

Yet must the mind woven of blood believe
An imaged vision scaled to an anchorage
In time, and watch eternities emerge
Out of the baseless dust: eternal spring
Conferred on land where cubicles of flesh
And thought must name themselves safe from the ardor
That walls apart all striving unities;
Admit no future fiercer than this river
Raging over cascades of ice the winter
Sun will soon take down.

The mind believes as much
As blood believes, nor grieves for surer purpose
In the immense star-endless curl of space
Than sea's or hill's or frail ephemeras'
Of air, but takes the earth and sun for truth
Eternal in a treasured now, and love
Its anchorage in time.

VARIATIONS ON A BAEDECKER

Five-past-six of a November dawn.
Penance for reaching Liberty too late:
I ride the tramcars dreaded by all workers,
The chill grey cars that move
Like roving ghosteyes through the black mill-towns.

Past the hard mile of sheds,
Alongside miles of freightyards, steadily
We travel while the heavy morning mist
Layered with the dust of coalsmoke, swims inside
Through broken windows of the shabby car—
Now all empty save for a few faces
Of other workers late on their way, like me,
Staring out of the dirt-streaked windows, wondering
If this before our eyes
Can be a place or some crazed mourner's phantom.

Flanking the freightyards: alleys, wooden shacks,
And hovels: a grim battalion
Of crouching rats covered down by the waters
Of fog that trickles down their slimy backs.
Near these: the blackened sheds
Of foundries, smelting furnaces,
And forges flanking the grey backs of the river
That stares so blankly this November morning.

We cross the bridge from Waterside then wind
Slowly through Clarksburg's ragged streets and alleys
Where sleek black chimneys leap
To spew their floods of orange smoke up, up
Into the low grey sky . . . showering the river
With sooty grime and slag . . . mixing new poisons
With those from other mills,
That change this stream into a torturing temptress
For children leaning from banks in blazing summer,
Longing for cool, green waves.

We wind through musty alleys and broken streets
Where freighters clatter by all night, all day,
Where lumps of children gaze from the steps of hovels
In a dead stare they learned from watching freightcars
Roll by before their eyeballs all year long.

Threading the streets at intervals a handful
Of whole or crippled children dressed in rags,
Playing together in greyness,
While some of their mothers labor in the hovels
With the new child to come—one more body
To keep from playing near the rails—or shiver
With wondering if the workwhistle
Will send her a man half-mangled or once more
A strong mate roaring for his evening meal.

Along another street: A Hun, his wife,
And children staring blankly at the roads,
Asking if they should turn to some other mill-town
Where he might pick up work enough to keep
His brood from starving through the nearing winter.

Hearses along some streets, taking the bodies
Of men who failed, who were not cunning enough
To dodge the swift wheels in the sheds; and the widow
And fatherless children wailing now inside,
Stunned in the grey, long morning.

And as we clank by I remember how once
On a hill across the river
A poet-teacher and his poet-pupil
Stood gazing down on Clarksburg through the fog;

Thinking they saw this phantom-land, and dreaming
What things they could not see. . . . But as I stare
Among these streets, I know
That all their vision and their farthest dreaming
Could never tell them of the heart I see:
The blood's unvoiced rebellion brooding under
This sorrow, this despair . . .

EARTHA

TO THE EARTH

Because a flame was wrapped in lonely skies
And hurled to sink into the deep-wind stream,
We cannot look at you with children's eyes—

For we are children of a buried dream.
Nor can we let our ways become too strong,
Nor be contented with the peace we found,
For you must always be a moving song
And we must always follow for your sound.

Nor might a man bring answer to our cries:
Men are of blood and bones that last not long;
They cannot know of fires that lie too deep,
Nor secrets lovelier than your face in sleep,
Nor why we still must follow for your song,
O secret farther than your windy eyes!

INSTEAD OF SWORDS

She begged of him to seek some noisy place
Where men rush by in roaring multitudes,
Clutching away the clothes from him who broods
Or whispers of a thing so curved as lace.
She counseled him to shrink away from space,
To go where spires alone know solitudes,
And people offer jeers to darker moods
Or mock a straggler's quiet-burrowed face.

Noise is too thin; gray chords and love too sharp
To smother under roofs of gashing sound;
The shifting quiets sawed too dull for pain. . . .
Instead of swords he clamored for a harp
To tease the rainwinds, and at last confound
The solemn insincerity of rain.

RESTFUL GROUND

I have known solitudes, but none has been
Such as I seek this hour: a place so still
That the darkened grasses wake to no sound at all
Nor float their shadowy fingers in a wind.

I have known quiet in places without dark trees;
But after this clanging of hours, I seek a silence
Where the only motion is the quiet breathing
Of dark boughs gazing on the restful ground.

FOREVERMORE

The clear white waters of the moon
Remember hills of earth-shadow more
Than the metallic flaming sun,
Or the most frozen star.

So, if you seek an altar-god,
Turn from the stars, turn from the sun;
Though suckled by the mother-sun,
Fly to the moon:

There you will learn the mystery
Whereof all lovely gods are made:
Beautiful coldness—and over all
A strange shade.

HER CROWN

Earth wears her crown of wreathed flowers so fair
That not a man can stand up strong and see
Her loveliness, and pass and dream him free
From the haunting of the flowers of her hair;
No man can see earth's crown, but he must dare
To steal away one petal jealously
To worship . . . thinking earth still rich with sea
And sun and moon and every star to wear.

Such be their grace! Their worship scars—with flowers,
They crush with love whose hands destroy. Strong birds
Alone evade the ardor that men raise. . . .
Better if they would only gaze, the hours
They spend consuming loveliness, the days
They burn in setting down uncertain words.

BLOOD OF EARTH

Weep not that some day suddenly our hearts
Will crumble into death by those strange hands
That crumble stars and turn all hearts to time:

Breath will still be breath, and human hearts
Must move together as before, when earth

Wove all men's hearts together in her song . . .

Nor weep that the trees of earth, the lakes and stones—
Companions of our living days—at last
Must turn to death like us, and like our ways

Rest but a living dream in sleeping hearts.
For, being of the blood of earth, like men,
Trees, stones, and waters cannot pass away:

They will remain with us and we with them—
We with our tongue they cannot understand,
They with their faces lifted toward a sky . . .

Parted from earth and seeking the last home.

Joy Davidman

TWENTIETH-CENTURY AMERICANISM

Lies have been told about this American blood
making it seem like laughter or like some animal
couched with a golden throat in the desert. Our roots
push apart the bones of an Indian's skull. Arrowheads
strike fire and flint sparks out of us. These lies,
these Indian rivers, these arrowroot sweet waters
seething in the blue flag. We have not drunk these rivers,
we have not chewed and eaten this earth. These ghosts
do not walk in our veins with painted feet.

Come now all Americans
kiss and accept your city, the harsh mother,
New York, the clamor, the sweat, the heart of brown land,
the gold heart and the stone heart, the beast of American blood,
the cat stretching out before a borrowed fire
beside the steam heat, in apartment houses.

We are not the dark cheekbone of the Indian
and there are no painted feathers for our killing
which happens grimly, beside clapboard and raw steel.
We are not the stone ribs underneath Manhattan
but we come and go swiftly in the sick lights of subways;
men with narrow shoulders, children and women,
Italians, Jews, Greeks, Pole, and even Anglo-Saxons
all worn down to the thin common coin of the city.
And our minds are made after new electric models
and we have no proud ancestors.

                              (Lost, lost
the deerskin heritage, the pioneer musket,
barn dance, corn harvest, breakers of new soil.
Lost the great night and thin assertive song

up from the campfire, lynxes drinking the Hudson,
bobcat in Westchester. What fish swim Manhattan,
what clean and naked rivers? lost and lost
the homespun and the patchwork quilt, the bread
risen in the home oven and smelling new.
Do not claim this for us. We have the radio.
We have the cat and the tame fire.)

                              Beside
   the bedroom window long trains ride,
   the harsh lights come and go outside.

And our minds
and the minds of our children. Give us the World Series,
the ballplayer with thick nostrils and the loose jaw
hanging heavily from a piece of chewing gum,
and when the baseball is over give us no time;
fill our mind with the Rose Bowl and Yale and Notre Dame
leaving no time for thought between the baseball and football seasons.
Feed us music to rot the nerves, make us twitch with music,
burrow with music beneath the comfortless brain and beneath
the aching heart and the worn heart and beneath
the honest gut and rot the gut with music
in the snake of nerve that sits in the knee reflexes,
wriggle in the dust with the snake's belly. All night
delight us with the yellow screaming of sound.

And give us
the smile, the glitter of rich houses, the glitter,
porcelain teeth and skin smoothed by diffused lighting,
(skin-cream, face-food, oil of Peruvian turtles
bright and grinning out of all the subway advertisements)
the dark movie house and old cigarette smoke
and the knee of the stranger sitting in the next chair.
If you close our burlesque houses, we will reopen them
and watch twelve hours long the one crude smile
and the same silk uncover the same thigh.

And from the film
borne home to bed with the familiar wife
weary and good, and burrowing into night
into her breast with the blind face of a child;
out from the bed to the familiar daylight

the invoice the slick glass desktop the worn counter
and madam these goods guaranteed not to stretch.
Borne from the bed to sewing machines, taxis, and the building
    trades,
and if you wear a pencil behind your ear long enough you don't even
    feel it,
just like eyeglasses. And we go home at night
bearing in two hands like the image of god
the dear shelter, the clothing, the bright fine food.
And daily, daily, we expend our blood.

  Give us this day our daily bread.
  Give the pillow the aching head,
  give Harlem midnight the hot bed.

  Let not the trespass keep us from
  the clean new streets of kingdom come.
  Forgive the sin, forgive the slum.

But when summer comes
we will bathe in the city waters, pronounced free of sewage
only the doctors who swam there came down with a rash.
And in winter we will go skating in Central Park
being sorry for the animals who live in cages,
and the trees will be blue. And the towers will look blue on the snow,
the wet fine street will shine like a salmon's back.
And we shall see spring bloom upon the tops of skyscrapers.
We shall be happy. We shall buy silk and new ties
walking in the sun past bright stone. This is New York,
our city; a kind place to live in; bountiful; our city
envied by the world and by the young in lonely places.
We have the bright-lights, the bridges, the Yankee Stadium
and if we are not contented then we should be
and if we are discontented we do not know it,
and anyhow it always has been this way.

PRAYER AGAINST INDIFFERENCE

  When wars and ruined men shall cease
  To vex my body's house of peace,
  And bloody children lying dead

Let me lie softly in my bed
To nurse a whole and sacred skin,
Break roof and let the bomb come in.

Knock music at the templed skull
And say the world is beautiful,
But never let the dweller lock
Its house against another knock;
Never shut out the gun, the scream,
Never lie blind within a dream.

Within these walls the brain shall sit
And chew on life surrounding it;
Eat the soft sunlight hour and then
The bitter taste of bleeding men;
But never underneath the sun
Shall it forget the scream, the gun.

Let me have eyes I need not shut;
Let me have truth at my tongue's root;
Let courage and the brain command
The honest fingers on my hand;
And when I wait to save my skin   ·
Break roof and let my death come in.

SNOW IN MADRID

Softly, so casual,
Lovely, so light, so light,
The cruel sky lets fall
Something one does not fight.

How tenderly to crown
The brutal year
The clouds send something down
That one need not fear.

Men before perishing
See with unwounded eye
For once a gentle king
Fall from the sky.

NEAR CATALONIA

We have the sweet noise of the sea at our back
and before us the bitter shouting of the gun;
and the brass wing of aeroplanes and the sun
that walks above us burning. Here we wound
our feet on metal fragments of the bomb,
the sword unburied and the poisoned ground.
Here we stand; here we lie; here we must see
what we can find potent and good to set
between the Fascist and the deep blue sea.

If we had bricks that could make a wall we would use them,
but bricks will break under a cannonball;
if we had iron we would make a wall,
but iron rings and splinters at the bomb
and wings go across the sky and over a wall,
and if we made a barrier with our earth
they would murder the earth with Fascist poison,
and no one will give us iron for the wall.
We have only the bodies of men to put together,
the wincing flesh, the peeled white forking stick,
easily broken, easily made sick,
frightened of pain and spoiled by evil weather;
we have only the most brittle of all things the man
and the heart the most iron admirable thing of all,
and putting these together we make a wall.

FOR THE REVOLUTION

This man, this ape with laughter in his mouth,
this ape with salt crusts stiffening his eyes,
this laugher and weeper, mongrel of grief and laughter,
spoiler of flesh, this breed of devastations,
this froth of blood and bone and passion and dreaming
corrupts on the earth; is rotten.

And when panic takes him
he will blacken the sweetness of the earth. And when hunger takes
    him
he will eat the members of his children.

He is full of shame; he is foul; he squats among bones.

But he has told me
(this man, this fine miraculous slime, this murder)
he has told me that he will give himself bread;
he has told me that he will make himself a fine house
and there shall be no hatred in it, nor lies.
I have heard his voice. He will have peace and bread.

The man will clean his own blood from his fingers.
He with his own hand will create himself.
He must come gilded with his own redemption.

Who else shall come,
what other shape, what more uplifted spirit,
wing at his shoulder, angel on his lip,
shall come to bury us;
                    and on this ruin
make the new earth out of pure gold and air
and the new city. For who else shall come;
neither the insect nor the son of god,
not the wise carrion-beetle nor the archangel Gabriel
annunciator of the kingdom of heaven,
nor the archangel Michael with the sword.
Nothing will be done that the hands of man cannot do,
nothing will be digged that he cannot dig with his fingernails,
nothing will be made and eaten without his teeth.

But he has said, this man. I have heard him speak.
He will come out of the black hell of the mine.
He will come out of the fire and forging steel,
the hell of the boiler room, the prison hell,
the whirring hell of the factory; and when he comes
we shall not need archangels. We shall need
only the salt and human loins of this man
and the sweat marking with grime the lines of his palm,
and he will make out of the angry storm,
the brutal stone, the sea, the supple water,
the iron mountains and the fertile soil
the everlasting image of this man.

IN PRAISE OF FASCISTS

What flowers come again
In the track of guns
Spring out of buried men
Whose lost blood runs

Thick and bitter in the root,
Sweet and thin in the stem;
The flowers underfoot
Give thanks to them

Whose numerous gift of death
Feeds liberally
Sweet purple to the heath
And honey to the bee.

And murder's hyacinths
Weave him a crown
By whose beneficence
The bombs come down.

APOLOGY FOR LIBERALS

Whether the greater or the little death
be more to fear; whether the ominous voice
and iron murder of bombs, the broken forehead,
the limbs left bloody in broken stone, the murder,
the sudden bursting of the flesh asunder
in a red scream, whether the last destruction
be the last degradation; or whether the spirit
stiff and encrusted with lying, the flinching eyes
poor shifts of daily death, the pride
resolved in filth, be a worse worm to bear
than any gnawing the eyeholes of a skull
lost on the battlefield; pity the little death,
fighters pity cowards.

The fear prevails the shame prevails the terror
weakens the cords of the knees and loosens the tongue

and we are wounded by any whisper of music
and we endure barely the weight of a word
and we turn aside. O then be merciful
to the soft hands the delicate torn fingernails
unarmored eyes. Forgive these cowards
for the weak dream; forgive them tremulous,
forgive them broken. Let them come upon
some easy corner of death. Pity these cowards,
you struck into fragments by the bombs, you perishing
under a scream of air and falling steel,
you fighters you fallen in battle.

Kenneth Fearing

DEAR BEATRICE FAIRFAX:

**Is it true that Father Coughlin and Miss Aimee
Semple McPherson and General Hugh
Johnson and Mrs. Barbara Mdivani
and Mr. Samuel Insull and Miss
Greta Garbo and Mr. Prince
Mike Romanoff?**

Foolproof baby with that memorized smile,
    burglarproof baby, fireproof baby with that rehearsed
      appeal,
    reconditioned, standardized, synchronized, amplified,
      best-by-test baby with those push-the-button tears,

Your bigtime sweetheart worships you and you alone,
    your goodtime friend lives for you, only you,
    he loves you, trusts you, needs you, respects you, gives
      for you, fascinated, mad about you,
    all wrapped up in you like the accountant in the trust,
      like the banker trusts the judge, like the judge
      respects protection, like the gunman needs his
      needle, like the trust must give and give—

He's with you all the way from the top of the bottle to the
      final alibi,
    from the handshake to the hearse, from the hearse to
      the casket,
    to the handles on the casket, to the nails, to the hinges,
      to the satin, to the flowers, to the music, to the
      prayer, to the graveyard, to the tomb,

But just the same, baby, and never forget,
   it takes a neat, smart, fast, good, sweet doublecross
   to doublecross the gentleman who doublecrossed the
      gentleman who doublecrossed
   your doublecrossing, doublecrossing, doublecross friend.

DIVIDENDS

This advantage to be seized; and here, an escape prepared against an
   evil day.
   So it is arranged, consummately, to meet the issues. Convenience
      and order. Necessary murder and divorce. A decent repute.
Such are the plans, in clear detail.
   She thought it was too soon but they said no, it was too late. They
      didn't trust the other people.
   Sell now.
   He was a fool to ignore the market. It could be explained, he said.
      With the woman, and after the theater she made a scene.
      None of them felt the crash for a long time.
   What is swifter than time?
So it is resolved, upon awakening. This way it is devised, preparing
      for sleep. So it is revealed, uneasily, in strange dreams.
   A defense against grey, hungry, envious millions. A veiled watch
      to be kept upon this friend.
   Dread that handclasp. Seek this. Smile.
   They didn't trust the others. They were wary. It looked suspi-
      cious. They preferred to wait, they said.
Gentlemen, here is a statement for the third month,
   And here, Mildred, is the easiest way.
   Such is the evidence, convertible to profit; these are the
      dividends; waiting to be used;
      waiting to be used;
   here are the demands again, considered again, and again the end-
      less issues are all secure.
   Such are the facts. Such are the details. Such are the proofs.
Almighty God, these are the plans,
   these are the plans until the last moment of the last hour of the
      last day,
   and then the end. By error or accident.
   Burke of cancer. Jackson out at the secret meeting of the board.
      Hendriks through the window of the nineteenth floor.

Maggots and darkness will attend the alibi.
Peace on earth. And the finer things.
So it is all arranged.
Thomas, the car.

DEVIL'S DREAM

But it could never be true;
How could it ever happen, if it never did before, and it's not so now?

But suppose that the face behind those steel prison bars—
Why do you dream about a face lying cold in the trenches streaked
        with rain and dirt and blood?
Is it the very same face seen so often in the mirror?
Just as though it could be true—

But what if it is, what if it is, what if it is, what if the thing that cannot
        happen really happens just the same,
Suppose the fever goes a hundred, then a hundred and one,
What if Holy Savings Trust goes from 98 to 88 to 78 to 68, then
        drops down to 28 and 8 and out of sight,
And the fever shoots a hundred two, a hundred three, a hundred
        four, then a hundred five and out?

But now there's only the wind and the sky and sunlight and the
        clouds,
With everyday people walking and talking as they always have before
        along the everyday street,
Doing ordinary things with ordinary faces and ordinary voices in the
        ordinary way,
Just as they always will—

Then why does it feel like a bomb, why does it feel like a target,
Like standing on the gallows with the trap about to drop,
Why does it feel like a thunderbolt the second before it strikes,
        why does it feel like a tight-rope walk high over hell?

Because it is not, will not, never could be true
That the whole wide, bright, green, warm, calm world goes:
CRASH.

NO CREDIT

Whether dinner was pleasant, with the windows lit by gunfire, and no
    one disagreed; or whether, later, we argued in the park, and
    there was a touch of vomit-gas in the evening air;
Whether we found a greater, deeper, more perfect love, by courtesy
    of Camels, over NBC; whether the comics amused us, or the
    newspapers carried a hunger death and a White House prayer
    for Mother's Day;
Whether the bills were paid or not, whether or not we had our
    doubts, whether we spoke our minds at Joe's, and the receipt
    said "Not Returnable," and the cash-register rang up "No
    Sale,"
Whether the truth was then, or later, or whether the best had already
    gone—

Nevertheless, we know; as every turn is measured; as every
    unavoidable risk is known;
As nevertheless, the flesh grows old, dies, dies in its only life, is gone;
The reflection goes from the mirror; as the shadow, of even a rebel, is
    gone from the wall;
As nevertheless, the current is thrown and the wheels revolve; and
    nevertheless, as the word is spoken and the wheat grows tall
    and the ships sail on—

None but the fool is paid in full; none but the broker, none but the
    scab is certain of profit;
The sheriff alone may attend a third degree in formal attire; alone,
    the academy artists multiply in dignity as trooper's bayonet
    guards the door;

Only Steve, the side-show robot, knows content; only Steve, the
    mechanical man in love with a photo-electric beam, remains
    aloof; only Steve, who sits and smokes or stands in salute, is
    secure;
Steve, whose shoebutton eyes are blind to terror, whose painted ears
    are deaf to appeal, whose welded breast will never be slashed
    by bullets, whose armature soul can hold no fear.

DIRGE

1-2-3 was the number he played but today the number came 3-2-1;
Bought his Carbide at 30 and it went to 29; had the favorite at Bowie
      but the track was slow—

O executive type, would you like to drive a floating-power,
      knee-action, silk-upholstered six? Wed a Hollywood star?
      Shoot the course in 58? Draw to the ace, king, jack?
O fellow with a will who won't take no, watch out for three cigarettes
      on the same, single match; O democratic voter born in August
      under Mars, beware of liquidated rails—

Denouement to denouement, he took a personal pride in the certain,
      certain way he lived his own, private life,
But nevertheless, they shut off his gas; nevertheless, the bank
      foreclosed; nevertheless, the landlord called; nevertheless, the
      radio broke,

And twelve o'clock arrived just once too often,
Just the same he wore one gray tweed suit, bought one straw hat,
      drank one straight Scotch, walked one short step, took one
      long look, drew one deep breath,
Just one too many,

And wow he died as wow he lived,
Going whop to the office and blooie home to sleep and biff got
      married and bam had children and oof got fired,
Zowie did he live and zowie did he die,

With who the hell are you at the corner of his casket, and where the
      hell're we going on the right-hand silver knob, and who the
      hell cares walking second from the end with an American
      Beauty wreath from why the hell not,

Very much missed by the circulation staff of the New York Evening
      Post; deeply, deeply mourned by the B.M.T.
Wham, Mr. Roosevelt; pow, Sears Roebuck; awk, big dipper; bop,
      summer rain;
Bong, Mr., bong, Mr., bong, Mr., bong.

C STANDS FOR CIVILIZATION

They are able, with science, to measure the millionth of a millionth of
      an electron-volt,
THE TWENTIETH CENTURY COMES BUT ONCE
The natives can take to caves in the hills, said the British M.P., when
      we bomb their huts,
THE TWENTIETH CENTURY COMES BUT ONCE

Electric razors;
I am the law, said Mayor Hague;
The lynching was televised, we saw the whole thing from beginning to
      end, we heard the screams and the crackle of flames in a
      soundproof room,
THE TWENTIETH CENTURY COMES BUT ONCE

You are born but once,
You have your chance to live but once,
You go mad and put a bullet through your head but once,

THE TWENTIETH CENTURY COMES BUT ONCE
Once too soon, or a little too late, just once too often,

But zooming through the night in Lockheed monoplanes the witches
      bring accurate pictures of the latest disaster exactly on time,
THE TWENTIETH CENTURY COMES BUT ONCE

ONLY ONCE, AND STAYS FOR BUT ONE HUNDRED YEARS.

DENOUEMENT

1

Sky, be blue, and more than blue; wind, be flesh and blood; flesh and
      blood, be deathless;
Walls, streets, be home;
Desire of millions, become more real than warmth and breath and
      strength and bread;
Clock, point to the decisive hour and, hour without name when
      stacked and waiting murder fades, dissolves, stay forever as
      the world grows new—

Truth, be known, be kept forever, let the letters, letters, souvenirs,
    documents, snapshots, bills be found at last, be torn away
    from a world of lies, be kept as final evidence, transformed
    forever into more than truth;
Change, change, rows and rows and rows of figures, spindles,
    furrows, desks, change into paid-up rent and let the paid-up
    rent become South Sea music;
Magic film, unwind, unroll, unfold in silver on that million mile
    screen, take us all, bear us again to the perfect denouement—

Where everything lost, needed, each forgotten thing, all that never
    happens,
Gathers at last into a dynamite triumph, a rainbow peace, a
    thunderbolt kiss,
For you, the invincible, and I, grown older, and he, the shipping
    clerk, and she, an underweight blonde journeying home in the
    last express.

2

But here is the body found lying face down in a burlap sack,
    strangled in the noose jerked shut by these trussed and
    twisted and frantic arms;
But here are the agents, come to seize the bed;
But here is the vase holding saved-up cigar-store coupons, and here is
    a way to save on cigars and to go without meat;
But here is the voice that strikes around the world, "My friends
    . . . my friends," issues from the radio and thunders "My
    friends" in newsreel close-ups, explodes across headlines,
    "Both rich and poor, my friends, must sacrifice," re-echoes,
    murmuring, through hospitals, death-cells, "My friends . . . my
    friends . . . my friends . . . my friends . . ."

And who, my friend, are you?
Are you the one who leaped to the blinds of the cannon-ball express?
    Or are you the one who started life again with three
    dependents and a pack of cigarettes?—

But how can these things be made finally clear in a post-mortem scene
    with the lips taped shut and the blue eyes cold, wide, still,
    blind, fixed beyond the steady glare of electric lights, through
    the white-washed ceiling and the cross-mounted roof, past the
    drifting clouds?—

Objection, over-ruled, exception, proceed:—

Was yours the voice heard singing one night in a fly-blown,
          soot-beamed, lost and forgotten Santa Fe saloon? Later
          bellowing in rage? And you boiled up a shirt in a Newark
          furnished room? Then you found another job, and pledged
          not to organize, or go on strike?—

We offer this union book in evidence. We offer these rent receipts in
          evidence. We offer this vacation card marked, "This is the life.
          Regards to all."—

You, lodge member, protestant, crossborn male, the placenta
          discolored, at birth, by syphilis, you, embryo four inches deep
          in the seventh month,
Among so many, many sparks struck and darkened at conception,
Which were you,
You, six feet tall on the day of death?—

Then you were at no time the senator's son? Then you were never the
          beef king's daughter, married in a storm of perfume and
          music and laughter and rice?
And you are not now the clubman who waves and nods and vanishes
          to Rio in a special plane?
But these are your lungs, scarred and consumed? These are your
          bones, still marked by rickets? These are your pliers? These
          are your fingers, O master mechanic, and these are your cold,
          wide, still, blind eyes?—

The witness is lying, lying, an enemy, my friends, of Union Gas and
          the home:—

But how will you know us, wheeled from the icebox and stretched
          upon the table with the belly slit wide and the entrails
          removed, voiceless as the clippers bite through ligaments and
          flesh and nerves and bones,
How will you know us, attentive, strained, before the director's desk,
          or crowded in line in front of factory gates,
How will you know us through ringed machinegun sights as we run
          and fall in gasmask, helmet, flame-tunic, uniform, bayonet,
          pack,
How will you know us, crumbled into ashes, lost in air and water and
          fire and stone,

How will you know us, now or any time, who will ever know that we
    have lived or died?—

And this is the truth? So help you God, this is the truth? The truth in
    full, so help you God? So help you God?
But the pride that was made of iron and could not be broken, what
    has become of it, what has become of the faith that nothing
    could destroy, what has become of the deathless hope,
You, whose ways were yours alone, you, the one like no one else, what
    have you done with the hour you swore to remember, where
    is the hour, the day, the achievement that would never die?—

Morphine. Veronal. Veronal. Morphine. Morphine. Morphine.
    Morphine.

3

Leaflets, scraps, dust, match-stubs strew the linoleum that leads
    upstairs to the union hall, the walls of the basement workers'
    club are dim and cracked and above the speaker's stand
    Vanzetti's face shows green, behind closed doors the
    committeeroom is a fog of smoke—

Who are these people?—

All day the committee fought like cats and dogs and twelve of Mr.
    Kelly's strongarm men patrolled the aisles that night, them
    blackjack guys get ten to twenty bucks a throw, the funds were
    looted, sent to Chicago, at the meeting the organizer talked
    like a fool, more scabs came through in trucks guarded by
    police,
Workers of the world, workers of the world, workers of the world—

Who are these people and what do they want, can't they be decent,
    can't they at least be calm and polite,
Besides the time is not yet ripe, it might take years, like Mr. Kelly
    said, years—

Decades black with famine and red with war, centuries on fire, ripped
    wide—

Who are these people and what do they want, why do they walk back
    and forth with signs that say "Bread Not Bullets," what do

they mean "They Shall Not Die" as they sink in clouds of
poison gas and fall beneath clubs, hooves, rifles, fall and do
not arise, arise, unite,
Never again these faces, arms, eyes, lips—

Not unless we live, and live again,
Return, everywhere alive in the issue that returns, clear as light that
still descends from a star long cold, again alive and
everywhere visible through and through the scene that comes
again, as light on moving water breaks and returns, heard
only in the words, as millions of voices become one voice, seen
only in millions of hands that move as one—

Look at them gathered, raised, look at their faces, clothes, who are
these people, who are these people,
What hand scrawled large in the empty prison cell "I have just
received my sentence of death: Red Front," whose voice
screamed out in the silence "Arise"?—

And all along the waterfront, there, where rats gnaw into the loading
platforms, here, where the wind whips at warehouse corners,
look, there, here,
Everywhere huge across the walls and gates "Your comrades live,"
Where there is no life, no breath, no sound, no touch, no warmth, no
light but the lamp that shines on a trooper's drawn and ready
bayonet.

Joseph Freeman

PRINCE JERNIKIDZE

Prince Jernikidze wears his boots
Above his knees; his black mustache
Curls like the Kaiser's; when he shoots
Friend and foe turn white as ash.

The movements of his hands are svelt,
Ivory bullets grace his chest,
The studded poignard at his belt
Dangles down his thigh. The best

Dancers in Tiflis envy his
Light Lesginka's steady whirl,
He bends his close-cropped head to kiss
The finger-tips of every girl.

Over the shashleek and the wine
His deep and passionate baritone
Directs the singing down the line,
And none may drain his glass alone.

When morning breaks into his room
He dons his long Circassian coat,
Marches to the Sovnarkom,
Knocks at the door and clears his throat,

Opens the ledger with his hand,
Bows to the commissars who pass,
Calls the janitor comrade, and
Keeps accounts for the working class.

SIX POEMS

1.

Rise to the surface, O my hidden strength!
Break down the barriers of these awful years;
Burn out all dullness, wipe away all tears;
Make me a man whom men revere at length.
Have I not paid enough for fate's caprice?
Sufficient is my penance for the sins
My forbears have committed. Now begins
The flaming dawn, the hour of release.
I brush away the fragments of the past,
Forget the cruel nightmare of my youth,
And dedicate my new-found power to truth;
And pledge my new heart to the world; at last,
Hope, blazing trails before my mind again,
Draws me to battle in the ranks of men.

New York
1924

2.

Our age has Caesars, though they wear silk hats
And govern vaster continents than Rome;
The bishops tend their bellies and wear spats
And lie like ancient oracles; at home
Circe, bored with triumphs on the stage,
Sets the table and pours out the wine,
Varies her smiling makeup to engage,
Bewitch and rob her smug enamoured swine.
If we have prophets calling for revolts
Who shake the skies until the old worlds crack,
For every hero there are twenty dolts
And Tartuffe's skulk behind Ilytch's back;
And Madame Pompadour and you, my dear,
Differ only in name and class and year.

The Ukraine
1926

3.

I accept the universe, which ranges
From absolute to relative, and changes
From closed to open, yet remains a mystery
With an obscure kaleidescopic history;
And I accept men, too: those keen, courageous
Beasts who strive to see beyond their cages,
Yet, in the midst of philosophic labors,
Sink their teeth into their nearest neighbors.
I am no better, this I learned at last;
Nor are my dearest and most noble friends:
Perhaps this savagery can serve good ends,
Building a new world on the shattered past,
If I accept that life can be less tragic
When pride gives way to battle and to logic.

New York
1931

4.

The hordes that battle for the world's domain
Sweat impatiently within each camp;
Once more the bloodsoaked earth roars with the tramp
Of armies thundering across the plain.
And now again the long eternal rain
Shall drum in darkness taps upon the damp
Cracked bodies, or the yellow lonely lamp
Of night glow on the entrails of the slain.
And we who once awoke from the slow dream
Of peace and childhood to behold he sky
Broken asunder by the flaming steel
Of shells whose death came with a monstrous scream,
Shall this time, having lived, know how to die,
Rifle in hand, to make a just dream real.

New York
December, 1931

5.

Between us lies the issue clear,
Though our silence seeks to mask it;
You pose the question through your fear;
I, knowing the bitter answer, do not ask it.

But clear are question and reply;
I hear the streets and houses shout them,
Bombarding the indifferent sky,
Far-off and blue, with long complaints about them.

Around us rises the new world:
I hear the tread of fighters roaring,
Their banners to the wind unfurled,
Their vast and glorious dreams before them soaring.

You stand among the vanguard, proud,
Ignoring time and place and season,
Firm where the battle rages loud:
And yet your iron face is lined with treason.

Your mind that bears the new conceals
Much that is savage, old and rotten;
Where your words burn, your heart congeals,
Your hands commit dark treacheries long forgotten.

Strange that two thousand years should pass
Yet Judas lives (the snake still hisses):
He combs his hair before the glass,
Preparing to betray his friend with kisses.

The past pursues us down the years;
Through our wise and mighty cities
The rivers flow with blood and tears;
A thousand, O a hundred thousand pities!

A hundred thousand pities yet to be
That man, who conquers arctics winds and torrid,
And harnesses the lightning and the sea,
Should bear the mark of Cain upon his forehead.

                                        New York
                                        Nov. 1931

6.

I grant you, then, the variants;
Dynamos roaring where bloomed fields;
The cannibal wears cotton pants;
Bombs rip the Yangtse; the old order yields

To new machines; and science breaks
The castles down of moldy creeds;
For ultimate historic stakes
The proletariat does mighty deeds.

To all the skies in every land,
The banner of revolt unfurled,
The worker with his iron hand
Crushes the rotten empires of the world;

Another age shall come, a life
Of work and wisdom, love and art;
Meantime a comrade slips a knife
Into your full and unsuspecting heart.

On the bright rim of worlds unborn
Dark seas of monstrous passion hiss;
Cain's bloodstained fingers greet the morn,
Judas moists his lips for the fatal kiss.

Be calm, I have not lost my head;
All bridges shall be crossed in time;
Until the ancient world is dead
There shall be malice, envy, treason, crime.

And I shall learn to disregard
The treacherous malice of a friend;
The crimes of lovers make me hard;
I shall be fighting to the very end.

Count me to stay: but I shall know
The secret suffering, the defeat
Of hearts betrayed; and every blow
I strike shall fall with unrelenting heat.

Man lives not by bread alone,
We shall give more than bread to all;
Those who are heartless as a stone
Shall fall when all these rotten empires fall.
                              New York
                              Feb. 1932

BALLAD OF TAMPA

When after dinner you smoke, gentlemen, remember
Tampa leads the world making clear Havanas: Mexicans,
Cubans, Urugayans, Porto Ricans are your vassals;
Ybor City, Palmetto Beach, West Tampa sweat, ache, starve,
For the azure smoke-ring exciting tonight's new lay.
Dull-eyed sallow elderly women stand confuted
In the factory-tomb banding, wrapping, boxing.
Machines monotonously clock the minutes;
Gossamer of cellophane automatically embraces cigars.
No, says the woman-worker, *I don't count cigars packing;*
There's no time, no time; we get used to it;
One look tells us how many there are;
No time . . . no time . . . no time.

Bastard houses, colonial and Spanish, lean
Over Ybor City's narrow Seventh Avenue, memorial
Of antithetic races flowing to the New World's shores.
Here the home of Tampa's proletariat winds its lank
Streets under balconies. Labor yokes all races; voices
And awnings shout Martinez, Cohen, Carducci! But O
Beloved flaming faces of Latin America, passionate
And stern, whose eyes burn with remembrance
Of a hundred battles with the world wide foe.
Going home, gentlemen, we find no architecture;
Home is an old broken wooden box patched
With tin or paper, naked within, maybe a hard cot;
Maybe, O petit-bourgeois luxury, even two; maybe
A decrepit icebox, a table limping on three legs;
Shacks whose faces grow black with worry.
Where will the rent—two bucks a week—come from?

The workers, having forgotten under the chronic
Fake smile of the Blue Eagle the feel of labor,
Do not recall the names of conquistadors
Who first touched Tampa's shores; let the Chamber
Trumpet to a posterity of tourists the memory
Of Pamfilo de Narvaez, Hernando de Soto,
The immense teeth and spectacles of Teddy.
We know only the third republic, the Roosevelt
Who flashes trecherous promises through a cataleptic grin.
We remember, gentlemen, the great strike of Thirty-One
When we marched to the factory of Sanchez y Haya,
And on the water tank high above Ybor City
Nailed the red flag with hammer and sickle.
We remember, too, the terror, the cops who wrecked
The face of our leader Hy Gordon, cracked their pistols
Through his wrist-bone, broke our Union.

Let us go, then Comrades, to the Communist meeting;
Go in silence; the forgotten man is forgotten,
The Reds remembered; they are here illegal,
Foregathering secretly in private homes.
Tiptoe up the stairway one by one.
Order, compañeros; Comrade Lopez has the floor.
The terror grows, we have no work, we starve;
Our wives and children hunger; those who still
Labor aridly in the factories (robbed
Of the traditional readers) face new wage-cuts;
The cops ravage meetings; jail, beat, deport
The bravest, wisest workers, those
Who know the road to freedom from this hell.
The factory gates are closed to Negroes:—
Let the black bastards die, let them all die,
Let the blessed Blue Eagle devour these rebellious worms,
But let it preserve our profits!

Compañeros, we shall not die; our ranks are but
A platoon in that vast army throughout
The world which carries high the proletarian banner
Fighting through blood and terror toward the goal.
We who once raised the red banner over Ybor City
Shall do our part indeed, striking the needed blows
For an America of work and thought for all,

Where soil, factory and machine; art,
Philosophy and science; love itself
Shall be with bread the portion of the people.

FOUR POEMS

In this black room, midnight and morn are each
Aeons away; the open window brings
The sea's insistent roar against the beach;
Loud in the night the hollow bellbuoy flings
Skyward its melancholy monotones;
Above the clamor of the breaking waves
Far off its lonely clapper moans
Like some despairing idiot who raves
Crawling on hands and knees through empty streets
To doors that seem familiar, there to weep.
While one unconscious twisted knuckle beats
For succor, for compassion and for sleep,
He rends the silence with a final cry
To which the stubborn night makes no reply.

New York
November 1931

2.

Mankind looks forward, but the hurt look back:
Broken of will, distracted and afraid,
They who have had no childhood but the rack
Shall yet be judged for what they've done or said.
And if their feet, once crucified, now drag,
We'll nail them once again upon our scorn:
When mankind marches, let the weak not lag,
Cursing the time and place where they were born.
The past dies, save for those whom it has broken;
They will remember whom the world has maimed.
Let them be silent! Things must not be spoken
Which hide deep in the thought of man, ashamed:
Or, if their lips are bitter and inflamed,
Let them speak all by symbol and by token.

New York
1925

3.

Still young, our faces may deceive
Your eyes, ironic in their gaze:
Since we have learned no more to grieve
We must have entered a maturer phase.

We must be growing old; indeed,
We must, since we accept the fair
And foul, the open heart and greed,
Goodness and malice both without despair.

There was a time we pounded gates,
Called down interminable stairs,
Denounced the treachery of the fates
Who sit in darkness spinning deadly snares.

We knew the iron teeth of guilt,
Were twisted on the rack of shame,
Lived in a night that nightmares built,
Were loth to place and glad to take the blame.

O happy youth, O happy age
To whom these poisons are remote;
Whose voices, ignorant of rage,
Babble forever on an even note.

The world is not to bless or curse;
In rain and wind, in sun and shade
Take it for better or for worse—
While we shall strike the blow that you evade.

New York
November 1931

4.

Drums of the world, beat!
beat a loud call for war against this madness!

Blue for a billion years, the sky
having seen at the world's dawn
man crawl up from slime,
still beholds the terror,
indolence, stupor, robbery, superstition,

blood and lies from age to age;
bones of butchered men cracking in the fields,
diplomacy's crooked smile,
the oppression of peoples,
cries of the poor in all times and lands,
the hatred of parents and children
(boys and girls twisted at life's gates
by the poison of unconfessed jealousy and revenge)
the struggle of nations, classes, factions, individuals;
hands that come empty into the world and leave empty.

Beat, drums of the world!
let the workers storm from the factories,
the peasants from the farms;
sweep the earth clean of this nightmare,
build new cities, a new world,
ringing with the clear voices of new men!

New York
1931

Sol Funaroff

UNEMPLOYED: 2 A.M.

The park lamp in reverie.
The nervous leaves rustle in palegreen light.

Here on a bench an old woman is sleeping.
Her head droops limp against her breast
rising and falling like the bow of the fountain
all night long whisperweeping:
sleep   sleep.

And the men with bared feet in the grass:—
their tired, heavy bodies hug the earth;
they mutter strange words in far away voices.
The cool soft grass is soothing:
hush ah hush.

The waterfront nearby smells like a black restless wind.
A horn uneasy calling moans far off—
outcries of unrest in a dream.

UPROOTED

The lamp-post pokes out of the dark street
a bare toe from a torn shoe.
He stands, at the age of twenty-two, in the shadows.
He thinks he is worthless.
What has he done
that men will be glad to remember him by?
His friend's humor hides a sneer:

"In the trenches, buddy,
you'll be good enough to stop a bullet."
And his girl:
"You make me happy. I love you.
That's all I care about, dear."

But, unhappy between kiss and kiss,
what is there to do?
He wants something to do, to work machines,
to be joyful among fellow workers,
to write beautiful songs and stories
they will understand and remember.
Tormented by the world and his desires,
he dreams upon the lips he kisses
and the dreams are lies.

The shadows of silent machines
spread on the walls of the city.
Amid uptorn pavement of the broken street
a blanketed steamroller,
stranded, waits.
Hands in pockets, he stands at the corner, waiting,
or walks, a brooding figure, through the streets.

TO THE DEAD OF THE
INTERNATIONAL BRIGADE

Let me break down foundations of the earth
and speak to you in the dust
as the wind speaks in the dust,
as the dust is carried in the wind
and the wind makes a speech of it.

Listen to me who hold you in memory
as a sky holds a cloud tenderly,
as the earth holds you eternally,
bearing each Spring green remembrances.

THE LAST SUPERSTITION

"Death is the last superstition."
Heinrich Heine

Put off your public faces,
people of Egypt—
put off the mummy's wraps,
reveal the heart's places,
how beauty is life
and these are not the living.

Put off your public faces, Death—
a people's mummery,
a Book of the Dead,
the psalms of empty phrases,
the incantations of the day's trade,
the priests' business,
the cruel grimaces, the distorted faces of fear
that exhort with howling mouths.

The city pyramids above the tombs—
embalmed in oil,
wound in ticker-tape,
encased in subway steel.
As he travels in his coffin,
his life disintegrates towards his destination
among the molecules.

In the x-ray light his head glows bald,
his mind is emptied by time,
his life strangled in bindings of tape.

Beneath the garbage and the ashes,
a pipe, a filament of hair,
a porcelain filling, the tooth of a comb,
coins encrusted in clay,
the car, the portable estate;
handyman and his tools,
bonded egyptian,
he lies bound with the maid, the chauffeur,
the wife and beautiful mistress buried alive
beside the heaped bones of the master.

From pulpit and platform
soothsayers contend for his soul.
The radio voice intones the Sunday prayer,
automatic screen devices
unburden his spirit of anxieties.
The cinematic ritual done,
he is prepared,
receives the blessings of the bill of sale,
prepares the token for the blinded eyes
that do not see behind the blinding screen
the religious merchants,
death's dealers in the dead world.

Under the sign of the coin and the contract,
under the mask of the two-faced double-dealing dollar,
under the fetish of the document, stocks and bonds,
the parchment faces trade in securities.

But the stock and bond king
markets no sureties against death.
No salesman, no charm,
no calling card in the dead kingdom,
no cross upon the gold seal
contract to deliver the goods,
can destroy fear's faces,
the primitive mask,
the dead spirit's traces.

Put off your public faces, Death,
before the heart is bitten by bone,
before the flesh is eaten by stone,
before the face and mask are one.

Life, put on your private faces,
unafraid.
Put private hearts in public places.
How the death-mask cracks with passion
and pyramids fall like a great empire!
The tombs open, the people smile,
free men live among fraternal faces.

WHEN THE EARTH IS COLD

Voices in the air and in the earth,
the voices of men—
workers, scientists, philosophers and poets,
their life, work and thought—
truths and beauties discovered, fought for,
and built,
for ourselves and for those after us;
the voices of trees,
voices that leaf by leaf gather volume;
now the thunderclap of histories;
and then the swirling of wind and the dust,
rain and the seasons.
And the brown leaves, like letters, vanish in the snow.

We shook our fists at the sun.
We dug our heels into the mountains.

THE SPIDER AND THE CLOCK

(FOR A NEW YEAR)

> *A University biologist has been studying the battle of a hairy black
> arachnid to harness the moving hands of an alarm clock in its silken
> web.*—NEWS ITEM

1

Here weaves a spider, and here a clock,
man-fashioned, for man weaves, but not the whole cloth,
time's tapestry, history at a midnight hour,
last hour of the last midnight of the year
when the year's first dawn begins.

Hunger marches on the capitals.
Congress is in session.
The ambassadors from France and Berlin
shake hands; the borders bristle with cannon.
And parliament burns. The House is on fire.
Fires flame on the frontiers.

Through smoke and flame and ashes,
the general rides on a coal black horse.

Four limbs crossed hatchet-wise about the face of the clock,
old wisebeard spins his mathematical web.
Forward and back. Forward and back.
                                    Forward or back?

Oh here's a Joshua set to tame the sun!
Blow your horn Joshua!
Blow!
Congress will open with a prayer,
the House will be in order, . . . and the priest's ideal
make irresistible public appeal.

The Senator from Wall St. speaks.
Tin-horns, lip-farts, rattlers, confetti.
The leader, dressed in rags, slums among the people.
But his paunch shows, his stink is not earthly.
He pats the guileless head of a child;
he smiles, and the guns of his warships roar.
Cheers. He is beneficent. He is kind to his people.
His smiling bust is in the best boudoirs.
Toot! Toot! The calliope grinds an old tune.
The card sharp offers a new deal.
His barker's voice. Take a chance, folks,
bring home the kewpie to your wife and kiddies.
Jazz-band touted heroes, promises listened to,
last year's vomit regurgitated,
retched in your face.
                        You win the cigar.
But when the last tune fades and the lights go out
and you grope your way, in fear, through the dark?
After the last attraction, walk home. And find:
crumbs in the breadbox, the landlord at the door.

The friend of caesar's friend murders the friend
who murders caesar. The juggler of knives
slits his own throat. Tight-rope walkers
find democracy in public urinals.
Black-robed ministers stand with hatchet crosses;
the headsman hacks a worker's life to bone;
within an idiot's laugh a people's tears;
within the victim's courage a people's fears.

You are the headless victim, you the white-faced
buffoon with damp eyes, pleading for work,
for a loaf of bread, kicked by the donkey,
strung by the tight-rope, struck by the axe.

Streamers of joy—the ticker-tape weaves
through the city, curls in wind-blown loops,
winds with the wind through moonlit streets,
spins colored threads among the populace,
designs a fluttering New Year's.
The ticker-tape falls.
                    Toll, bells, toll!
Dust in the grease cups, the engine still,
webs across the broken panes, a torn time-card,
splintered glass, and scrap in the factory yard.

The nickelodeon sprinkles perfumed
nickel sentiments with a western air.
Art?
The sounds of leaves, books, burned in the brown season;
the silver bullets of metallic nightingales;
and the diplomatic notes, the bowing,
the scraping of generals and foreign corps,
the war bonds floated by financiers;
and all the instruments,
guns, flame-guns, machine-guns, gas-guns,
manoeuvres, charts, letters of state and
cannon drawn by mules, make death too an art.

Toll, bells, toll, a midnight mood and hour,
death's carnival, bomb in a boudoir.

2

The moon is a spider's eye. The moon
makes of an ashcan the golden grail.
And hungry hands dig in the holy pot
and find an age's mediaeval rot.
Here is alchemy at a moonlit hour.
Down atomic orbits, science tracks an electron
and finds god's footsteps pacing the universe.
Oh here's a knowledge to make
fools wise, thieves honest, heroes of rogues.
Science, indeed, is miraculous.

Step right up, folks, and see
the mathematician pen on an atom,
three hundred words to the cubic millimeter,
universal law, the ninth psalm of the bible.

And acclaim cries: "Sir, you are superb,
you have rendered everything meaningless!"

* * * *

Where are the more magnificent,
the men with labor in their hands,
the hand's touch that renders things their meaning,
the spade, the seed, and sowers—they who bring
to green altars marriages of spring?
Will cold winds nip nuptials in the bud?
Is man's mastery of earth a mystery?
And man's wealth, abundant, so penurious,
a plenitude in rags, famine-fattened?
How long do mansions built on hovels stand?
Who played with flames and cannot quench the fire?
What fool blows a false horn?
What trumpet breath of what false dawn,
what false wind wills the fire out?
Can all the holy waters of christendom
drown this conflagration in the east
where morning's firelings flame?
Does man walk upward down a hill?
Will the sun
                    stand
                          still?

DUSK OF THE GODS

1
OVERTURE

I am the hammer,
I am the anvil,
I am the flame, the sword and the song;
the valkyrean rider of battle steeds

whose cloud banging hoofs
strike flinty cliffs of sky,
stinging lashes of light;
nostrils breathing the wild air
where stormy wood winds blow.

I am the hammer,
I am the anvil,
the violent blue leap of electric:
song of the motion of work and wheels,
of the motor's hum and charge of voltage;
song of the warbling of birds in the forest
when the sun sifts through the leaves
and the song is all sunlight, harmonies of sun.

2

Childhood to youth,
as from half-dreams,
I awoke from play,
from the laborless world.

I learned sorrow
and for my labor, hunger;
misfortune pursued me,
woeful and a wanderer.

I toiled twelve hours,
they took the work of ten,
I toiled ten hours,
they took the work of eight.
They took my bed
and they took my books,
the clothes from my back
and the crust from my table
and I walked, holes in my shoes,
on the damp pavement.

Evicted, my bed, bedding,
books in the gutter,
scattered in the drizzling rain,
the crowd shuffled past me in the street.
Pity, pity, their eyes wept,

and I heard their pity fall like coins,
tearless, drop, drop, in the tin cup.

3

I saw there, standing at the corner,
guarded by the policeman,
the landlord, god of property;
as in a dream, I saw the old dog:
his haunches gripped the land,
and when he roared,
Cave Canem,
I have and hold,
his breath was poison gas,
his jaws like cannon flamed;
and where he pawed the earth
like an ancient beast,
the earth smoked and baked;
stones in the field
marked the dead land:
coins taxing the earth,
marking the drouth.

Howl, Cerberus,
hell-hound of war
defend your hell,
howl and hiss your hate.

Of those who have power
I have hatred.

You, thieves of to-day,
what can you steal
from those whose possessions
are in the future?

4

From bitter roots,
parched, thirsting,
the black blooms of poverty
gripped the brain like opium.

My mind, so used to wild imaginings,
lover of beauty,
beauty for beauty's sake,
learned its lesson from realities;
blonde aphrodisiacs,
beauties I adored,
who fed and glutted on my heart,
bite now,
and break your teeth upon its iron core.

And you, wish-woman,
virgin, crucifix, whoring nun,
you have been at the death
of too many syphilitic poets.

Where is the priest now?
Upon the bed,
trousers on the floor,
the virgin in his arms,
inside, searching for the truth.

5

As a lover's hands evoke desires
from the body of his love,
I, too, with fruitful fingers,
touch with tenderness,
as twilight a city,
till electric blooms flower from steel and stone.

I grew and understood growth and desire,
the love of a woman, the love as one.

New skies I saw with their many horizons,
new horizons with their many visions.

My hands like hammers,
my mouth like iron,
I crushed mountains,

I consumed fear,
ate darkness.

Look!
The day is aflame!
The night is on fire!

On singing wires,
like notes of music,
choirs of birds
telegraph their song.

I heard their voices
issue from the forest,
hum in the power lines,
at the hour when factory whistles warble
and light sifts through the panes
and the song seems all sunlight,
harmonies of sun.

6
SONG

I heard them, in the city,
their voices, amid evening traffic,
tumult of people, drills,
workmen, on the roadways,
in the foundries,
the words bubbling
in lead in the printshops,
boomed in the press-rooms,
folded in sheets, the news carried,
shouts in the street, homeward,
on the lips of thousands;
sounds of the city, their voices, blended,
I heard them, knew, their voices, gather,
grow, and machines, horns, gongs, whistles,
songs resound from the city.

7

I heard an army of toilers
and their tread pulse in my heart,
I heard the measures of my heart extend
and beat like drums the march of their lives.
I embraced them all, I knew all,
I loved them with great passion.

What I build, I thundered with a city's voices,
I build by will, I need no gods,
and in their voices I heard my song.

I am the hammer.
I am the anvil.

8

Of my deep hunger
great dreams grew,
and I made of my ideal
my bread.

I stopped my tears
and god's wells ran dry,
of my disbelief
a desert bloomed.

I made of the truth
my sword of need,
I made of my anger
a battlefield;

and in my need
I knew no fear:
I swung my hammer,
their structures fell.

I stopped my labor,
machines were still,
and I made of their laws
a broken staff.

I drove the lender
from the land.
I gave the tiller
back his soil.
I gave the toiler
back his toil.

My field of war
was a growing field
where all my victories

were sown,
and I made of my joy
a harvest's yield.
My joy, it rose,
a new found land.

9
FINALE

Descend, descend,
unlamented and damned,
the long line of conquerors
in the fading dusk.

You are gone forever.
You are dead forever.

New heroes arise
and they do not know you:
land without leaf,
shadow and no sun,
they do not know you.

As the living the dead,
the thirst without water,
the gun without death,
they do not know you.

They touch the springs
and pour forth power,
in life without labor
they do not know you.

Their strength is a city
and masters power,
and its doors are open
in streets without fear,
for they do not know you.

You are gone forever.
You are dead, forever.

WHAT THE THUNDER SAID:
A FIRE SERMON

*Where are the roots that clutch, what branches grow
Out of this stony rubbish?* —T. S. ELIOT

A Cinematic Poem

The Communards, they are storming heaven!

A damp gust of March wind
swirls and scatters papers.

And the hot, critical July days!—
tense wireless bristling with flashes,
stammering, stuttering,
awaiting what code,
what code to translate
Capital, Famine, Predatory War,
into what dialectic odyssey
the machine gun's riveting shall inscribe—
the Leatherjacket fatally indite?

In the Smolny:
the decisive delegates,
drawn faces,
burnt cigarettes, telephones,
wires, leaflets,—
telegraphic congresses:
and in the chill streets
armed workers, soldiers,
add fuel to the street fires.
Rifles ready. Waiting, Deciding.
Who are the riders?

When the thunderheads hammer,
the palaces reverberate,
the napoleonic columns fall;
the cracked plaster of paris Narcissus
drowns in his fragments.

The Thorthunder speaks:
Workers! Soldiers! Sailors!

We are the riders of steel storms!
We are the fire-bearers!
Ours the heritage of the first flame-runner
racing up the steep dark slopes,
lightning in the night!
Created and creator of fire!
We are the riders of steel stallions—
we are the fire-bearers,
the kinetic synergy of factories
snorting flambent plumes,
charging,
rushing up the tracks beacon-eyed!

And scarlet ships of space
wing time's fires
cataclysmic bear
earth's heirs
the communists with battle shouts
rumble over the skyways,
scatter cannonades of stars,—
flowers of life and death,
flowers of revolution
rocket amid acrid clouds!

The Thorthunder says:
(rumblin crumblin)
Da!
Da Da!

All Power To The Soviets!

The Spring rain blows over the steppes.
In October
lightning ripples in the windwaved wheat—
great streak of silver whistling scythe!
And tractors bloom in the wheatfields!
They rumble,
they crumble the earth to their powerful wills.
They speak:
Gigant!

Overhead—
soft sunsetwinds blow rosegold odors

twilightly descend with their first young star.
Over the bridge strong hands on wheels and levers skim.
Over the bridge trains bead red stars
weld through fire and iron
five years!—
electric songs of speeding lights!
A blow torch simmers sparkles
and the Leatherjacket welds
stars over the waters below.

Red coals toss in torrents
in waterfalls of the Dnieprostroi,
and the Dnieper sows her banks with rubies.
There spring up socialized cities . . .
Workers of Magnitogorsk, with huge blast furnaces,
write in flame,
through fire and iron,
steel statements of steel deeds:
armored trains of revolution
dynamic steel drilling through black rock
dynamiting tunnels
mining blackgold ores!
Subways without christbeggars
whose blind eyes beseech a penance!
While the bursting sun flings from chaotic flame-pits
the synthesis of new worlds . . .

Far into the night, far into the ages,
the burning worlds whirl and shine . . .
. . . City towns . . . worker palaces of art and culture . . .
. . . Workers! We are at once the makers and the made!
Across transition belts of time and space,
tools in hand, we mould the human race,
we lay the base,
assemble and rivet bolts and parts
of marxist machinery,
and build mighty structures,
higher forms of social union . . .
. . . classless society . . . Gigant!

* * * *

Here are the blazing windows of iron mountains

in an electromagnetic sunset.
These are the heights men reach.
Still higher—
the Communard soars like a comet,
until the world is small tinder
for such a blaze of space!

Yes
the world is burning
and the stormwind's big bellows fan the flames
and the hammer pounds stronger and stronger
and the anvil rings in answer
Thalatta! Thalatta!
and her all-conquering legions
shout and clash and clang their armor
and scarlet seas surge
exultant upon new shores
flowers of revolution red and gold bursting
the magniloquent red battlehorses of
plunging plumes in the thundering wind
paced with the lightning
. . . roar . . .
a song of flame
and the world in the embrace of the flaming flood
and the hammer heard clanging
clanging upon an anvil
clanging and shaping world october
and they march and demonstrate
and bright banners of faces cheer
thorthunderclapplause!
and they shout through the streets of the universe
yes
and the sun like an executed head falls
and the whole sky bleeds
dripping over church and skyscraper
and arms like hammers strike stars
forge new worlds shoot upwards
yes!

Robert Gessner

UPSURGE

1

Look! We are the depression bastards!
You of America, our fathers, look at us!
We're grammar school kids with smudgy knees,
High school boys in long pants,
And college graduates with whole alphabets of sweaters.
We're in our twenties; we're under twenty—
We're any age, year, month, week you can think of!
See our faces and our bodies—we're older, you say?
Well, Sirs (and Ladies, if you're so damned nosey):
We are the youngest old men in the world.

We've eaten tin-can stew, tin-can java, tin-can soup
Inside the jungles of America!
We've slept in rain-soaked gondolas, across ice-caked bars,
              on top of wind-beaten boxes
Hitting the dirt and pavements of America!
We know El Paso's yards like we know what's inside your hat,
Know to take the Texas out, not the San Antone,
       know to catch the Mopac east from Fort Worth;
And the bulls in Barstow who chase us from the Santa Fe to the U.P.
       and the U.P. bulls who chase us back;
And the tank towns out of Council Bluffs, Pontiac, Baton Rouge
Where shotgun constables meet all freights to see we don't
              unload for grub.

When will you stop this runaround?
You older brothers, you big-hearted cousins,
When will your stinking charity stop?
We've been given the run across your private continent

Three times, four times—ten!
A muddy sewer across your God-damn continent!

We don't steal your railroads, or harm our pullman floors
            (we love our comfort even when we're found
            locked in after a three-day run froze stiff
            as your heart)
Our bodies slam against roaring manifests when we grab rungs
            and have the strength to hang on;
Our tangled legs are kicked in sleep, eyes dazzled by flash-
            lights, brains battered by questions—
They separate us, rape the girls in overalls, and chain-
            gang us—
And so does Death.
Yes, we're killed. The wheels are magnets—suck in
            toes, crunch ankles, chew off knees;
And the cops got guns that answer any backtalk.

We don't try your highways because our thumbs are sore.
(do you think we look like white-collar passengers?)
We see our ghosts, damn you—right in the boxes with us—
Your age, plenty lousy, getting by since Grover Cleveland;
We don't wanta be pop bums, grandad hoboes;
Or like the crazy ones, the sex nuts, hungry for feeling,
            who get us alone in box car corners;
Or the sugar ones in the street who want us, show us
            clean beds and warm food and dough.
Or like the real crazy ones who mutter to their hands;
Yah, you bet we'll go bugs, just like them.

Well, Patriots, you've had 1620 and the Rock;
Now see what we're getting, thank you:
Why, we're a damn sight more cuckoo than the shell-shocked
            guys,
And we get no pension for syph contracted in or out
            of service.

Maybe you've had enough, and would like to hear a movie.
I haven't started, Mr. Democrat, for we are a million over.
We're from all your God-damn states, every one;
None's blessed without us, even the D of C.
We've run away from families on three-buck-a-week doles,
      from fathers whittling sticks, mothers cooking bones.

Christ! We had to go, didn't we?
Away to Idaho for beet-thinning when there wasn't,
      for grape-picking in California, oranges in Florida.
No strangers allowed, the Good Samaritan said.
Hasn't every house a laid-off mug?

Say, Captain, any room in the CCC?
Scram, kid, we got no bunks for runaway rats.

We were proud all right, when we ran away from homes
                  shamed under a cloud of relief.
Today, you bet, we're not too swell to stand in lines for you
                  passers-by to hurry past, heads down,
And you certainly got a look on like you're ashamed of us!
No, I'll say we're not picky over beans and bread and slum.
But we'll be damned (as if we aren't) before we'll sing
"Jesus" for sleep and keep, and give up coin for
                  pie-in-the-sky.
God's no delouser—no more than you got guts to cure
                  our ills and yours.
Maybe you're expected over at the Elks for poker
                  or at Susan's for bridge,
Perhaps you got a date for dancing and some hot jazzing after;
But we're an army moving, huddled in the night.
We are an unseen army moving over America.
You with your dates, you don't see us—only the whimpering
                  stragglers at backdoors, the scratchy beggars
                  in the streets—
But never the endless hordes flooding over America,
      the endless line of starvation stretching over America.
You don't see our villages of jungles, running beside the rails,
                  across and up-and-down America.
You don't see our comradeship over footsores, eaten shoes,
                  blood-spit, matted hair, rotten teeth, and
                  dirty bodies stinking;
Our giving and receiving of each other's food begged, bought
                  or stolen, of clothes and songs;
And the kind of silence the stars have.
And the jokes over lidless toilets in crappy cells not
                  fire-proof but good enough for bums;
And the dumb lice eating like they thought we was already dead;
And the hot air of flop-houses, air for shadows limping
                  in muggy long-legged underwear.

You think we're all the same because we dress alike.
Fools, split shoes don't mean cracked spines like the old-
              timers of '30 and '31.
Yah! Two years more and we'll be there!
You can't beat the road, kid.
We know.
But we're not an army of defeat;
We're twenty and under-twenty:
You won't see us taking it below the belt with our mouths shut!

2

Look closer! I am your cousin, uncle, brother—YOU!
I thought you'd recognize that college glow—
Sticks out, eh what, in a queue of job-waiters?
It makes a man stand up and hold his shoulders back,
That economic knowledge about diminishing returns,
And who's the head of Industrial Recovery,
And how to score the bouts of railing bulls and cotton bears;
And know, by God and Babson, that toboggan slides are rounded
Always (patience, Harvard) scooting up to snowy peaks!

Yes, even minus English collar, Knox-snapped brim,
I just felt you'd realize I know
Surface blasting's cheaper than a mile-down shaft,
That nitrate sprouts potatoes quicker than potash,
And cable stresses are divided, girders lengthened, lime
              for redwood,
That this motor displaces that more men—
Well, boys, let's run to Owen Young,
Ask teacher what is knowledge for.

This numbness of the flesh from sitting long,
Your dulling drug of we-had-to-take-ours-now-you-take-it,
This fret and muscle-twitching—
Christ! these hands breathe life; buttocks, legs still
              shape of youth; bellies taut; heads generate—
Give us the world! We'll fix it!
What are you waiting for?
We're hungry for life,
We got years to go and centuries to climb!
We gotta get going
Before we're sick and sit on curbstones.
Brother! Bootstraps pull boots up!

CROSS OF FLAME

"Torgler and Könen left the Reichstag that evening between 8:10 and
8:15 P.M."—"The Brown Book."

Six days before election—not a poster up!

We sat in the Fraction room, bouncing our pencils on the blotter

I've gone each day to Braschwitz, stuffed in his uniform,
Sitting in Alexanderplatz as though he were Hitler.
"Herr Commissioner—" Paugh! I hate repeating his name—
"The party's not outlawed, you have no legal right . . ."
And he'd sit smiling officiously.
Some day the sides of that desk will be exchanged and then—
Well, we went to Karl Liebknecht surrounded by detectives;
Ach, Torgler, you should see what they have done in there.
The desks apart lie hushed among the papers
And the rooms unsprung like when schoolboys had tinkered with a
        clock;
What kids—swooping on themselves (they held the fort).

Well, this time he let the comrades tie some bundles up,
Small parcels hardly enough for Wedding alone.
I asked him where the catacombs were that Göring saw
And, Torgler, as the flag is red, he struck his finger
At the hole in the porter's place.
                                            A comrade laughed:
"Man, that's the trapdoor to our old beer cellar!"

"And the instructions to burn down museums," I asked,
"The flames to signal for a Bolshevik reign of terror?"

He had no answer.

Our pencils hit thoughtfully and the echo died.
On numb November we had felt the pulse of the polls:
Eleven quickened ours; theirs fell off thirty-five.

And now

Six days before election—not a poster up!

I stood by the window while he talked. It was dark already
And the fibers of his voice swelled, rising with his plea.
This begging—paugh! When will the vote be cast with lead?

The porter struck his head in with our coats—fine skull
He had, old Franco vet, shaven as smooth as his big buck teeth.
At eight I heard far below the sound of the door
Closing, the massive frame-bone settling down for the night.

So, Torgler, ready now? My stomach's angry, come,
The Aschinger has *Hasenpfeffer*, comrades, talk;
There, *Fräulein*, your coat . . . it's not as frayed as mine.
You limp, sciatica? It's the plague of the times we walk.
Well, we will move forward slowly down the corridor of this tomb;
Look how plush the curtains hang and carpets close.
Stuffy, isn't it? The chairs sit quietly.
The dim light here seems pregnant like the street's in here.
Six days and we will know who holds this Bastille prize.

Goodnight, porter; here's the air. Smell, comrades, now:
Do you not feel the night, the fog there brewing?
Last month it was a chimney fire in the Berliner Schloss
Yesterday a railway near the Corridor
And now the catacombs in Karl Liebknecht.
Paugh! Tell the Press. They know it! Tell the Sportpalast:
Assassination Coming! Admission Free!
Starring Hitler in Christ-on-the-Cross!

The night stood ready and the sound of autos died
And swelled along the street.
We stood, heavy on the top step, like three ocean divers
And descended slowly,
The frame above us looking down without farewell

Goodnight, *Fräulein*, we all go Underground tonight;
Bathe your leg in salt tears and tomorrow run.
Friedrichstrasse's overstrolled with three-mark girls;
I wonder if they feel this air—vital now—closing in

There, Torgler, are the comrades at the corner table.
Beers around! Where's the *Hasenpfeffer*? Come,
You sit like three old maids at a wedding; life is hope.
They haven't nailed our coffin yet. Let's eat—*prost*!

The table tops got white toward ten; two comrades left.
Hans shifts his corner to Otto, so we called the bill
To let the fellow buy coke lumps with his ten percent.

Then Otto came up running, his new apron starched,
Looking like the puppet waiter in the play:

Herr Comrade, have you heard, the Reichstag is on fire!

We sat stiff, we hired sitters in the play,
Sitting in our electric chairs, strapped in and masked:

Man, are you mad?

No, it's true—his eyes reflect the flame—*the taxis say
It's true. Thousands are already throbbing there!*

Outside was the glow and the distant hum of men
Near Königsplatz black snakes of hose wormed on the street
No general call and the fire-brigade was fumbling late.
The building looked as though it wanted now to burn.

But above stood Hitler smiling from his cross of flame

Torgler saw and marched erect.

                              No! I cried.
His grin of victory is a trap of blood-toothed hate!

He knew and his voice was steady in the rising roar:

My life's a step; let it display our innocence.

He moved forward, my eyes glazed with the fire and tears
And the mouth expanding closed on him and Germany.

TWO SALESMEN IN SEARCH OF A COUNTRY

Being an imaginary monologue of
David Windsor to Charles Lindbergh

Here we are, old chap, at the Café de la Paix,
Star salesmen temporarily unemployed.
See Alfonso over there and the fat boy Otto
Waiting with Kerensky, whisky eyes that pray
For the people to petition slavery?
You and I were never such small fry;
We, my man, sold empires, grass and sky.

My face with Zulu chiefs, eyes lost
In the jungle, so the poor will eat their poverty
And natives die for God and Monarchy.
No offense—we sold the same encyclopedia
From planes and trains and other media.

My ride to Berlin was a housing tour;
You flew directly for an insomnia cure.
Now Bertie and Betty are stealing my show in the States,
But then your labor's free, you know, and smarter;
They'll have to sell the cure as a Dionne sponsor.

Well—drink up, old man; keep upper lipped—
Mustn't let Alfonso think we've slipped;
We're star salesmen just temporarily unemployed.
Front is the word for royalty, old fuss-fuss—
Hope Bedaux doesn't stick stop-watches on us!

HYMN FOR OCTOBER

Hey LOOK!

Today's my birthday
Today I celebrate
Close the factories, stop the trams
Today I'm eighteen
Tall and handsome, jaw bone clean.
Today in Leningrad
Eyes were opened, brown and sad

The sky hung black with pain
Blood lay on the ground like rain.
I fired my first-born cry!
Crack in the iron, the sun is seen!
I struck my roaring feet
Split in the pavement, grass is green!
I fired! I struck! I laughed!

The fields are flowing rain
And the sleet is bearing snow
The steppes as smooth as a floor
Awake with the storm and roar:

Today I celebrate
March the roadways, shout my song
My feet are mountain snorts
Toward the Red Square, great with pep
My body uniformed
Red and beautiful, step on step.
My body fits a horse
Swift with rhythm, clicking stones
My body rides in a tank
Strong as heart-beats, pulse and bones
In autos, trucks I drive
Sit at ease, smooth as dreams
I sail the sky in a schooner
Climb with wings, swoop with screams
I float in the air with Gorki

My body is the proletariat of Russia

Today's my birthday
Today I celebrate
See me marching, wind in my hair
This is my factory flag
Rise up floating, flood the Square
My slogan marching bobs
Words that rumble like a fight
My arms extending shout:

Workers of the World, Unite!

See these my banners—yours
These my tractors, farms—all yours

Shops and schools, bread and tools
I give all of these to you
These my birthday gifts when too
Eyes are opened, earth is felt
You fire, you strike, you laugh!
The day you celebrate
The day you shout with me

Today's my birthday
Today I came to life
I am the Revolution

Today I'm eighteen!

THE EXILES

[A CANTATA]

My people are as a people of grass,
uprooted and scattered,
fugitives of the earth.

They are a people of exile,
a people of all nations, yet forced apart,
homeless ones, wanderers in waste places,
refugees on a road of ruins,
refugees on a road of mourning.
In a world without refuge
desolation is their dwelling place.

They march—
on the long road of exile.
How their banners are fallen about them
like beggars' garments!
The sorrows of my people are rains
that fall on the sands of the desert
and are barren.

My people are a people of grass,
uprooted and scattered.
In a world without refuge
desolation in their dwelling place.

1. THE GARDEN

I had a garden, a lovely garden,
a tribe of flowers in a garden of nations,
a people of many-colored grass.

I had a garden, an oasis,
a well of living waters,
a well of learning.

I gathered out the stones,
and planted in the garden,
as a seed made bread
were the plants in the garden,
as a people of grass
grown up from the plains.

In a garden on a hilltop
I kept my lodging.
The pillars of my house were of precious trees,
a tree of love, and a tree of peace,
a tree of life and a tree of knowledge.

I had a garden, a lovely garden,
I nurtured with care each root, each branch,
flowers in the sun, words of gold,
a lily, a song, rich fruits like poems,
golden scriptures like leaves of a story,
of a tree of life, of a tree of knowledge
of a people of grass.

2. SONG

I went down to the garden,
to the beds of spices,
to glean in the garden,
to gather the lilies,

I gathered the fruits
like ripened grain
and the granary is full.

My fruit is better than gold,
Wisdom has builded my house

and furnished my table,
"Come, eat of my bread,
and drink of my wine,
and walk with me in the way of understanding."

3.

They have come up from the plains,
They have come down from the mountains,
The many nations walk in the garden
They feed among the lilies,
like a flock among the lilies.

Their swords are ploughshares.
Their spears are pruning hooks.
There is ploughing and planting.
There is pruning and paring.
They break forth into singing.
And the nations rejoice.

How beautiful among the hills
are grown the roots of the people,
a family of flowers, a garden of nations.
a people of many-colored grass.

4. THE DESERT

The beast is in the garden,
the beast with claws of iron,
the beast with breath of fire,
the brown pestilence in the land.

The walls of the garden are fallen,
swine feed in the ruins,
The bark of the tree is leprous,
the tree of life is leprous,
the wise man is become a leper
and wisdom a disease.

The branches are slashed with swords,
the limbs are lopped with terror,
there is burning instead of beauty,
there is no green thing.

O people of grass,
you are as a heap of stubble,
a heap of refuse.
Beauty has fled your dwelling,
and desolation is your dwelling place.
The beast of nations lies down in the field,
the garden is a desolation,
a place for beasts to lie down in.

5. THE ROAD

Awake and sing, you that dwell in the dust.
Gather yourselves together,
gather together, O people not desired,
blow the trumpet.

Blow the trumpet,
cry, gather yourselves and go,
gather yourselves in troops
against those who besiege you.

The brown beast shall perish,
the cities of his pestilence crumble,
you shall rise in the dust of their cities
as a people of grass,
as roots out of dry ground.

Awake and sing, you that dwell in the dust;
take root in the earth,
O people of grass,
and rise again.
Awake and sing,
prepare the way of the people,
lift up a standard for the people.

Set up your banners,
O people of grass,
wave them in the fields,
gather them in the fields,
gather in the hills,
roll in the valleys,
from the crevices of earth
go forward,
march.

HEARD AT DNIEPERSTROI

Who has sung the Dnieper?
Who has caught his currents in rimes,
Made his eddies echo on since saga times?
Who has pulled his beard through rapids
Heard him scream like scampering kids?
Who has seen the moon upon Dnieper?

Herodotus heard Borysthenes,
The Romans Danapris
And the Tauri grunted Usu
Did the Byzantine remember Allah?
Did the Normans swim to Athens?
Who has sung the Dnieper?

Pushkin pulled the river to the ocean
Gogol sat beside its lake
Cossacks rode its waves like mermaids
Did Deniken write rimed verses while he swam from bank to bank?

I have seen the Dnieper waiting for a song
Standing in his strength like a wading fisherman
Holding between his feet the harness and the chain.

The song of the Dnieper is the gallop of a million horses
Along the shimmering wires strung from town to town
Galloping into farmyards where there are no horses
Trotting into city streets where there were no streets before
Carrying workers from homes to factories and back to homes
Erecting the factories and charging them with sparks and thunder.

These are the Wild Horses of the Dnieper tamed and powerful
Theirs is the song of the new-born Dnieper,
Dnieper of Ivan, worker and farmer and owner of a million horses.

DECLARATION

I

I'm the face this side of the microphone
The eyes on the senatorial debate
I'm the razzberry row in the balcony
The quizzical ear in the chambers of commerce
I'm the young man with the old-man smile
  you want to know
  listen I'll tell you
Under the street lamp, the corner idle
Under the harvest moon, the fields denuded
By the juke box in the boomtown tavern
I whistle Broadway's lonely melody:
  Winter winds off Erie, heat blasts in Texas
  The tugs in 'Frisco, clank of cranes in Spokane
  The midnight bray of a mule over the bayous
  The indifferent cars on the highways out of camp
  you want to know
  listen I'll tell you

II

Calloused hands that never wore the velvet
Feel no hankering after Coolidge and the dividends
No song to echo boots on the thirsty road
No memories of this side of paradise
Disturb our dreams, sweet alabaster
  Born without umbilical cord the milk of
  Human kindness is for us in cartons
  Fourteen cents, no bottles to return
O empty hands that crowd the empty streets
Of youth, harsh echoes on the hollow ground:
What shall we use for love when the heart is dry
  you want to know
  listen I'll tell you

III

We know each second of this hour
The midnight clock in the canteen ticking
The half sun poised in the old horizon

Don't speak to us in slogans: we're the slogan
We're holding the mortgage on the nation

We love this map called home
This screwy continent is us
   you want to know
   listen I'll tell you

IV

For a Bill of Rights unblotted
We fight
This is no war of selfish preservation
For us who die
No restoration of the dollar
When we're busted
No watering the beef we eat

We want a many-shingled house to get married in
The time for love, the years to stretch our grasp

Our voices
In the pursuits, in the battlewagons
Our voices clamoring with the tanks
In the factory whistles rising
Young voices over the farmyard
Over the camp in silent song:

Not for the maintenance of our liberties
But for their expansion

V

The new life's in the old payoff this time
The many-shingled house, the years to stretch

They can rub our bodies out but not the heart
That will beat forever on the treaty table

We would destroy the dead in Spain, in China
Break the lifeline weaving under the captive countires

Verify the lie if we fought otherwise
Friends, unknown faces, we tell this truly

Give us the pledge or we will write it
Give us the word for the page we own

Fathers, O mothers, believe us now

Our future's your past—what we will of it
In the crucible where flesh is recast
In the flame where the earth revolves forever

Michael Gold

A STRANGE FUNERAL IN BRADDOCK

Listen to the mournful drums of a strange funeral.
Listen to the story of a strange American funeral.

In the town of Braddock, Pennsylvania,
Where steel-mills live like foul dragons, burning, devouring man and
    earth and sky,
It is spring. Now the spring has wandered in, a frightened child in the
    land of the steel ogres,
And Jan Clepak, the great grinning Bohemian, on his way to work at
    six in the morning,
Sees buttons of bright grass on the hills across the river, and
    plumtrees hung with wild white blossoms,
And as he sweats half-naked at his puddling trough, a fiend by the
    lake of brimstone,
The plum-trees soften his heart,
The green grass-memories return and soften his heart,
And he forgets to be hard as steel and remembers only his wife's
    breasts, his baby's little laughters and the way men sing when
    they are drunk and happy,
He remembers cows and sheep, and the grinning peasants, and the
    villages and fields of sunny Bohemia.

Listen to the mournful drums of a strange funeral.
Listen to the story of a strange American funeral.

Wake up, wake up! Jan Clepak, the furnaces are roaring like tigers,
The flames are flinging themselves at the high roof, like mad, yellow
    tigers at their cage,
Wake up! it is ten o'clock, and the next batch of mad, flowing steel is
    to be poured into your puddling trough,
Wake up! Wake up! for a flawed lever is cracking in one of those
    fiendish cauldrons,

Wake up! and wake up! for now the lever has cracked, and the steel is
      raging and running down the floor like an escaped madman,
Wake up! Oh, the dream is ended, and the steel has swallowed you
      forever, Jan Clepak!

Listen to the mournful drums of a strange funeral.
Listen to the story of a strange American funeral.

Now three tons of hard steel hold at their heart the bones, flesh,
      nerves, the muscles, brains and heart of Jan Clepak,
They hold the memories of green grass and sheep, the plum-trees,
      the baby-laughter, and the sunny Bohemian villages.
And the directors of the steel-mill present the great coffin of steel and
      man-memories to the widow of Jan Clepak,
And on the great truck it is borne now to the great trench in the
      graveyard,
And Jan Clepak's widow and two friends ride in a carriage behind the
      block of steel that holds Jan Clepak,
And they weep behind the carriage blinds, and mourn the soft man
      who was slain by hard steel.

Listen to the mournful drums of a strange funeral.
Listen to the story of a strange American funeral.

Now three thinkers are thinking strange thoughts in the graveyard.
"O, I'll get drunk and stay drunk forever, I'll never marry woman, or
      father laughing children,
I'll forget everything, I'll be nothing from now on,
Life is a dirty joke, like Jan's funeral!"
One of the friends is thinking in the sweet-smelling graveyard,
As a derrick lowers the three tons of steel that held Jan Clepak.
(LISTEN TO THE DRUMS OF THE STRANGE AMERICAN
      FUNERAL!)

"I'll wash clothes, I'll scrub floors, I'll be a fifty-cent whore, but my
      children will never work in the steel-mill!"
Jan Clepak's wife is thinking as earth is shoveled over the great steel
      coffin,
In the spring sunlight, in the soft April air,
(LISTEN TO THE DRUMS OF THE STRANGE AMERICAN
      FUNERAL!)

"I'll make myself hard as steel, harder,

I'll come some day and make bullets out of Jan's body, and shoot
        them into a tyrant's heart!"
The other friend is thinking, the listener,
He who listened to the mournful drums of the strange funeral,
Who listened to the story of the strange American funeral,
And turned as mad as a fiendish cauldron with cracked lever.

LISTEN TO THE MOURNFUL DRUMS OF A STRANGE
        FUNERAL.
LISTEN TO THE STORY OF A STRANGE AMERICAN
        FUNERAL.

EXAMPLES OF WORKER CORRESPONDENCE

BIRMINGHAM, ALA.

This is a troubled time in Alabama
I took my boys out of school as they had no shoes or clothes
I can hear the Klan mutter about Scottsboro
And if our boys are lynched there I shall never forget or forgive
So I am studying to join your party.
Having been born and raised in Birmingham
I find it now the most damnable spot on earth
After eleven no Negro must be out of doors
If seen the Slingshot Squad will shoot him
They shoot wire staples at his legs and feet
They hunt us like wild animals in the brush
So I am studying to join your Party.

INDIANAPOLIS, IND.

We held a red funeral for a child who died of hunger.
We marched in thousands to her grave.
Red roses came from the Communist Party
A wreath of lilies from the Unemployed Councils.
Our banners flashed in the sun
But our hearts were dark with anger.
When at the grave like red soldiers
We swore to end the world's poverty
Brave comrades were seen to weep
Fathers and mothers of hungry children.

ASHTABULA, O.

I am resigning from the American Legion
It reminds of a dog I used to have
That picked up toads in her mouth
And was sick of the yellow acid in their glands
But did it again and again, the dumb fool
And the more misery and famine and bunk
The more the Legion seems to like it
But I am not a dog and can understand
That now is the time to end capitalism

FLINT CITY JAIL, MICH.

Arrested as a picket in a recent strike
I have found my cellmate here an Indian chief
His name John Thunder of the Ottawas.
Once his fathers owned America
But now after ten years at the Buick plant
Working under Mr. Crowder as an expert fender finisher
Chief Thunder is destitute and can find no job.
His family scattered, his children in the orphanage
So the Chief worried and was low in mind
And drinking in a saloon fought a Ku Kluxer
And beat up the 100 percent American
So now is in jail waiting his sentence.
He talks of days when his fathers owned this land
The buffalo days when food was shared by all
When no one was hungry and there was no rich
He has asked me to write and tell his tale
He wants us to remember the deep wrongs of the Indian
I have given Chief Thunder a pamphlet by Lenin.

ODE TO WALT WHITMAN

Walt Whitman loafed under the trees
Leaned on his cane and observed
In a slow and sunburned Manhattan—
But now they've killed his God
His love and horsecars and old trees—
Hear the shriek of the killer babbitts

God is the smash of two taxis in a hurry
God is a skyscraper house of money
Where crazy little benitos murder love
And ring cash registers all day—
God is hate dollars chromium speed—
And no lilacs bloom, Walt Whitman—
No hope no grass no quiet
Nothing to love but Coney Island
Your ocean now a garbage dump
Where millions of young greenbaums sport
And must swallow colon germs B
Americanoes at twelve a week—

2.

And me a son of Walt Whitman
A son of Manhattan the bitch
Born on Rat and Louse street
Near Tuberculosis avenue—
In my unfortunate cradle
A tenement fell on my head
A double-crossing rotten Tammany tenement
A shylock tenement that devoured dreams—
People tramped the hospital streets
Sick with the dysentery of life
Cowards without a flag—
And me a son of Walt Whitman
Kicked into a basement to die—
Eddie Greenbaum, skinny shipping clerk—
Americano at twelve a week—
Nietzsche packing pink lady's underwear—
Pale, goofy young poet of hardware—
Department store intellectual dope—
Soaring with Keats above the gum-chewers—
Doped by a priest named Walt Whitman—
Why did I mistake you for the sun?

3.

Love love love on the Bronx Express
Ten seconds to gain and a world to lose
O sweet unfortunate Baby
Phoney in five and dime jade and rayon

Constipated under the woolworth roses and lilies
You smelled bad, poor girl
Of swollen feet, rouge and cash registers—
My chest touched your little breasts—
The subway crush married us—
I dreamed among the gum-chewers—
"I sang the body electric"—
You were the kind and lovely woman I had sought
In my long, long Walt Whitman dreams—
But you divorced me with loathing
At the Simpson Street subway station—
Why didn't I shoot myself
Goofy young Greenbaum rooting for love
In the garbage of my New York—
And yours, Walt Whitman—

4.

O Pioneers, our foreman was a nervous little rat—
And all day like a third degree
Down in the basement hell with democracy
Commercial madhouse from 8 to 6
I knew the clatter speedup and gangrened air
Electric bulb sweat and coffin fears—
Above us the macy gimbel millionaires
Plotted bargains in young greenbaums and kelleys—
Hell hell hell and low wages
And little salesgirls puked among the rayon—
Such was our life, O Pioneers—
Until I gagged at Walt Whitman
His son of the open road and splendid silent sun—
Lies, lies, a lazy poet's lies on a printed page
Meant for rich college boys—
No winds blow, no sun shines, America is my prison,
Don't mock me with your tales of the free,
Give me time, I want real love and fresh air,
Poetry is the cruelest bunk,
A trade union is better than all your dreams—

5.

So on April 14th we struck
A miracle like your lilacs, Walt Whitman—

Spring, spring, Rocky Mountain spring and democracy
Out of the basement greenbaums and kelleys—
And me, the dope, the factory fodder and jailbird,
Actually singing on a picket line—
Cops sneered and slugged and the millionaires went nuts—
But my heart glowed with proud happiness—
And Lenin said, scorn not the dream—
See, see new skyscrapers for Manhattan
Communist factories for human love—
A pure ocean, and sunlit homes not tenements—
Streets for sun and friendship
And no more Tuberculosis avenues—
And no more hell in a basement—
Son of Walt Whitman, to strike is to dream!

6.

O Pioneers we build your dream America—
O Walt Whitman, they buried you in the filth
The clatter speedup of a department store basement
But you rose from the grave to march with us
On the picket line of democracy—
Sing sing O new pioneers with Father Walt
Of a strong and beautiful America
Of the thrushes and oceans we shall win
Of sun, of moon, of Communism and joy in the wind
Of the free mountain boys and girls—
It will come! It will come! The strikes foretell it!
The Lenin dreams of the kelleys and greenbaums
Deep in the gangrened basements
Where Walt Whitman's America
Aches, to be born—

TOM MOONEY WALKS AT MIDNIGHT

1

The prison sleeps! A murderer moans. A boy insane
          fingers the bars.
Down the long corridor flickers a sick yellow star to
          light the dreary acres of steel and death.

And a guard paces the tower under a powerful moon.
    And yawns!
They sleep!
Wife-killer, bankrupt, fool and rogue.
Children of the poisoned social womb.

2

Does Comintern live?
Are the workers marching?
These are the thoughts that ache and burn
In the heart of a class-war prisoner
Alone in a cell at midnight.

3

It is the dark hour.
Tom Mooney paces his cell.
At midnight battles are lost and won.
Tom opens his door. Glides through the steel and concrete.
Unlocks the gate to the world.
The guard cannot see:
Tom walks the hills to his world.

4

Two pale miners from the Ruhr lie on a straw bunk in con-
    centration camp.
"Is it well with you, my comrades?"
"It is well, Tom Mooney!
In Berlin streets our songs are sung by bloody lips.
    Hitler will end!
In steel mills our teachers stoke the furnaces of a red tomorrow.
    Hitler will perish!
On every ship our navigators steer the course to freedom.
    Hitler must die!
Our factory forts are still unconquered!
Fascism is the last frenzy of a dying ape!
We have gained the last terrible clarity. All or nothing!
It is well with us, Tom Mooney!"

5

Tom Mooney walks the world at midnight.
A sentry raises his blittering bayonet. The moon lights his
      calm young face. It shines on tents and a trampled
      ricefield.
"Who goes there?"
"Tom Mooney."
"Welcome, comrade, to the Red Army of Soviet China!"
"Comrades, is it well with you?"
"Well! Our Soviet is a symphony of hope rising from sixty
      million broken hearts of proletarian China.
We are building the beautiful world of brotherhood, peace, and
      rice.
One race—one class—one dream: Communism!"
Cannon boomed from the Dragon Hills,
The sentry woke the vast army,
Red flags saluted Tom Mooney in China.

6

Tom roams the Arctic shores. Fishermen greet him: Swedes,
      Lapps, Finns.
They report to Tom Mooney. All is bitter. All is well. The
      ocean has its ebb and flood. Comintern is never still!
In Africa the drums beat. Voodoo priests make the old mum-
      mery. But in the mining camps Lenin speaks.
A secretary of the African Laborers' Union is reading a
      pamphlet on imperialism.
"Comrade Mooney, the African race is a young giant reaching
      for the Marxist key that unlocks all jails."
The two embrace, and know that all's well.

7

Paris! Belgrade! Barcelona! Hamburg!
Rome! Athens! Lisbon! Tel-Aviv!
The planet turns, the moon is a lamp for secret building.
Among Australian ranches and Hindu mountains Tom finds
      comrades who tell him all is well.
In Tokio a secret conference of workers, peasants and students
      elect him to their presidium
And red poets of Japan chant their solemn ballads to Tom.

Moscow! Kharkov! Tiflis! Baku!
A brigade of young shock-troopers report:
"Comrade Mooney, for each year you have suffered in prison
        we have built a hundred monuments: Red factories!
Member of the Moscow Soviet, it was Lenin who nominated
        you. We elect you year after year.
The Pacific Ocean does not separate us. It is our leader who is
        locked in San Quentin!"

8

Havana! In a sugar mill stands a Red Guard in ragged overalls.
        He smiles at Comrade Tom and salutes.
Lima! Bogota! Buenos Aires! All is well!
The planet turns, the earth bears fruit, Communism marches!
Battles are lost, but the war is being won!
Vera Cruz! El Paso! Galveston! It marches!
Chicago! A proletarian tide sweeps the streets clean of their
        century of capitalist filth and blood!
New York! In Union Square fifty thousand workers shout the
        great name "Mooney!" in a challenge to the skyscrapers!
Alabama! In the mysterious pine woods Negro and white share-
        croppers weld their union and greet Tom Mooney!
The South awakes like a long fallow field! The ice smashes
        up in the farthest north!
Tom Mooney is inspecting his world!
San Francisco! His mother:
"The blood of the proletarian centuries is in you,
The voice of the famine, the heart of our poor, hungry Ireland.
It is better to be in jail for the Working Class
Than in the White House for the capitalists,
With all my eighty years of sorrow and labor
I say to you, all shall be well!"

9

Tom Mooney in his cell at midnight—
It is then battles are lost and won,
It is then a worker reviews his world,
Tramps the dangerous roads of birth,
Finding the far-flung comrade-armies,
Who tend the flame of Comintern,
And fight and bleed and will never rest until truly all is well.

A WREATH FOR OUR MURDERED COMRADE KOBAYASHI

"On February 20, 1933 comrade Takiji Kobayashi, one of the most gifted revolutionary authors of Japan, was tortured to death by Tokyo police. Cause of death was given as heart failure—a lie often used in these cases. He was 29 years old, but had written much—notably the novels, *Crab Fishing Boat* and *Absentee Landlord*. Last year in Japan 6,000 revolutionary workers and intellectuals were arrested and tortured."

Cabaret lice with clever eyes and loose sucking Mouths
And fat liberal frogs defending the swamp
Befoul our life with false theses—
Said the sheriff's gat to the miner's guts
Communism
I'll blow yuh to hell out of this perfect world
But the strike was a Kentucky sunflower that dying left immortal
  seeds—

A dark cloudtorn night we slept
While Judas the polecat murdered his brother
Yet from Roman graves rang the proud *International*—
Yes, yes, despite Gallifet, the Czar, the Horthy slime
All the museum of horrors
Duces, Jack the Ripper rhetoricians
Hitler butchers and bombastic pansies
Corpses sucking at tomorrow's throat
Hollow T. S. Eliot-Ezra Pound-men
History's bad dream
Shrill queer poisoned scurrying fascist rats
Despite, despite
Communism lives

2

Though they murdered thee in a mean Tokyo hell, Kobayashi—
Burst the strong skull that held our passion
Thou Kobayashi lover of this world
Born to be free, grateful to her
At whose burning breast we drink joy—
Born of grace like the deer on fragrant nights
Thine was spring, the wild plum and blue star—
But in Otaru no rice for thee

Thy sister died in factory lava-dust
They father was a tenant farmer
Thy father was a tenant farmer
Thy soul a clear mountain lake
Where labor's grief shattered the fine stars
O the grim lost young Shakespeare
Dead on a railroad track in Montana
O, the holocaust of our proletarian genius
But thou wert saved—
Thy days grew magnificent
The great seawind filled thee
And in New York we swear revenge—
In Paris Canton Prague we say—

3

Long Live the Communist International
Because near a green canal fascists have flung another corpse
An old bloodsmeared Berlin Jew
Killed to be a fascist document
To prove men are not brothers
His large face ripped by the Aryan bootspikes
And children laugh at comic gore on his white wool beard
Under his nails they stuck phonograph needles
In his tall forehead gouged the hooked cross of Jesus Hitler
Still he does not die
Stares with Hebrew majesty at the heaven
Patient to ask, are not men brothers—
They will never die
Trapped young beautiful Negro in a swamp
Hangs from a florida liveoak by torchlight
Of Benito's whooping ku klux klan
Stretches his long useless neck and forever, quietly asks
Are men brothers—
Yes, yes, in Kharkov we swore to avenge thee
Jew, miner, German, Negro and proletarian poet
Men are workers
Men are workers
War on the war makers
On those in Tokyo who murder thee
On those in New York who murder thee

Horace Gregory

ADVICE

You can't fight God,
I know the facts, I said
to Mabel: I know what's going to happen,
it always does. You might as well be dead
if you get violent, he gets you.
I've seen him work before,
I said to her:
You wake up at night violent—
you wish to Christ the Woolworth Tower were
ten thousand stories high
and you on top nude naked, shouting at God,
shouting, 'Get out of my sky.
It's mine. I went the limit with Jake—
it's my affair.
I don't know where he's gone, or if he's dead,
or if he goes
to hell.'

'I'm going to jump. I'm going to make a splash
and spoil somebody's nice clean suit of clothes.
This sky is mine.
I got a right to jump.
I'm tired of my eyes and hair,
my arms and legs, I've seen them all
since I was born.
They're going to fall
in one grand smash. I got a right
to tell my boss to go to hell this way
and get some other fool to take my job
and wait a week for Saturday'.

I said, 'God's watching you:
they'll call the wagon then,
they'll run you into Bellevue,
fighting like tigers in a crazy zoo
to get you into bed and hold you there
with a strong arm doctor feeling you to see
what's wrong and ask you where
Jake is and calm you down.
And the screams
of crazy women in the halls
will be like whispers in your dreams.
They'll make you go to sleep in sleep that seems
like sleep forever'.

'And when they let you out
you'll be quiet, you won't try
to take a drink of lysol for they might
get you again. Until you die
you'll keep yourself a secret,
talking to yourself in the streets,
fighting God on Broadway.
I know how God works,' I told her,
'when you fight his laws.'
I saw what was going to happen

and it always does.

HOMESTEAD

This house rises into a metallic sky
a brilliant iron lake under its porticos,
under its balconies and watch towers multiplied
beyond reason and (one, two, three, four) exact calculation.
An institution for the blind,
a sailors' rest (home from the seas)
not quite, but the specific hiding place where John
McCumber Bluethorn, millionaire, sleeps (falls asleep)
after a dozen cocktails.
                    Expects to die
in the inevitable stronghold for his nerves and tissues.

The bright machinery that was his mind
falls silent.
    His factories (men in the street
crying against him and the quick rifles of the State Militia
are quiet now)
     Here is the last retreat.
The legend of his wives, his children safe,
locked in iron waters.
      His mind, fallen inward, stirs no more,
only the house rises;
count the bricks, the stones
and estimate their power
against wind and rain, time and dissolution.

THE MEEK SHALL DISINHERIT THE EARTH

Darkness in rain:
traffic in asphalt mirrors on the Square
gathers before it mounts Fifth Avenue
north through the white-arc'd Victory in stone
toward Five O'clock.
    A voice in air:
"Come talk to me at 61, my attic
an antique stairway-landing in the sky:
'Loaf and invite the soul,' the deer that strays
into our hands, the silver beast
with wary, child-like eyes, yet innocent—
we'll talk until another day's begun."

And through the rain I saw his house loom up,
an old ship harbored into alien time,
dry-docked in broken timber, the bricks fallen,
steel hawsers giving way, the cornice sprung:
and as one stepped inside, one heard the wind.
I saw him leaning from the top-flight floor:
"I have been ill, been poor, yet when night enters
this room that holds the hours I lie awake,
something like youth returns: there is a tumult
of warmth within my veins . . . and then the tide,
music inspired by a golden bird—

that winged bough whose day is always spring
whose fiery chariot is the song-unheard
leaping the ashes of Time's Illium
from dark to dark, that lives in fire,
climbs fire that flames upon an iron tree,
takes flight within a dream,
and is the hurricane in deepening calm.

I sometimes feel that I have lived forever in this room:
the rent unpaid, yet I am fed and watered
like a geranium on that window sill—
by landlady, charwoman, or foolish girl
who disappears at noon
leaving her alms behind.
But if I leave the room, wherever I go
I hear a whisper: 'Don't come again;
your face is too well known:
you are Herman Melville of the Customs House,
bright in oblivion and yet unseen.'

In a far reach of the room I sometimes hear
Shakespeare and Dante risen from the shades:
perpetual oak and olive sheltering
the delicate laurel of middle-aged spring,
May in October and an early frost:
the grasses changed to glittering white hair.
No, I'm not bitter: I am always friendly.
I always threaten meekness everywhere,
my face the preternaturally calm
forgiving smile . . .
                    Last night I saw a flame
pour out of darkness over eastern heavens:
the earth had perished on the farther shore,
an ocean wilderness on either hand . . .
The sound of that sea shall be my requiem."

UNDER THE STONE I SAW THEM FLOW

Under the stone I saw them flow,
express Times Square at five o'clock,
eyes set in darkness, trampling down

all under, limbs and bodies driven
in crowds, crowds over crowds, the street
exit in starlight and dark air
to empty rooms, to empty arms,
wallpaper gardens flowering there,
error and loss upon the walls.

I saw each man who rode alone
prepare for sleep in deeper sleep
and there to ride, sightless, unknown,
to darkness that no day recalls.
Riderless home, shoulder to head,
feet on concrete and steel to ride
Times Square at morning and repeat
tomorrow's five o'clock in crowds
(red light and green for speed) descend,
break entrance home to love or hate
(I read the answer to the door)

the destination marked "Return,
no stop till here; this is the end."

DEMPSEY, DEMPSEY

Everybody give the big boy a hand,
a big hand for the big boy, Dempsey,
failure king of the U.S.A.

Maybe the big boy's coming back,
there're a million boys that want to come back
with hell in their eyes and a terrible sock
that almost connects.
They've got to come back, out of the street,
out of some lowdown, lousy job
or take the count with Dempsey.

When he's on his knees for the count
and a million dollars cold,
a million boys go down with him
yelling:
            Hit him again Dempsey,

kill him for me Dempsey,
Christ's sake Dempsey,
my God they're killing Dempsey,
It's Dempsey down, Dempsey, Dempsey.

The million men and a million boys,
come out of hell and crawling back,
maybe they don't know what they're saying,
maybe they don't dare,
but they know what they mean:
knock down the big boss,
O, my little Dempsey,
my beautiful Dempsey
with that Godinheaven smile
and quick, god's body leaping,
not afraid, leaping, rising—
hit him again, he cut my pay check, Dempsey.
My God, Dempsey's down—
he cut my pay check—
Dempsey's down, down,
the bastards are killing Dempsey.
Listen, they made me go to war
and somebody did something wrong to my wife
while I was gone.
Hit him again Dempsey, don't be a quitter
like I am Dempsey,
O, for Jesus Christ, I'm out.
I can't get up, I'm dead, my legs
are dead, see, I'm no good,
down for the count.
They got me and I'm out,
I've quit, quit again,
only God save Dempsey, make him get up again,
Dempsey, Dempsey.

HAGEN

Hagen is dead.
His girl remembers
his quick, bright head,
his well-washed hands

and his lean fingers
and how his cough stained
her bedroom floor.

He'd cough the moon
and a gallon of stars
red as fire torn
from a hundred wars.

All that could cure him
was "faith, hope and charity"—
she couldn't pay his
doctor bills
(and he wouldn't take pity
from her, nor tears).
There'd be no money
in the wills
he'd leave if he lived
a thousand years.

Hagen is dead.
All you can do with him
is dig up his coffin and
look at him there:
he wouldn't be changed much—
he looked like that anyway
and he'd still have
neat, red hair
and a quick, bright head.
That's all you can do.
Hagen is dead.

HELLBABIES

Hellbabies sitting in speakeasies
trying to make a million dollars come to life
out of a shot of gin,
trying to make love again
to a new girl,
trying to get out of the way
of sleep and death.

Hellbabies (another brood)
walking through rain,
electric signboards,
in subways,
at shop windows,
their brains filled with tears,
trying to get out of the way
of wives and children
because there are
                    NO JOBS, NO JOBS
no work, only walking.

Maybe God is waiting for
these hellbabies,
surely, hell is waiting
for them to come home:

come home, there will be sweet hell tonight,
always ready.

O METAPHYSICAL HEAD

The man was forever haunted by his head,
this John Brown's body head—
John Brown's body lies—
John Brown's body lies—
John Brown's body lies—
Its head goes marching on—
triumphant, bowing to its friends,
lost in a crowd, then bright as dawn
found again, shining through streets,
laughing, happy by god, drunk, merry old head,
two cocktails and a bottle of champagne
lighting the dark corners in its brain.

A taxi. Home. O metaphysical head,
the world is too small for it,
barefooted, naked in a bedroom. Bed.
It is awake, remembering, thinking:
(I have seen this head too often,
this too-familiar head, yet it changes, changes. . . .

I have seen this young Caesar head
rising above a summer hill, bland and omnipotent,
to meet its love, to see her rise
to this head and with closing eyes
and open lips drinking
the head down until
its brain enters her body
and its will
becomes her will.)
And now, the head goes rolling down the hill,
(uxorious head)
rolls into darkness, sleeps:
grows large in dreams, serene, awful,
becomes God, opens its mighty lips
crying, Let there be light
in this dream. Let
all the women who have not worshipped
this head come naked and ashamed before it,
suffering their little children
to come unto it.
Pity for little children,
conceived in sin,
not fathered by this head
but from the needs
of other men.

Awake again, rising from the dream
into the bedroom, eyelids closed,
the head lost in space,
fixed in ecstatic peace,
senses warm, fluid in the body,
but the head, the winged, haloed head gone,
gone where all godheads go,
singing, Heaven, heaven . . .
                              No,
found somewhere in a gutter,
pitiful, blind, sallow.
(And curious friends examine it,
saying, It shall never rise again,
poor fellow,
put it away.
It hurts us.
Poor fellow,

no words were made to say
how sad we feel. An ugly head—
see what's become of John—
we're sorry, but we must be moving on.)

The head gone. Irrevocably gone,
no longer magnificent, the speaker of the word,
divine, exalted, tilting backward in a barber's chair,
august, revered,
floating above a glass-topped desk,
making its power heard
roaring into a telephone,
then brisk, attentive,
meeting its clients and its creditors,
then finally tired, meditating restfully
on the flat bosoms of its stenographers,
on the undetermined virginity of its stenographers.

There would be no offices for headless men,
no girls, nor wives,
only the subway entrances where one may stand
unseeing (almost unseen)
with right arm raised, the index finger of the hand
pointing where the head had been,
the left hand catching pennies.
John Brown's body goes
begging underground,
John Brown's body—
(No one would dare look at the creature;
it could stand,
a monument for years,
headless, quiet,
forever catching pennies
in its hand.)

Alfred Hayes

IN A COFFEE POT

Tonight, like every night, you see me here
Drinking my coffee slowly, absorbed, alone.
A quiet creature at a table in the rear
Familiar at this evening hour and quite unknown.
The coffee steams. The Greek who runs the joint
Leans on the counter, sucks a dead cigar.
His eyes are meditative, sad, lost in what it is
Greeks think about the kind of Greeks they are.

I brood upon myself. I rot
Night after night in this cheap coffee pot.
I am twenty-two I shave each day
I was educated at a public school
They taught me what to read and what to say
The nobility of man my country's pride
How Nathan Hale died
And Grant took Richmond.
Was it on a summer or a winter's day?
Was it Sherman burned the Southland to the sea?
The men the names the dates have worn away
The classes words the books commencement prize
Here bitter with myself I sit
Holding the ashes of their prompted lies.

The bright boys, where are they now?
Fernando, handsome wop who led us all
The orator in the assembly hall
Arista man the school's big brain.
He's bus boy in an eat-quick joint
At seven per week twelve hours a day.
His eyes are filled with my own pain

His life like mine is thrown away.
Big Jorgensen the honest, blond, six feet,
And Daniels, cunning, sly,—all, all—
You'll find them reading Sunday's want ad sheet.
Our old man didnt know someone
Our mother gave no social teas
You'll find us any morning now
Sitting in the agencies.

You'll find us there before the office opens
Crowding the vestibule before the day begins
The secretary yawns from last night's date
The elevator boy's black face looks out and grins.
We push we crack our bitter jokes we wait
These mornings always find us waiting there
Each one of us has shined his broken shoes
Has brushed his coat and combed his careful hair
Dance hall boys pool parlor kids wise guys
The earnest son the college grad all, all
Each hides the question twitching in his eyes
And smokes and spits and leans against the wall.

We meet each other sometimes on the street
Sixth Avenue's high L bursts overhead
Freak shows whore gypsies hotdog stands
Cajole our penniless eyes our bankrupt hands.
"Working yet?" "The job aint come
Got promised but a runaround."
The L shakes building store and ground
"What's become of Harry? and what's become
Of Charley? Martinelli? Brooklyn Jones?"
"He's married—got a kid—and broke."
And Charley's on Blackwell's, Martinelli's through—
Met him in Grand Central—he's on the bum—
We're all of us on the bum—"
A freak show midget's pounding on a drum
The high L thunders redflag auctioneers
Are selling out a bankrupt world—
The hammer falls—a bid! a bid!—and no one hears . . .

The afternoon will see us in the park
With pigeons and our feet in peanut shells.
We pick a bench apart. We brood

SINGLEMAN

I have been thinking here again tonight—
What if tonight I, Singleman, should die?
I am a poor man.
This home, this narrow downtown furnished room,
The picture of my mother on the dresser,
My business suit I wear for everyday,
My Sunday suit I rarely wear,
These theatre stubs, my blackened brair-pipe—
These are my possessions.
I have kept them against an evil day.
I have neither son nor heir
Nor any living kin.
I have always been alone, too much alone.
I leave no will behind to be disputed,
Nor racing stables, nor any large estate, nor shares.
If here now as the clock goes now
I should die tonight—
A dawn tomorrow find me cold here in the cold room—
Only the Frenchwoman coming up the stairs
To hang the towels and make the bed,
Bringing into the room her cheap perfume, her laundry scent,
Would shriek once—then hasten to remove the dead.
Tomorrow night she'd have my room for rent.

I think of myself asleep and dead forever—
Buried or burned and laid in some large Potter's Field,
No tombstone and no iron separating railing.
No one would come in summer or in spring
To see how my poor grave was faring;
I would have no share of someone's tears
And no remembrance of my living days.
My death would be as unimportant as my life.
There would be someone to take the ledger in the office,
Someone would have my table in the automat,
There would be someone else at twilight in the rush hour
Pressing a coin down into the turnstile slot.
Only perhaps some small unobtrusive flower
No taller than my hand would come up there where
I, Singleman, would rot.

Yes, I have heard them often in the office
Dutch telling of a Swede he had seen the night before,
Harris of bicardi he drank in Cuba,
Milt of freights and lice and New Orleans.
I think how I would act in similar circumstances—
In county jails, in swell cafés, in hot Havana,
With waitresses, with black girls, burlesque queens.
I think of their adventures and romances.
Yes, you have heard me laugh and chuckle with the boys,
You have heard me boast above cigars,
But somehow they never asked me to their friendly dances—
I always paid for drinks we had at bars.

All my life I have been aware of failure—
I sucked it with my mother's milk.
I have dreamed and I have desired—
You have seen me with my face pressed to haberdashery windows,
You have known me when I studied law by night.
Do you imagine I have not wanted my name in electric light,
Or seen myself descend from limousines?
Do you imagine I am not aware of my disgrace?
If I had been born from a different mother,
If I had been reared in a different place,
If there was time enough to start all over,
I might have won against the world and scheming men,
I might have had cars as fine as that one's
I might have become the screen's great lover. . . .

Do not think I am not a sensitive man.
From the corner of my eye I glimpse their sneer.
I hear the cruel laugh behind my back.
I hate this room. I hate this life.
Do not think because you see me dressed in my business gray,
Smiling and pleasant and obedient among you,
I have no thought of suicide and death,
Iodine or a rope from the chandelier,
A razor swiftly drawn across my throat.
Do not think because I seem so meek among you
I have no thought of murder once alone.
The ox does not suffer humiliation,
Disgrace is never felt by a stone. . . .

But I, Singleman, yes, sometimes I lust to see the whole world
        overthrown. . . .

Yet change dreamed of brings no change.
Tomorrow the Frenchwoman may find me dead,
But still tonight I raise the window shade.
There are no stars, the sky is overcast,
The evening papers talk of snow perhaps, or rain.
Each of us has some secret grief, some private pain—
I, the Frenchwoman and the prison of my life,
The mystery that is my unfamiliar name.
Then wind the clock. Good night.
Tomorrow work again.

TO OTTO BAUER

Go Bauer praise their patience now
Walk in the ruined gardens of the Karl Marx Hof
Speak to these dead speak to them now
Next year this court may blossom iron trees
Flowers of steel spring up to trim the future lawns
Old corpses underground the Heimwehr plants
Next Spring may rise as shrubberies of bone.
But Spring can wait. These dead belong to February alone.

Listen. Beyond the waltztime river the city glows
Ascend your ministerial balcony again
Apologize to all these gentlemen
The shopkeepers forced to shut their shops four days
The ruined business in the street cafés
Her ladyship disturbed the maid in tears
Assure her she can wear her jewelry tonight
Then right the chairs and calm the chandeliers.
Behind the last of windows the last sniper falls
The trolleys run the provinces subdued new order reigns
Except for that routine the dark night hides—
The quick and muffled hangings in the prison yards
And here—the burials with black holes through their brains.

Yes, Bauer, Austria has need of you
The speculator businessman the summer bride
The daughter in the private school the dancing master
The lovers in the drawing rooms the cupids carved in plaster
The president of banks the little Richelieu
Who juggles class and state—have need of you.

But not these dead, not Florisdorf, not Linz, not Steyr,
Not the women with drawn faces, not the men with fire
In their unbeaten eyes, not these,
Who walk upon their feet, Bauer, not upon their knees.
They are not crushed, Bauer. The corpse upon the barricade—
Behold! is that of the betrayer not the betrayed!
The feet that dangled when the trapdoor clanged
Behold! is of the hangsman not the hanged!

In the ruined gardens of the Karl Marx Hof
These dead keep here their final discipline,
The iron front, the last republican defense,
That Heimwehr bullets now have locked them in.
No proclamations on the city's walls repeal,
No parliament can outlaw or suppress,
These unions of the dead, these cadres formed by steel.
You taught them patience, Bauer, to wait, wait,
Until the clock was over-run, the time long past
Until the hour when they struck, they struck too late.
But in the end these sightless eyes saw clear
Upon the barricade before the machine gun belt ran dry
In that huge moment, in the hot and reeking hour,
They knew at last how gun and hand grenade
Prepare the last great pathway into power!

All honor to them, Bauer! For you
History prepares a shameful grave
A nameless spot buried under weeds and stones
where creeping jackals shall come down to howl
Stirred by an ancient kinship with those bones!
But they—they sleep with Communards,
Their brother Spartacists lie at their side,
They marched forth Social Democrats but Bolsheviks they died!

A FRESCO FOR A. MAC LEISH

They are all dead: our reaching hands half a century long
Cannot restore them: a heap of bones there: a buffalo's whitened
    skull:
A buried tomahawk boys dig in a lost cave in the mountains:

A rusted wagon wheel with no spokes rotting in the sand in the sun:
These remain: these they left us:

$\qquad\qquad\qquad\qquad\qquad\qquad$ What shall we restore

Restoring them? Those stuffers of animal skins:
The museum men with field glasses: the bone-lovers:
The scientific ghouls: they stiffen the corpses:
They fix the representative stance: the correct pose: the historic
$\qquad$ gesture:

These antiques inspire memories not sad: not without glory:
They pushed back mountains: they took plains in their stride:
Their homesteads peopled a continent: their sons are with us:

Not the museum: the sunburnt face is produced with
A little lacquer: it is a fine art: children are impressed:
Also hollywood directors:

Abide with me awhile: there are always pioneers:
They are saddling new horses: buckling the cinches: waving goodbye:
Who's going along? they're saying out there there's new lands yonder:
Paths to be broken: and those higher mountains: new divides: new
$\qquad$ frontiers:
They resemble the old: but they're different: and they speak all
$\qquad$ languages

THE PORT OF NEW YORK

> This was the Promised Land, and still it is
> To the persuasive suburban land agent
> In bootleg roadhouses where the gin fizz
> Bubbles in time to Hollywood's new love-nest pageant.
> —HART CRANE

Magnificent to tourists and to tradesmen come,
Loaded with luggage, from voyage oversea,
Between shrill swoopings and the cabled air
White buildings lift a cue for praise.
Far out, upon the ocean's level rink
Where gulls are skaters, freighters and steamers,
Cunard liners, queens of the voyage,
Down on the world's curve curl one smudge of smoke
Farewell—and sink.

                    And now the port
Swells up to meet you. In the huge sunset,
Crowded with chimneys, terraces, grain elevators,
Ignite a million windows to the widened gaze,
A world afire—the city burning
In a towering architectural blaze.
                    O stranger welcome,
Feted with fire, but longing for the land,
Turn by the rail and see, where tall she stands,
Iron and green, and crowned with liberty,
Erect upon the bay, the rigid greeting of her hand!

Descend now gangplanks to the dock. Taxi
And hotel suite awaits you, who command
Bellhops and brilliance. Actress of screen,
Chief of staff, Minister or Financier,
You come upon us in a bitter year
Of bank failures and breadlines in the public squares.
Down South Street in one-arm joints
Sawdusted, crawling with flies—or in the Doghouse
Reading the shipping news—bronzed sailors,
Tattooed with blue anchors, naked women
In a Shanghai hophouse or maybe Samarkand,
Wait for a berth—who know all knots, riggings,
The wheel's kick and the gloryhole—ordering coffee and.
But still up Whitehall drape shipowners' flags
And hunger has not changed Trinity's known site.
Locked in their vaults, the gilt-edged shares repose all night,
And pigeons alone assault the Treasury's bronze doors.
Through bankrupts, panics, crashes, the Exchange,
Though shaken on its pillars, knows no change.

Safe in your room, unpack and watch the evening fall.
The lamps come suddenly to life, as though
Touched by a secret hand to tungsten glow.
After your supper, served in the hotel grill,
The night awaits you; sightseer's bus will take you round the town.
The barker will explain each famous sight.
The Mission of the Holy Name, the Bowery and Chinatown,
Hung with gold lanterns, tong wars—and further down
Through twisted streets to little Italy
And garlic smells—perhaps in Cherry Street you'll see
The celebration of the feat of Maria Negre, the black Mary,

Worshipped with white candles and pushcarts on the curb.
Peer through the smoky window, remember all the names you've
        heard;
Back home you'll quiver the persimmoned souls
Of village aunts with murder dives, gin mills and opium holes.
Up through Delancey smile at the derby hats and rabbi beards.
But through the motor's purr is still unheard
The sweatshop's hiss of steam . . . the Hoffman's pressing roar . . .
When drunken laborers come lurching through the swinging barroom
        door
Down on Third Avenue, under the El's shadow, think
What terrors the barker has not spieled has driven them to drink.
Then rumbling through Fourteenth you hit the Square.
And now Broadway again . . . this is the terminal, the end,
Lights! lights!—Times Square.

Through midnight throngs, under the dancing signs,
Among the tinhorn sports, the small time gamblers,
The hoofers out of work, the stenos taking in a show,
The restaurants with flapjacks and the Roseland Ramblers
Playing the latest dance hit—with thousands go.

Past stage entrances and billiard parlors
Where bookies pass out business cigarettes, the thousand faces
Shift, vanish in a neon fog, glimpsed once and gone
Rise up anew upon the tide, new eyes the flood replaces.
And glimpsed among the lights' hallucination
Pleasure laughs out of a trombone's mouth
Lifted in the Circle north or in the thunderous Square.
Hands grope to clasp her, but she eludes them there,
Though always they return to seek her vanishing face that soars
High above the Paramount clock or laughs from haberdashery stores.

Slow metropolitan bells empty the late theatres,
The richest to their homes upon the Drive.
But midnight sends the clerks and stenos home
By the last trains and nodding in their seats
In interborough slumbers, to dark and obscure streets
Where locals lurch and stop at silent stations.
Along deserted pavements where the thin moon leaks
Into quiet garbage cans, the feet awaken echoes.
Slip into the lock the hushed key quietly . . .
Slow snores gargle from hot rooms . . . here the bedroom

And the same bed . . . neatly fold the clothes on chair . . .
Pick out the office dress you'll wear . . .
Wind the stopped clock . . . the head sinks down in weariness,
Remembering the alarm, the muffled chorus of a song,
A face seen . . . then dark and sleep swallows the pursuit of happiness.

Tourist, turn in—or will you go
When watchmen on their rounds
Flash searchlights into shuttered department stores?
The lean cat bounding from the fence slinks
To the pool of rainwater, eyes warily about, and drinks.
The crosstown streets run both ways to the rivers
And trolleys empty trundle to silent barns.
The ferry hoots and sails the Jersey side.
The pilot trains the splayed beam on the tide.
You go now, leaning on the rail, to ride
The quietest of waters, downstream,
Past slaughter house and ironworks, the cattle yards,
Past viaduct and park and amusement place,
Until the river bending to the bay, lifts
To the sight the electric hand and the illuminated face.

Now from the brooding ragged men who nurse
Their sores in the grass on the small public lawns
Or seek the river's wharfed and warehoused side,
Yesterday's papers about their feet—what dreams
Awaken seeing across the slow and darkened tide
The apparition where her tall face gleams?
Once was she haven, harbor and desire,
Europe's better. Who knew the double eagle and the crested claw,
North England's hunger, or the pogrom's fire,
Ireland's landlords, or the great floods, sought her shore.
Cunningly she lured them, cunningly—
Who came in the ship's depths and in the land's depths died—
Some mine exploding explained their liberty,
These warehouses shelter all that's left of pride.

But brightly to the stranger lifts her hand,
And ragged though it is, her myth survives.
White buildings still amaze the visitors who land,
And lies conceal what hungers wreck our lives.
Who sought her as the sickened seek the sun,
No longer on her towering falsehood blind our sight.

Now in the iron shadow of the piers—swept
By the North Atlantic—though tall she stand—
Brightly as ever—with myth and hand—her myth is done.

IN A HOME RELIEF BUREAU

So it has come to this
In spite of everything it has come to this
This that did not figure in your dreams
This that had no place within your pride
Or when you labored to perfect your private schemes
A morning now like this when you would stand
A morning now like this public and ashamed
In the broken sunlight of a children's grammar school
Trying so hard to understand
Trying to grasp how it could happen to you
Trying to understand how this that could not happen
And seemed somehow always less than true
Has happened now at last to you.

That virgin's face before you
That face that shifts and tames its cold distaste
That thin nose saddled with distrustful glasses
Which invent smells, decays, dirt
That charity which is careful of its tweed skirt
Its polished hands, its manners, its uptown grace,
It does not recognize, accept, pity, or distinguish
Between these faces here and your face
Between their beggary and yours
Between their humiliated eyes and yours.
Neither this virgin's face soured over slums
Nor the faces of the guards who guard the doors
Nor that face glimpsed beyond the hall
Which waits for a scream, a shouted word, the spit of hate,
Which is alert to call
The riot wagons we are all aware of, wait.

And the minutes. And the hours.
But you have time to wait
Now there is nothing left you have but time.
What you were when you were not this

What you were before time brought you down to this
(Before the last policy was cashed
Before the last ring was pawned)
Now you have time enough to recall.
Think now of the profit and the pride
The ambition fed in furnished rooms
The nails kept clean against the imagined day.
The pressed suit, the manner honest and assured,
The undeceitful face,
Survives for this that once was not to be endured,
This charity, this disgrace.

To be signed. To be filed away.
To be referred to later by a girl or clerk.
To be remembered every day
To be remembered with the potatoes and the meat
With the canned milk and the landlord's knock
By that Italian combing his graying hair
By the aproned housewife with the kid in her arms
By the tired Jew in the interviewer's chair.
Age. Religion. Weight. Experience. Sex.
What once we were, what we have been is there
For the virgin to paw, for the faces frozen in smiles,
For a senator's speech, for a caught vote
To quiet the children when they scream
To keep the bones from breaking through the skin
To nourish what is left to us of life
This or the streets
This or the gas
This or a rope
This or a knife.

I ALWAYS COME HOME

The pretzel man ugly with warts and a crippled hand
The blind newspaper dealer in the fur cap at the newspaper stand

The hunchbacked clerk and the dieting girl whitewashed with powder
The counterman and the customers and the halfeaten clam chowder

What was expected? Angels in pressed tweeds?
This is how the beast looks. This is how it feeds.

You however must be drawing the bath naked in steam
On the toilet shelf the mascara brush, the polish, the cream

The bath salts, the hand lotions, the mouth rouge, the dye
Your hair screwed in a dark knot loose and pinned high

About you the smells of stoppered bottles and that other smell
A woman in a hot bathroom naked early in a big hotel.

I wait for the bus. The bus is late. The bus is always late.
Delivery trucks back up to freight entrances and unload freight

Will Dr. Abrams the dentist have a patient in the chair?
Whose pillows are hung out? Who has left his garbage on the stair?

I always end up home. Mail box is empty. What did I hope to find?
Telegrams from heaven. Love letters in longhand. And checks, signed.

SUCCESS STORY

Ride me around in your big blue car.
Where shall we eat tonight? At Maxie's.
Afterwards, the premiere. The dress-suit applause.
A quick scotch. And fast taxis.
Then Geraldine, smiling between the doors.
Thus our lives.

O the freedom of a thousand a week!

But those bigeyed on the curbs,
Those flattened against the restaurant windows,
Would they suspect
The agony of this wealth,
The soul hiding here and suffering under the starched shirt?
And the headaches, the constant depression,
The terrors of failure between rehearsal and opening night?

Of course there is my lawyer. 5 percent
    My agent. 10 percent
        My broker's fees.
The sleeplessness at night. I took a room with a river view.
    And the pains here, my heart, you know.
I'll leave. I must get away. What shall I do?
    Do you think I would like it in Mexico?

Let us unearth restaurants with mama's cooking
Drive the big cadillac through neighborhoods where we were young
Exercise the simple heart under the expensive tweed.
Nevertheless we must shave twice a day
Nevertheless we must have three guest rooms and a car
Nevertheless, despising these,
    There are our agent's,
        Our lawyer's,
            Our doctor's,
                Our broker's fees.

Joseph Kalar

WORKER UPROOTED

The slow sleepy curl of cigaret smoke and butts
glowing redly out of moving smiling mouths;
now a whisper in the house, laughter muted,
and warm words spoken no more to me.
Alien, I move forlorn among curses,
laughing falsely, joking with tears
aching at my eyes, now surely alien and lonely.
Once I rubbed shoulders with sweating men,
pulled when they pulled, strained, cursed,
comrade in their laughter,
comrade in their pain,
knowing fellowship of sudden smiles
and the press of hands in silent speech.
At noon hour, sprawled in the shade,
opening our lunches, chewing our sandwiches,
laughing and spitting,
we talked of the days and found joy
in our anger, balm in our common contempt;
thought of lumber falling with thump of lead
on piles geometrically exact; of horses
sweating, puffing, bulging their terrible muscles;
of wagons creaking; of sawdust
pouring from the guts of the mill.
Now alien, I move forlorn, an uprooted tree,
feel the pain of hostile eyes
lighting up no more for me;
the forced silence, the awkward laugh,
comrade no more in laughter and pain.

And at dawn, irresolutely,
into the void . . .

121

PAPERMILL

Not to be believed, this blunt savage wind
Blowing in chill empty rooms, this tornado
Surging and bellying across the oily floor
Pushing men out in streams before it;
Not to be believed, this dry fall
Of unseen fog drying the oil
And emptying the jiggling greasecups;
Not to be believed, this unseen hand
Weaving a filmy rust of spiderwebs
Over these turbines and grinding gears,
These snarling chippers and pounding jordans;
These fingers placed to lips saying shshsh;
Keep silent, keep silent, keep silent;
Not to be believed hardly, this clammy silence
Where once feet stamped over the oily floor,
Dinnerpails clattered, voices rose and fell
In laughter, curses, and songs. Now the guts
Of this mill have ceased their rumbling, now
The fires are banked and red changes to black,
Steam is cold water, silence is rust, and quiet
Spells hunger. Look at these men, now,
Standing before the iron gates, mumbling,
"Who could believe it? Who could believe it?"

AFTER THE STORM

(AUGUST 23, 1927)

Humbly to be now walking and talking,
Speaking low to men in black derbies,
Smiling now, laughing a bit, smiling,
Eyes gliding by gold tooth mouths,
Frog mouths twisted in cigar leers,
Spitting, talking, talking, talking,
Smirking, sneering, smirking:
Humbly now and sadly, walking and talking,
Tickling children under downy chins,
Drinking maybe, sleeping under warm bedcovers,

Feeling thighs and soft warm bodies, maybe,
Walking always, talking always, reading,
Eating breakfast and dinner, buying shoes,
Yawning sleepily over newspapers, writing
Letters, talking to men, running with boys,
Seeing with glad, warm eyes the suns and stars,
Feeling wind, hearing wind in the trees,
Counting grass blades or stars, maybe,
Living on, life flowing through and around me,
Certain, steady and low, with no ripples,
Pushing me, urging me on. Thus am I
Who shouted mad anger to the skies and spat
Most foully on walks in thought of that
Senile puppet who ruled that they should die,
That these two men who brought fresh winds
To heal the aching heart of the world
Should die; thus am I, who ground my teeth
In thought of fat men who ruled that gold
Should win, and that these two men should die.
Remembering them, forgetting them never,
I walk the streets, talking, talking, talking,
Hoping for something, having lost something,
Knowing that never will I be the same, yet
Talking always, walking always, living
As always, knowing that forever now
That cup shall be filled with remembering hate,
And I shall live on with love for two good men
The senile living corpse ruled must die.

INVOCATION TO THE WIND

O sprinting of the wind over land
like a colt galloping swift
pounding over grass, neighing
to the sun, snorting howdoyoudo
to the clouds, with a flying mane—
O wind coming over the lean land
like a fatness of green in spring
or flowers blooming in Mojave
blow, blow into all dusty corners,

reach cool fingers beyond cobwebs
festooning this dark room where
throats are choked with dust and
beauty shrivels like mushrooms
in dry cellars—blow, blow, blow
into factories with windows of dust
and a shuffling of feet tired
in silk stockings, and fingers
red at the tips—blow, blow into
jail, come like a draught of spring
water to faces hungering against
steel bars—blow, blow into slums,
cleave the darkness festering
in mines, coal and iron, glide over
pale children bowing in beetfields—
blow wind, sprint over the land
like a colt pounding over grass—
rattle the shutters of this dark room
where beauty whimpers softly like a child—
O surely someday we'll fill the fields
with our dancing and laughing and singing,
O wind coming over the lean brown land
or flowers creeping over Majove!

NOW THAT SNOW IS FALLING

O the sky shall crack with laughter
now that snow is falling,
and all small timid things shall scent
frozen petals of white and feel
knifeblades of cold sink into fur;
yes, the bear shall suck his toes,
and ants will sleep.
If the sun, coming slowly after,
warms flies from frozen lethargy
to crawl again upon window panes,
and you and I, hand in hand,
shall make tracks in the snow,
woollen gloves, and necks bound warmly
against knifeblades of cold, and we
shall say: O most surely is the snow

beautiful, and ask, what can we say
now that snow is falling, and all
the world is white, and clean, and beautiful,
what can we say but that snow is beautiful
and cold tingles the sleepy blood
into new surging awareness—what can
we say if the sky is most suddenly rent
with laughter, trees crack with mirth,
and sparrows chatter in derision, as
a man walks by us clad thinly, shivering,
hungry, vainly searching for bread,
a job, and warm fires; what can we say,
if such a man passes us bowed against
the wind, and another, and yet more,
until he is as a multitude, a sad parade
of hungry, cold, vague faces? What can we
say, now that snow is falling?

THUNDER IN A MOMENT OF CALM

O lightning! slice the sky
with sudden amazing grins of flame.
O thunder! shout hoarsely from the sky
your deep black throated challenge
to all small fragile trembling things.
O thunder! beat upon us,
have no pity for us,
who stand idly in the street
with dust in our eyes
awaiting rain
talking softly now or smirking
over nothing and nothing,
fumbling secretly for the wounds
of the week's unbeautiful toil
(bitterly sterile)
while there before us
the warm friendly earth
smiles and beckons and commands:
Comrades: take me, I am yours.
O thunder! chastise us
that for one instant

we should be humble
before these foul derbied men
flipping frayed cigars
into the street
from autos passing.
Enter into us hugely.
Give us of your roar
that we may have speech
for what we really mean to say.
Teach us your mad splendid fury.
Bring to us tokens of the storm
that shall bring the long awaited rain
to ease the parched aching throats
of men standing sullenly in the streets.

BANK

Be proud be proud whimpers
the bank be proud with
compound interest and
mortgages on farms lean
and not so lean . .
O blueprint under eyes
manifestly curves pillars
burglaralarms O eyes
warm with wine of massive
granite . . .
Addingmachines, ledgers,
president with black cigar,
and bookkeeper scanning
stockexchange reports have
a beauty too . .
Be proud be proud workmen
glance at surplus fund
deposits receipts with eyes
warm as eyes gliding over
what must not be said . . .
Be proud be proud whimpers
the bank be proud to a bum
with crooked legs and cinders
in his eyes be proud to a bum

diffidently picking at his nose
and with blunt nails,
scratching at his ear.

POOLROOM FACES

Faces floating in a poolroom fog,
faces flowering out of collars
and shirts like greenhouse cabbages,
faces with eyes tired, eyes like pools
filmed over with fog, sad and vacant eyes
like bright coals burned to grey cinders.
Men sitting on poolroom chairs
staring at the floor with vacant eyes
blinking as the last billiard ball
rolls smooth as hell into the right pocket;
seeing and not seeing, seeing phlegm
glistening like jewels in the yellow light,
smoldering cigarette butts, gum wrappers,
cigaret packages; hearing sharp sudden click
of billiard balls, low loving entreaties
of players finding life concentrated in a cue.
Faces, now so unlovely and sad,
were you ever wise and resolute? O corpse faces,
pasty faces, dead faces, did your eyes
ever smoulder with creative hate?

Faces growing on that evil sour apple tree,
withered fruit of sour poisoned stalk,
sad harvest of work and looking for work,
harvest of mine, harvest of factory,
harvest of lumbercamp and sectiongang,
poolroom faces gazing at poolroom floor,
waiting, thinking maybe, wishing a little,
praying for strong men to plow the sour soil!

REPENTANT JUDAS

When the five o'clock whistle blows
he comes to stand beside the iron gate,
faint hunger in his eyes and twitching shame
in his hands, lips mumbling old stories
known as lies. Pressing against a car,
glancing at the men swarming from the mill
with swinging dinnerpails and a walk
much too stiff for buoyancy, not an eye
that sees him but grows hard and cold,
not a lip but tenses into a sneer,
not a hand but twists into an iron vise.
He stand there monument to our shame,
ugly echo of the day we lost our fear
and felt it fall from us a heavy weight
and STRIKE! felt the power in our hands
thrust toward the ceiling in a chorus of ayes,
yes, by god, STRIKE! and saw eyes shining
with remembered purpose, knew again
the proud magic of a clenched fist. He led us,
his words were the mirror to our hopes.
Day after day, the net of his phrases
spun craftily, unbeautifully encompassing,
water drenching clear flame to cold ashes.
Then one day, a conference held secretly,
the nodding of heads, the scratch of a pen,
and cigars chewed quite powerfully
by sleek sullen jaws. And we went back,
knowing again the old story forgotten,
some with feet leaden and the spirit dark,
some thrusting a finger into every wound,
and some braver for defeat, pain and hate
generating visions of a new dawn. While he,
he stayed outside. Alien eternally to our dreams,
our suffering, and our hope, to die at last,
potbellied and alone, brother only to contempt.

NOTHING TO LOSE

As piles of sand disintegrate when sucked
by the wet urgent tongue of the sea—
as one about to die finds life escaping
like rush of air from a punctured tire——
as a house gnawed by red teeth of flames
falls at last to ashes and ashes——
so now the land we love, comrade,
so now the dreams we dreamed,
so today and all the hours. . . .

Hunger is with us.
Factory smoke is sour
with the memory of work
to be done
and a wild look in the eye:
no work today, buddy, no work. . . .
Hunger is with us, it is a rodent
that chews flesh from us
that drops dung on our joys
that dogs our steps blackly
a shadow you can't outrun,
hunger is waiting,
hunger loves you,
hunger is with us, brother.
O now the grease will surely
leave your fingernails
and cinders will surely
leave those eyes alone
for a wild look in the eye:
no work today, buddy, no work,
no, no work, no work, buddy,
the old system
can't squeeze out another job for you,
can't find a loaf of bread for you;
that for you, brother,
a fig for your pains,
a sneer for your love
and spittle on your dreams.

Nothing to lose anymore,
gone now the lies

the beautiful lies
the red white and blue lies,
nothing to lose anymore, comrade,
nothing to lose now but your chains.

This is a new day, brother,
come gird your loins with me,
spit on your hands——
(no more time for dreams)
a big job is waiting
hard work needs completion——
a big job is waiting
and is tired of waiting,
for men like you, brother,
who find Hunger a comrade
with a lean embrace——
and for you too, brother,
with smoke in your eyes
and grease on your nails
and a paycheck smaller and smaller
and hours that seem
never to end
and a boss that demands of your strength
till it seems to snap——
a big job for us today
a big job for us today
Nothing to lose anymore, comrade
nothing to lose but our chains.

Don't you remember the days
that left us rotting with sleep
and we lay as one etherized
thinking that dreams could last?
don't you remember the days
when that flag meant something
and the blood thrilled
to the red white and blue?
Listen, comrades, have you forgotten
the lies we embraced,
the lies that offered us dugs
full of milk
to soothe our anger
and embalm our wisdom?

Have you forgotten, comrade,
the finger of scorn we pointed
at comrades who shook us from sleep
and told us a big job was waiting
and sang the wonders
of the workers' fatherland?
Gone now, all gone, brother,
gone now the lies
the beautiful lies
the red white and blue lies——
nothing left us but this hunger
nothing left us but this hate
nothing left us but these hands
and a job that's tired of waiting. . . .

Nothing to lose anymore, comrade,
nothing to lose but our chains!

NIGHT-SHIFT

Sleep aches deeply in the eyes; taste of ashes
dryly sands the mouth, while lips are cracked
with mouthing gobs of stale brown plug;
hours have no periods, no precision, they
are merely hours, stretching into dawn
like a haze of fog greyly lifting over lumber
to warm compulsion of the sun; they are merely
the aching cry of the body for sleep, sleep,
sweet, sweet Jesus, sleep, sleep, the far cry
of drowsy tired blood: sleep, sleep, sleep.

Into the night, body a hunch against darkness,
jostling and bouncing on a wagon rigid
with stiffness, permitting no dreams of cotton,
creaking, groaning, a clot of shadow urgently
propelled down dark canyons of lumber, poking
fragrant load of pine between rows of piles
darkly reminiscent of western canyons of stone,
thoughts swarm drowsily behind the eyes of this man
who stares vacantly at the giant swell and roll
of horse buttocks dark and heaving before him,

thinking no more while muscles bulge terribly
like pistons moving smoothly under hide,
and the body is only a remembered cry for sleep.

In the morning when dawn has crept over the sky,
lips are a thin line not curving into the glow
of a smile, eyes are a lesson in brooding and vision,
and hands clutching at leather reins are ominous
with significance; tho sleep is a phlegm of weariness
clotting his mind, hate is knowledge incandescent,
bright illumination for a mind busy with planning,
and hands are rich with promise of a tomorrow
in which dreams will sprout beautifully into action,
and throats harsh with cursing will shout terribly
the word that will give meaning to hours,
precision to time, significance to bodies
now but a far painful cry in blood for sleep.

H. H. Lewis

UNHOLY ROLLER

Of those who muck in Mammon's total mess
For various little lumps to overstress,
Who damn the morsels but condone the maker,
Bellows a certain sacrilegious faker.
    A one-time Socialist, not quite so punk
About *the* most entrancing *bit* of Bunk;
Then on the ship that needs a bolder crew
Than simpering bastards of the parlor hue,
He craned at eddies. . . . One, Agnosticism,
Whirling upon the route to Socialism,
As foxes whirl beneath the roosting prey,
Enthralled his weakness,—got the stowaway.
    Full-windedly he's floating yet, a spoil
Calming the *status quo* with ooze of oil. . . .
    Why pound its flea then give the cur a hug?—
For "capitalism works"—to feed the bug!
Why boot the shade then kiss the fact, of Pelf?—
Only to make sensation, further self!
Vile hypocrite, all unction when it's due,
A fascist-hearted liberal through and through,
He's Mammon's court-diverter, very odd
With the mauled old dummy known as God.
    His Atheist Church, avowed to set us free
As rational souls amid demockracy,
Has comfy tenets for the bourgeoisie.

They come, mere futile puffs of literate pride,
To clap his BUNK, amen his Godicide.
Here swells a convert who, if born to need
And lammed to work before he learned to read,
Had never known these sacrilegious thrills
And the "poised breadth of mind" above the "nils."
Now see him scorn the "rabble"—yet he owes
As much to leisure as a dude to clothes.
And here's a college kid *almost persuaded*,
Tugged by the schismic ghosts, by each upbraided;
He doubts, he dampens: oh, the trial's intense
"To make the world safe for intelligence."
    How many spirits can caper on a pinpoint?
As many as there are Atheists at the din-point!—
Fanatic nothings who can only scoff
And jig likewise to keep the others off:
Proving that metaphysics can result
In either a Christian or an Atheist cult.
    Through *here* the Wolf, quite godless for the scene,
Drags Destitution in and all between;
Though cynic Vultures darken like a cloud
To batten *here unhated*; though the loud
Maniacal laughter-clap and hoot of Mars
Peal from his paper-prison, mock the bars,
Resound above this "rationalism,"—though
Heaven's the *consolation*, not the woe.
    How does it help the social situation
To worship either GOD or GOD-NEGATION?
Can more "free thinking" drive the fascists out,
Put hunger, war, and millionaires to rout?
Why throw up barricades against the Lord?
To clown for the pleased plutes ho-hoing hard?
    Is Mammon not proprietor of the show
And God his dummy? Answer here below.
Say it, you scotched avoiders, yes or no!

I'LL SAY!*

Plowin' undah cotton,
Plowin' undah cotton,
Gee, yeou 'fraidy hawah,
Helping "man fuhgotten."

Uh needs a paiah o' britches,
Mirandy needs a skuht,
Lil Da-Da needs a diddy
Aroun' its nekid butt:—

Dis donkey, uset tuh middles
En' 'fraid o' ruinin' rows,
He needs tuh luhn dat cotton
Ain't really meant fuh clothes.

Plowin' undah cotton,
Plowin' undah cotton,
Haw, yeou 'fraidy geeah,
Sumpin' sho is rotten . . .

*"Haw" means "come to the left," "gee" means "come to the right."

ROAD TO UTTERLY

Such a dismal lot to see
On the road to Utterly. . . .

Hill erosion-ruined by Spoil
With deluging sweat of Toil,
Not a tree surviving, no
Grassy green forgiving-show,—
Ever blaming, boding ill,
Monumental mummyhill.

Now Depression's added pall
Glooming over hill and all;
Sown the bad and reaped the worse
By the evolving Mammon-curse.

Weeds unsickled on the lawns
Of evicted woe-begones,
Windows ever pining there
With the shadeless stark stare.

—As a native can but see
On the road to Utterly.

On the ridge that grayly runs
Through the South of Native Sons,
Past the cotton-minded ones,
Toward the town of Utterly.

(((Where, beyond the eye and ear,
Indians prospered, even here)))
On the road,
Now the road,
This the road of hunger-fear . . . . .

Nordic living hand-to-mouth,
Beggared by a little drouth.

"Nigger Ninteenthirtyfoured,
Working for his bed'n board.

Workers stooping in a clump,
Black and White and all a-lump,
Grayishly blended by the Slump,
Men and women, "vag" and "frump,"—
Picking at a garbage dump.
See:
Now an old "retired" Hump
Limping
Back to
Utter-
Ly.

Worse the Load,
Sharp the Goad
On the road to Utterly.

II

Road beside which I was born
At a century's hopeful morn,
While as yet each dawning day
Cast a forward future-ray
Gilding well the *status quo*
With an aural glamor-glow,—
Rousing up the fortuneless
But to dreamings of SUCCESS.

Road that lured my feet afar
As beneath a guiding star.

Road that mocked me crawling back
Hopeless in the *cul-de-sac*.

III

From that old-portentous hill,
Through the plowing-under ill,
Even to the Bank-head Bill,

Year by year and day by day,
Whether Hyde or Wallace pray,

Worse by every mad decree,
Worse since Nineteen-thirty-three,—
Bitter road to Utterly.

IV

Course that blindly forward wends,
While another Hope impends,
Through the worst to be;
Trending as a river trends,
Even with the backward bends,
Toward the sea;
Till the profit-system ends,—
That's the road to Utterly.

GONE WEST

I

   The old-time Yanks, becoming poor, oppressed,
Got as by instinct ever hopeward—West!
Like the moon's pull then flow of habitual tide,
That cosmic uplift: Out to freedom's wide!
Were wages low and Wealth above the laws?
Then lifeward, whee! away from social flaws!
From rented farms and Moloch-rumbling mills,
From deadly slums and all gregarious ills;
Thus brightly toward the vistas trailing far,
Then airily through the prison door ajar—
Away, away, awa-a-a-a-ay beyond the hills!
With whoops of soul-expansion
In space profoundly good,
With great uplift of backbone
On breath of hardihood,
With a brave, glad bound to what unfurled:
Oh! . . . O World!
   Not like the jobless meanly after bread,
But like the strong lion nobly fled
He came. Two Sturdy Hands opposing all,
And shoved his ego through the forest wall.
The *individual*:
To log a cabin "good enough for me"—
Far from the manor of the mortgagee!
To burn the brush and plant a fertile plot,
To reap—his harvest whether good or not,
His weal and woe, one everlasting cheer,
"A dang-long-ways" from the profiteer!
   Nature's Olympic view of sky and ground,
Anarchial freedom privately refound,
And the grand sweep of ownership around—
It sunk to bone and there intensified
His-to-the-youngster's *self-dependent pride*.
   Then came two "fureign fellers" acting droll
With a look-through dingus and a painted pole—
Then gangs of Irish, fond of exercise,
Filling the lows and ditching through the highs
Twelve hours per day beneath a boss's bawl—
Then spike to rail—and then, with a loud toot,

The Age of Steel, the loco-motive brute!
Like clangorous Cæsar forcing into Gaul.
   Until the hoary settler learned again
The ways of money with the ways of men,
The hard-souled competition and the squeeze—
But from his own view now a mortgagee's
   From which the tide of proletarian quest
Was moving, moving, moving, farther, farther—West!

II

   As the last smoke curled from the cannon's mouth
And the gash flopped shut along the red suffusion—
After the slaves were "freed" and that pretence
Had drummed enough for industry's moral sense—
The working-bleeding stiffs of North and South
Both faced defeat, hard times, and disillusion.
"Go West, young man," resounded full of aim.
Then like our solar parent when she hurled
That seething essence forth to form a world,
Pent disillusion shot a creative flame
Far out to freedom, *individual claim*.
   And here the Germans, Britons, Swedes and more
Were also coming, faster than before—
Washed from the gaunt hills of feudalism,
Down from the serfdom of democratism,
The real old peasant marl, good for ground,
Eager to spread itself—Amerika-bound!
   That day was epic: the symphony of life
Awoke from trait bound deeps of destitution,
Awoke and shattered its bars,
Quavered eager and rife,
Sang to the sheer mountains and the stars,
Thundered for the escapist revolution.

III

   Well, here we are, ha! bumping fate again,
Millions, millions, millions of idle men!
There's no escaping *now*: from shore to shore
That individual trend can move no more. . . .

FIVE MINUTES, OLEO

Ole Olson,
"Prominent farmer of this community,"
Paused at the bottom rung of the ladder leading from the hallway of
     his barn, up through the loft, up toward a rafter.
Many a time he had mounted that total height to throw hay down
     from a crammed harvest.

But now—
His purpose very different.

Forty rungs in that ladder,
Worn glossy by the callouses of as many years!
To climb now,
Pausefully,
Reluctantly,
Was to epitomize it all . . .

Never had he been called lazy.
In Minnesota, across the flat visibility of the Swedish township, his
     woman's kitchen-light had always been the first to appear at
     morning, his lantern the first to go swinging barnward;
Five miles away some Erik prompting, "Greta, Greta, time to get up,
     that Olson's at his cows";
All the local Knutes pillowed conveniently beside windows that faced
     the *center*:
Ole the free alarm clock,
Ole the pace-setter,
"Pushing on the reins."

Never had he been called extravagant.
"Oleo" becoming "Alarm Clock's" other nickname after a gossipy
     neighbor discovered him selling all his butter and eating
     oleomargarine.

Never had he been called a poor manager—
"Keeping books" for the Extension Service of the State College of
     Agriculture, filling the blank spaces in big annuals, achieving
     more than a mere-factive ledger, a heartfelt diary of his
     heydays
From the World War to the World Depression,
Till *loss* became too remindful.

Now once more upon the ladder,
Up to the crossbeam holding the framed parchment MASTER FARMERS
      OF AMERICA, his own name gorgeously calligraphed hereunder
      as one of the 48 so honored for 1927—
He extended a gnarled finger,
Fondlingly,
Tremblingly,
Rubbing away some fly-specks . . .
Up to the roof at last,
He opened his eyes again, facing the cowled hay-entrance, and peered
      out upon the familiar landscape shimmering in earthlight real;
And he gripped the rung tighter,
Holding on,
Holding on,
And he rested chin upon it, looking . . .
Could Heaven itself be dearer?
But could Hell be worse than banishment alive from *this*?
Ole Olson,
Not praying to God and Frazier-Lemke any longer,
Removed a coil of rope from his shoulder, tying one end to a rafter
      and the other around his neck.

II

"Scratching like a mole,
Dusty old soul,
Oleo, Oleo-Ole."
Ole, Ole, Oleo-Ole, *
Longest-houred clodsman in the country whole,
Worst to hirling roustabouts from Pole to Pole,

Had he jumped,
Was he dead?
Satan taunting him with that old ditty?

No,
Worse yet,
Sounds like Nels Nelson!
Mortification at death's door—

---

*Concocted years ago by a Yankee harvest-follower, this being doubly vicious because
Ole does not rhyme with whole, the mispronunciation still parroted by certain local
Swedes for pure damned meanness.

His former hired man, the belly-aching Bolshevik, the organizer in
        the Farmers' Holiday Association,
That fellow at just *this* time
Popping into the hallway below!

III

Two hundred pitchfork-men waiting yonder,
Tines sharp as the logic of Lenin,
Courthouse-bound to prevent a number of foreclosures by threat of
        low bidding:
Nelson announces,
Palming his timepiece with a flourish toward the one who has stopped
        trying to de-noose himself quickly enough.

"All right now,
If you can decide to be saved dy 'damn Reds,'
Five minutes, Oleo" . . .

NOW WHAT GOOD THAT DO?

Today on the folly-made desert,
Where the greenness once grew tall,
Where the bison roamed and the tribesman homed
With food enough for all,—
Out there on the ruin of Kansas,
In the duststorms grown severe,
Came a Voice profound from the wind around
And spoke against my ear.

"White man shove off Red man,
Start plow work like hell,
Want put mon in bankhouse,
Got grow worth crop sell.
Dang wheat dry out subsoil,
Then come no-rain too . . .
White man shove off Red man,
Now what good that do?"

Downtown in the ruins called Denver,
Where the "hoboes" stand and stare,

Where the eyes would glaze in the deathlike daze
At sharkboards mocking-bare,—
It seemed like a Touch at my shoulder,
Like a Shade to haunt me then,
Till the mood could hear, on the scene so drear,
That same old Voice again.

"White man build great big burg,
Heap few glom much roll,
Rest make fun 'bout Red man
Wash in town crap bowl.
Then come this here layoff,
Bad kind joke on you . . .
White man build great big burg,
Now what good that do?"

THE SWEETER OUR FRUITS . . .

It was said that oranges could not be
      grown in the Soviet Union.
But there they are—
A new strain
Developed by cross breeding Horticulture to Socialism.

Where Wrangel's army was to defeat the Reds,
Now the citrus groves,
Triumphantly fruitful,
With golden death-rays,
Vanquish the ghouls of another wish-prediction.

There, O Massman,
Lift a festival beaker,
Drink
This tart sweetness of revenge
To the health of your comrades all over the world.

Behind clenched teeth
In hells of "democracy" and fascism,
We taste
What you taste,
Your joy

Is our joy—
Of the inspiriting example.

Before 1918 we were "visionaries,"
Socialism "against human nature,"
But now
We point
        To Red Russia.

The sweeter our fruits,
The bitterer to profiteers.

THE MAN FROM MOSCOW

The American workingclass is a big-boned charmaid
Muscled like a man;
Direct, simple-hearted and vulgar:
An Amazon
With great passionate dugs and a potent womb,
Whew!
A real man's woman!

The Knight of Labor was a wan boy and passed off before coming
        into his own.
The Anarchist never did know how.
The Wobbly was game, he plunged right in for direct action, but soon
        petered out and went haywire.
The A. F. of L-ite has been fixed so that he cannot create
        abomination against respectability.
The Proletarian, strumming the Marxian uke and singing one
        manifesto after another, gets no farther.
And the queer Socialist—shame forbid!—dress-suited and manicured
        and nice, nice, the queer Socialist!

But the Man from Moscow!
Ahah!
The international villain,
The international hero,—
Young Lochinvar from the whiskery Left!
Aha-a-a-a-ah!
The MAN from Moscow!

The impotents sulk off into the background and lurk forlornly.
William is Green with jealousy.
The Proletarian slumps to the ground and distractedly mumbles pure
        theory.
And poor Nor-man Thomas, a minister, tsk, tsk, God help him!
All in the background
Relegated to a blur of undistinctiveness,
Fading, fading out. . . .

Hark!
Do they not hear Gastonian cries of conception?
Has not the Man from Moscow
Started something?

JUST FOR PROPAGANDA

No unemployed in Russia now
Because of communism?
No hungry at the pauper's vow
By rule of bolshevism?
No aged out of pensionhood,
Nor youthful forced to pander? . . .
The Wrong Idea "doing good,"
It's just for propaganda!

It's just for propaganda, pshaw,
It's just for propaganda,
Outraging economic law,
It's just for propaganda;
Ulterior purpose driving Reds
To stunts appearing grander:
A *hoax* to turn our muddleheads,
It's just for propaganda!

A renaissance for world-acclaim
From Poland to Pacific?
Where art can serve the social aim,
And proudly does, prolific?
Where culture rears the dreaming boy
To live a life of candor? . . .
Too Red, too Red, the Russian joy,

It's just for propaganda!

It's just for propaganda, pooh,
It's just for propaganda,
Whatever fine the Russians do,
It's just for propaganda;
The darkest motives urging them
To lull our righteous dander:
This all-so-peaceful *stratagem*,
It's just for propaganda!

STAR RIDE

Though it seemed, to childish wonder,
Even then somewhat bizarre,
Once I heard the preacher saying,
Hitch your wagon to a star.

So I put a length of plowline
To my wagon's pulling-bar,
Stood at night upon the smokehouse,
Trying to lasso me a star. . . .

Preacher, preacher, what the dickens,
Just a spoofer, that you are,
Telling me to hitch my wagon,
Hitch my wagon to a star!

But with Lenin as the preacher,
After childhood, after war,—
How my freedom-loving spirit
Has been
Lifted
By
The
Star! . . .

Star in the East,
New faith released,
While the most of mankind lingers in duress.

Star to rebirth,
Brotherhood of earth,
Future ringing, ringing, ringing out redress
Till the most afar
Hail the freedom-star
Over their U.S.—
S.R.!

Norman Macleod

NEWSREEL

1

Magnolias of the south were a silver fragrance
In the blackbloom of the sun and the white
Hearts of the people were quiet with warmth
And the beer was a conviviality for the mouth.
The mammies were its legacy and were shed
Like shingled roofs of rain; and the pickaninny
Sound of the weather was a growth
For the soil until the black bucks came
Like factory funnels to a human drouth.

2

The hunger of our hearts was lost in the jungle
Of metropoles and we slank like jackals
(Forest footed) in the alleys
Hunting for refuge: there were none
To find us relief and the constant desire
Was paled in the image of day
And we were blinded: the staffs of our life
Were insufficient and our thought
Decrepit: we were a lost cry in the canyons
And the arroyos of sound were echoed back
To refute us. There was nothing for us to gainsay
That could offer security
(From hour to hour we were a brood
Of sorrow) and the pulse of the streets
Was a fever of sickness.
The deathbeds of our hearts were lost
In the linger of dying: we were single in our pain
And cold: we could not hunt together.

3

Cries of the peddlers were a market in the city:
The wares of their life were commodities
For relief and we knew them by a scale of prices.
We often bought them for an assimilation
Of experience but found that they fouled the air
And our hearts were lost in the welter.
We haggled with the poverty of their speech
And found it had overshadowed their homes
And left them penniless of grief.
We could never find sympathy in our hearts
To believe them: we chose to be
Outside the pale of their sorrow
(Having enough of our own
To know occupation): we never left for the country
Because we paled in the distance and the sun
Was no orb of fire to warm us
Who had so long been cold and unidentified
In the heart of the city (but nevertheless
We slept in the sound of their commerce
And we woke to the selfsame cries).

4

The cinema of individual life (before us)
Was a stretch of indeterminate years:
The continuity of sorrow was interspersed
With 'laughter and tears'.
We were assured by the boards of censor
That the end would be happy
And that the marriage of our hearts would be
A denouement not without standing.
We were reckless with the expenditure
Of our souls and our hearts were given to many.
The characters of interloper were forgotten
(We knew that none had died
Until the memory had fouled him).
Our hands were clenched with whiteness
And our brows were ridged with sorrow.
Many episodes were deleted but we often
Remembered: each reel was an overlap
For another. We strained our eyes
But we could not see ahead.

5

We admitted the plight of our hearts in the city:
The harbors of night were so far remote
As to be an excursion: from travail in the womb
Of the metropolis.
We never went to the top of the buildings.
The thought of our lives was lost
As the captions of relief from dying.
There was nothing we could do
That others had not done before us
We were pale as the spit of light
In the facet of waters.

DEATH IN THE CITY

The city had no color for our hearts:
Amazons of light were shafted upon our brows
And our eyes were facets for indiscretion
To gimlet the mind with ice.
The experience of our single bodies
Was denied and we sought
For the universal thought
In the mind's alleys: always
We went beyond the curtailment of night
And wandered in the canyons of concrete
And steel.
The sound of former death
Was indistinguishable as light
Cresting the skylines.
There was nothing to do but die
In the tenement districts
And the thought of tomorrow was effaced
From the crystallization of any hour.
We were lost as much
Through the single birth of a child
As the concession of death to the homeless.
We were not wayward because we knew
We were not staunch enough
To battle the walls of the city.

DESIGN IN COTTON FABRIC

The children are born with the taste of cotton root
In the mouths of their mothers (desperate
With the thought of more to feed with starvation
Already a boarder). And they grow up to see
Their fathers slave picking cotton until
Their heads are whiter than any field in the fall.
And they grow up to the facts of their poverty
And with hope they enter the mills to be spinning
And weaving (and they manage to live by the grace
Of a god who is absent of memory and a hell of a distance
Away). And they die and are buried with a solemnity
Unwitnessed and the lint
Of cottonwoods (which has no commercial value)
Covers their graves.

NOT STEEL ALONE

After so many years of desperate quiet
and silence has grown, knitted with midnight
in the heart, in bone,
into reverberations that the mind shadows
beneath the transit of the sun
swung in a long arc across the desert,
After sudden distance from mountain heights
and hunger for snow against the sky
and people, the warmth of flushed proximity
to men and children, women and men,
here in this closely intricated metropolis
there are complications of steel and stone,
life more perpendicular
leaning upon smoke and the sound of factory,
and the frenetics of living, working
hurrying, starving
and in the welter of lost humanity,
Santa Claus comes once a year
with a bedtime story
in shopwindows, on street corners
clanging a bell for pittance. . . .

And I think of the desert of silence once again
where life is tensed to earth and quiet,
not steel alone.

STEEL MILL REVERSAL

That year there were many communications
From the revolution: a steelworker
Bared his brawny heart, breatsed with strength
And furred with the hair of his sweat
And his labor: he said what we all feel
And I won't repeat it. You have seen the dawn
Come up in the scarlet way of a red factory
And the burnish of steel: the barbwire there
And the uniformed thugs and the piles of brass
In the background. The blast furnaces are
Running like the time of the era, and the workers
Have been swept along with their leaders.
Their revolt is latent and hoarded
Against the year beyond convalescence.
They presume to suppose the fixity of definition
In the class alignments and are readily
Informed of their enemies. It is not too much
To seek the end of this supposition: the armed
Of their mass in arsenal reversion
Will be a field of bayonets with the conquested
Audible airplanes flying above them
And their bombs exploding as reports of a new day.

COAL STRIKE

The darkened hills around the mine at Coverdale
Curled like a blacksnake whip to break us
But our picket line was dangerous
As white hot cables of steel in the factory
Of our revolt. The shaft of the coal mine
Was a black silence in the early morning.
There were no scabs could penetrate the cordon

Of strikers. The deputies were yellow faced
In the grey dawn: it was too early for them to be out
With the dark brown memory of debauchery
Before them. For courage they needed
The tin hats mounted behind them. Their rifles
Were rested up the horns of their saddles
And their faces were unwashed of their adolescence,
Too young and yet weakly brutal.
We were stronger than the coal operators
And the mounteds and scabs, because we had many years
In the mines to harden us. Shoulder to shoulder
We had come to know our common purpose.
We were not fuel as the coal but a welded metal
And we could flash death like any steel.

SHADOWBOX: IN A MILLTOWN

Always he shadowboxed himself on Sunday evenings
when color ran riot into the evergreen
that hedged the sunset horizon to the west.
There was within his eyes knowledge of geraniums
(how futile red and what they meant to railroads.
how could a railroad be other than it is
with no flower pots around dim desert stations,
wrapped in deceitful silence and wind in the shadows falling
where mournful color was the echo of all sound
penumbrous, prone upon evening).
Flowered in his brain were fetishes of evil
. . . saying no sin was ever quite like this
and none existent, rather a euphony of sad illusions
built upon the evidence of mind decaying
clad with survival emblems of a pseudo-beautiful disease.
He wrapped himself forever in the garden of his mind
showered with golden cataclysms, sun-explosive
and shadowboxed all patentcy of death.
Drunk with wine or with being, he would go
when dusk was an archaism of the night
and the shield of dark was pierced with phantom light
(yellow as the point of myriad sun-fire)
and knock upon the door of some good neighbor

to ask for Casanova or his present whereabouts—
only to be met with disapproval, the eyes set querulous
or the blank face of an empty door.
This was matter for hilarity or secret mirth
and he would blaze with laughter in the street,
bent double by improvidence of all mankind
(such humorous repartee). And the wine within
would flush his brain and countenance until one thought
the very image was satanic but reft of any threat contagious
(and in this be deceived). He moved within a cultivated circle
wherein he figured multiplicity and shadowboxed
himself into the night.
He worked by day as checker for some lumbermill
(heard the blue machinery that whined throughout his sleep
or woke to see the fire on the sky
or heard the creaking of the belts or some whistle blowing),
but when he knocked off work sufficient to the day,
he went back to his room to curse the maid
for ordering the chaos of his books or shuffling the manuscripts
he annotated with sidereal comment
(that no one could decipher or guess the meaning of).
He would fume and fret and finally withdraw
the wine from out the cupboard to drink into the night.
(the *Dial* was always in such prominent display,
and Schnitzler's *Casanova's Homecoming* was the handiwork of god.
Rupert Brooke was pretty and read upon occasion,
but to remark upon the futile idealism of the youth
slaughtered in life and war).
But mention should be made of women, the damaging of goods
to spice a dreary life. Always there would be
some wench behind the door, tittering and rumpled,
and breathing in so audible and this despite
practiced confusion (and perfume would be reeking in the room).
All this for years (except those moments when so close to tears,
the ministerial self pity upon times he recked his lives
and saw no good therein though little harm,
a weak and yet so glumly glamorous with pattern of the days
with time and tedium expunging with nothing left
but memory of spent desire and his travels with
decadents of all eras from mankind, and then . . .
something not he himself and yet more native
would tremble for explanation and relief, and he would give
free rein to phantasy and such poetic tears

that would engulf with sure defeat the listener—
who could not figure in his personal indulgence,
the Waterloo of mind) . . .
But this was so infrequent. Most of all he rioted with maxims.
libidinous and humorous withal or shadowboxed
upon the streets of midnight, in converse with Casanova . . .
Now, he is dilution of a memory of adolescent years:
faded like withered petals of pathetic flowers
(and he must be old . . . nothing could be much worse),
a phantom of the brain.

PROLETARIAN VISIT

Enter the toney tenement district
And visit us casually in our homes.
We will have tea for you or coffee
(If any remains). Beautiful
Curtains over the cupboards—
For we are not poor. Stacked
On economical shelves
Are boxes of rice and oatmeal.
Whatever heat is conserved
Of an early morning in bed,
Overcoats about us—frayed
And frazzled, the tapestries
Of the workers. Cosmopolitan we are,
Educated in the languages
Of the world. Pick us out:
Italian, Polish, Russian,
Portuguese—speaking English.
Our homes are condemned
By the Fire Commission, but
No one can condemn the fire
In hearts constructed of hunger!
Our fever is scarlet (a semaphore
From body to brain): And we think
Of barricades in some red dawn
On the East Side of New York City.
Get in touch with our block
Committee or, better yet,
Test the quality of our speech
In councils of the Unemployed.

THE TURN OF OCTOBER

We were alone on the prairies and mountains:
There was no brotherhood to know us by
And our passage was a lonely cry in the arroyos.
The desert would not hold us nor the cities:
Machines were turnstiles for our thought
And our labor was treachery to others.
We were fools to have been bat eyes in the darkness
But October has shattered
The chains of our slavery.

What will you do when your factory funnels
Are no longer plumes to shout you a windy song
In your own weather, when wheels of your wealth
Whine to a revolution and your carriage
Is a funeral in the streets of the city?

Our hearts will assault the citadels of power.
Our hands will be a noose to throttle your throat.
Your children will be with us workers
And will not know the sound of your name.
Your death will be a hearse in the factories
And no mourners will be bearer for your pall.

Forgotten as your crimes will be history,
And biographies
Will murder the saints of your fame.

THE PASSING OF JOE WILLIAMS

From the battery of progress and punchdrunk with defeat,
The case of Joe Williams requires no special
Attention as he walks down Delancey street—
But the cop on the corner will greet him,
The panhandling bums will think him elite:
He is kind to his countenance (Joe Williams still washes his feet).
But the phaetons sleek in their passage
Will knock him from pillar to post;
And sirens will sometimes accost him
When he lies in a pool of his blood—

For even the well-dressed indigent
Will take to smoke to forget, and the bleak
Blue jowls and lean line of Joe Williams
Will lie a hollow cadaver on the white Bellevue sheet.

A RED DAWN IN THE EAST

The flags of autumn are mutinous as the tide
Of the season with scarlet upon the edges
Of scudding clouds, moving like an entrainment
Over the western horizon to be curving under
To flow back to the east and emerge
As a new dawn upon another day: in such a manner
Does the old revitalize the new
And turn with color of metamorphic revolutions
Into the sound of a scarlet year.
The trumpets of a riotous birth
Now come from the east where the steppes of winter
Have frozen the vestiges of grief
And burst with spring
Into a promise for equality of economic return
For the workers of all the world:
The west is dying like a brood of aged birds
In the nests of their decay
And the east is a flaming message out of Russia
As bright as the sun (hammered like a gong
In our hearts) and as sure as the sickle
Of the moon, dispersing the color of night.

AFTER THE BOMBING OF BARCELONA

I am waiting for my honey to return
With news of the antiseptic rape
And the mechanical murder,
For the time is secure in violence
And the execution is exact
When the sun comes over
And daybreak falls like an axe—

But we did not know
The city or what people
Would next be exploded
And the rain of legs and churches,
Banks and eyeballs
For the harvest.
We tossed a coin and I it was
Who fastened by terror
Remained with the radio—
Now I am waiting
For her to come back
With words of the slaughter.

Ben Maddow

ACTS OF GOD

1. THE FARM

Before morning the dark western valley of the continent,
the obscure Dakotas, Kansas, and the wheat-withering plains
dream the deep plush of rain on early fields, and when
the night like a tin reflector dewless has pivoted, wake at
          sun: a hatred.

Their farmer scrapes with his hoe the uniform heaven: drought,
drought; dust boils to his shack on the noon-burned hillock.
No flowers. His starvelings stare by the twisted doorway; and
    mother
grinds from the pump, while the hot nails start in the boards,
         her few tears.

The beans counted on dry plate, the dole from the barrel's acrid
    staves,
may God grace. Last week from black pasturage the cattle
    stooped to
rasp the last mud; now between the dead horns sing
wild blue-green shiny flies; and gnawed bark cracks along
         the dead tree tomorrow.

But open the air-cooled humidified the courteous doors
whereto the prosperous motors haul up linen paunches
at evening glad or sorry from the screeching Pit.
Wheat sharply up, chilled soup down; with shriveled beef,
         waiter, the ices!

Puzzling by scanty lamp, dusty, sun-swollen, a man's
hands may turn furious and massacre a sheriff; therefore

at 9 P.M. let F. D.'s national smile be hooked
up coast to coast to offer across mahogany
                cold cream gratis.

"Dear Mr. President: Out here we heard your kind voice
        promising.
But August is bad in a mine town. Bread is high, meat not to
        touch.
Them the Co. evicted have no windows, or flowerpots to put
        in them.
That one day a week my man finds work in the pits is like one
        leg—
                who can stand on it long?"

2. THE MINE

Gleam on forehead, working the staggered day in the earth's
absolute evening, in the hot places or over the knee in icy rush,
cracking black from black while the battery jolts on the buttock.
Skinny rats attend at lunch, and—"Look't that big one!"—
                writhing in a faint!

The child's scream, the rescuers masked, class-solid, the folk
watching into the earth. The young thigh of whose love
burns meanwhile in a splitting tunnel? What father drowns
        in stone?
"The air-pump had T.B."? For whom, hoistable from deep
                grave, prepare a shallower?

Just at lunch the life-thirsty carbon monoxide coughed,
from the bad pockets left unbricked by the new dividend,
into a hundred miners' mouths, forever open.
About those busy with flame, succor, hand to eardrum,
                rock folded rock.

Outside in the old sunlight each woman watcher gripped
the concentration of her vacant hands, the desolate summer;
food and hope dear; terror outliving prayer; at last
in the tipple yard these stretchers parallel, where smiles
                horror, the acrobat.

"God's devastation," calmly God's minister in pure collar
among the uncomfortable dirty tombs, sanctions 63 dead,

"God's hand and compensation. Moved like David in its heart,
our Co. sends green wreaths to each and $25 scrip.

> God's will be done."
Men, O drillers, plowers, workers of the actual ground, we,
our will be done! Our picks must pierce in Washington
the plaster falsehoods. Miners' local, farmers' league
can, to strangling courthouse or the marble shaky bank, apply
> the probe of many bayonets.

Always were we impaled upon the spines of the inhuman seasons.
Headed with frightful feathers, gold-knived, the Aztec
> millionaire
slaked heaven with hearts fountaining naked on the elaborate
> stone.
Thus now the priests of finance consecrate us naked to
> the planet's brutal stone.

From which we rise with bloodied knees, we wide as America.
The rivers are our race. Each corn sprouts from an exploited eye.
Were not of Quetzalcoatl the gross and costly pyramids
split with explosive leaves? Our class already stands,
> burning with growth.

On fresh tables can lie flowers and the heavenly grains of the soil.
Yes, from the shining mines propped with our incollapsible
strut of mutual arms, we can, on god-abolishing rails,
condense our power to propel the tremendous irrigation,
> the communal Mississippi.

IMAGES OF POVERTY

1: CAMERA IN 9TH AVE.

The derelict who groaned in the dry gutter;
signs stamped on the eyes: unbearable afternoon.

Those heaps of plaster in the condemned house,
where the evicted slept last week; the nailed doors.

Or the barber drowsing with flies on his lids;
or the grills where the dried beer decays.

Beams of the tenement famous for 20 burned; left
in charcoal like the jointed bones of the lynched.

Voracious eye, stay, stay to see
in a steep hall boys standing with
the strengthening finger of their fresh sex,
eager,—(the word chalked on the shoddy wall)—
how some will smile toward the old syphilitic.

Dust, iron, shouts, ethereal exhausts.

The cardiac baby cries on the highest floor;
the relief potatoes boiled and blue
served on oilcloth; and the blue milk, rocking.

The rocking L; and the long cripple
vendor of lemons from white bag; and the sunburned drunk
head yelling, hands forward, adrift in the L's
regular shadows, cursing a life locked
in bars of the enraging sun.

The crowds twisting over the maimed cement;
the unemployed with bars of the L in their eyes.

2: THE SUBWAY

Sleep on the way home, 6 P.M., and each one shaken to a stifled flat.
Sleep. The ads murmur: buy me, buy me. Hands hanging in a
net of veins; the sweated collar; feet unseen; heart sodden with a
full week's overtime. Heavy, hungry. Light scuds on the con-
crete. Our sleep is shaken like the shadow of vibrating chain.
Another hour toward another hour, another hour toward

Where. We're stopped. Who? Blue bulb steady in the tunnel. Wake
up, we're nowhere. Is it the end? What's up? Is the lottery over?
A girl stands staring from her nickel sleep. Nowhere. Who is it?
The bright walls still. Ask someone. Who jumped or fell under-
neath the

Two cigarettes for lunch. The suitcase remained on the platform.

Those were the last of the pack. Found crumpled. He jumped
here. Delay of ten minutes. Won't we go on? The split arm and
the mouthful of brain. Don't look. Don't crowd. Don't jump.

There's no room for all. Who'll ask to be first? The fouled? the
woman with the secret growth? the punchdrunk? the disqual-
ified? Shall we brake the trains with corpses? We've learned in
boyhood the routine of sorrow; losers mostly; heads harsh inside
with worry. Consider: if all jumped who remember the distrust
of affection, the morning when we were laid off, the broken cup
of gin, or the feverish child in the darkness; if each who bites the
internal knuckle of misfortune,—consider!—,shall all jump? Shall
we stop

These tunnels with suicide, sour the automatic draft with blood, neg-
lect rails wrinkled and the cities stopped? These are our halls;
courage; we spin the world. The first majority of mankind, only
a few we dare excuse to die. Our vigor rushes deeper than these
pits.

Anew! Ugly, shaking with dialectic, the train plunges our metal force.

A SUMMER NIGHT

The wind wheels over Manhattan like an enemy
storming, and we wake before dawn in the midst of bombardment,
turning our heads from the beams of lightning, searchlight of death.

Then like newsreel on the flashing wall, from Shanghai
floating in conquered creek toward the dark ceiling, the eyes
of uniformed soldiers, puffed with decay, the shocking smile.

Long rains of childhood return in the hush of rain,
and the morning twenty years gone, the shouts in the wet doorway:
War At Last and our men over cloudy ocean marching in parade.

Wavering years: the mind burning and our hands unsatisfied ever:
gripping from job to job, in escape or search;
the children grown out of war and restless to return.

Helmet and muddy cheek, the grenade poised to throw,

natural we'll stand at land, watching in the man-deep furrow,
the explosive fountains, the shrapnel flowers with instantaneous
          growth;

The hateful stance, the habit of bayonets, the doomed
gasping in deadly landscape, and the imagined wound
darkening the sheets while the pulse of guns still thunders in the
          shallow room.

You gave no choice, Oh shouting rulers, so we learned none.
brave by routine, we'll come to pollute your brilliant guns,
your stadia, and your microphones—with your blood.

GREEN IN THE HALLS

FOOT OF WASHINGTON BRIDGE

At deep evening, low by the tremulous Hudson,
in the palm of a stone we embraced with unhappy strength;
but footsteps warned us, wandering in gravel.

Oh love, oh where shall love have ease in this rocky city?
sawn by a shadowless river, while tin cans
raw from its shore evolve like savage leaves.

Spurning the sleek river, past the spindle
of the dead flag over Roosevelt Row, the avenue
of shadows nailed to house American hunger;

Searching in all that broken strand, nor in the park
lanterned respectably for dogs, was any lodge
to straighten secretly our distracted hands.

Expensive on the other sky we cursed the turrets
where gold-creased doormen would unlock boudoirs
to impotents sprawling with their silky cash.

The roaring wedge of our time strains us apart:
see there, troops on the wooded frontier? from a microphone
a smoking navy launched to murder lovers?

"Quick, to the dark heel of the speedy bridge
stooped in its huge cement, turn again
under a severed sky to mend our love."

Crossed with steel shadow, mouth on mouth
wrung together on the concrete pebbles,—"quick O
lovely, (now!)," the ravenous unison,—

Delicious with fatigue, we leaned to watch
from our quiet shoulders vaulting irresistable
the elastic bridge, as bright in the trilling river

As love should be,—not bruised with public grit,
still discontent, hasty as the parting subway door,—
but in a slanting field, complex with private sweetness.

ONE GARDENIA 50C

Intersecting early night
the stack of Faultless Shoe as sheer as horizon
two days per week vents up its vital smoke
The scant coin in our four hands flick it
soften into petals? buy a wavering movie?

The dirty Ave. plugged at either end
the families walking in monotonous worry

Some on the dry summit of their week sit gulping
at the quick screen whence romance may rebound

Others at the slick footwear forbidden by plate glass
brilliant as the covers of unread magazines

But tulips shine to our lips at the florist window

That staircase stale with yesterday's shoe
the key nervous to a borrowed room
where hours wait compressed

And we've already bought a dense small flower

Twin carnal arch and plunging kiss   spring!
machines of sex that skate an intense track

The heavy blossom is dismembered
we admit to our thighs the fresh the caustic air

Morning opens vertical and rusty
on the coarse floor love's naked feet must rasp

Rough these years in our hands but only a handful

Familiar comrade, pledge in this soiled day
not to be old when green is pinned up
in lovely halls and houses filled with brides
the first bed alive with flowers

THE DEFENSES

TYRE, PERGAMUM, AND TROY . . .

White sky, and moonlight famous in our eyes;
locked by the tree, self-turning, kissed,
lost in a fierce translucent love.

Then in morning heavenly the moon goes calm and transparent;
then we walked to our work,
speaking subtly or smiling,—

BAALBEK, JERICHO, AND TROY . . .

Writing in freedom, the thought moving among the papers
like a familiar bird; or looking, or asking;
the faces of everyone lighted almost with motives of love.

And then:—the endless radio ends in brass,
the wristwatch continues its simple seconds, and our hands
drop in the midst of lunch:—what was it?—
and feel the sick thrill of disaster.

THE CREAK OF THE WOODEN HORSE ON THE BOULEVARD . . .

Reading aloud in a room in the city and there came
extras at midnight like a violent heartbeat;
we, too, some time, must

Set guns on the marble sills of the university;
the strangers dead; the insane controlling the insane asylum

The pale eyes of our people; the bitter retreat;
defending the square of burned grass in the park;

UR, ANGKOR WAT, TROY . . .

And that night the open faces, the bandages black with wounds,
the alive going slowly back, entrenching by stones, by brook,
cursing the travel of the moon that brings bombardment.

Yes, by this elm we kissed, for which the shells are searching,
minute by minute, may find and may destroy.

O cities across an ocean,—

MACCHU PICCHU, BABYLON, TROY . . .

      —with dark fire
guard yourself, and you, lost capitol of our world,—
Madrid since your great trenches hold

Death back from love; and if they hold, keep safe
our trees, our harbors, and our happiness.

Or if they fail, this broken stone, this poem
endures unknown.

THE CITY

Children of the cold sun and the broken horizon,
O secret faces, multitudes, eyes of inscrutable grief,
great breath of millions, in unknown crowds or alone,
rooms of dreamers above the cement abyss,—and I,

who all night restive in the unsleeping rain,
awoke and saw the windows covered with tears.

I heard, like the noise of melting rivers, the concourse of the
     living:
all hours mingled, violent, murmuring, or bright:
the cheers; the radio; the metal shriek of the accident;
the whisper of hired affection, hit of the week;
applause; gunfire on the screen; and at night the tragic houses
issuing like voluble flame the outcries of the city.

Yet none pronounced the truth, no hand disclosed
the heartbreak behind the muted door, denying all.
I longed to read letters therefore which were never sent,
to pierce walls, covers, silences, part the sad lips,
to stand by warm bed and witness the instantaneous dream,
put my hand in men's foreheads and clasp the beating spring.

The girl in the park cried *Juan! Juan!* but it was not I.
None answered, but I felt the breath of unknowable love.
Dawn silent: an old woman climbed with dry hands
the iron stoop where her daughter feared to give birth.
None spoke, but waited to watch the discolored twins drawn forth,
wrapped on the bed, together, born to the extremes of neglect.

Light on the painful eyelids, agony of beginnings;
the assault naked against the edges of the world;
then the long childhood inexplicably kind or cruel;
the boy fingering himself, the flush and the blind pulse,
the maiden touching the first blood of sex;
still ignorant of desire, the double wilderness.

Life smiles with heavy breast: her children run
forward with shouts, hunger, the impulse of free affection;
but each gets punished for his open face, each falls
twisted, twisted returns, gets dreaded blow, and turns
back screaming into that room at last, into himself
obscure, restful with lonely forces, like the sea.

The young return,—but cold, with skin-tight mask,
seeing this city honors most the most false:
the lady behind glass, untouched by human hand,

with plaster pubis, thigh, and docile belly
lifting the admired fabric up for sale,—
while the living long to wear her enameled eyes.

Within is dearer merchandise: men and numbered words
cold, vehement, or admiring, as the price demands;
where the painter hangs for sale beside his work;
the critic, the peddler, and the smiling acrobat;
toady and plagiarist for the price of one;
and a masked surgeon offering jars of happiness.

The sheen, the glamour, and the marvelous fanfare,
the alluring neon and the porcelain smile,
the arranged caress of furs, the forearm blazing with dollars,
the headlines bought in advance for the subnormal beauty;
and all life long the shoppers with laboring hearts
desire and possess at last: the corpse in cellophane.

Black halloween! I walked with the crooked nun;
heard the cruel father sob in the empty room;
and households dining together in daily hatred;
the posed hysteria, and the idiot calm; and those
whose love was poisoned with delay, I saw still smile,
—and felt in myself forever the anguish of understanding.

O lost people! O vendors of desperate myths!
Who prints the cold path of stars that promise voyages?

Who markets the daydream to the tubercular,
puts obscene clothing on the frigid wife,
makes woman its soft automaton, and man its bed,
and brands the false face on the living flesh of the child?

I read the smooth journals, but they gave no news of this.
Who rents the cells of this city? Whom shall I learn to kill?
The mysterious pencil? The dealer in abstract food?
Or past the chrome-steel and the politeness of corridors,
with row of buttons summoning tears or flattery,
at his old powerful desk, the immaculate imbecile?

As I walked on the glossy avenue, and with morose fire
thought the immense proud fraudulence to vivisect,

I heard the derision and the girls' duet of laughter
of two who stopped before me with flaunting hair,
insulting the photo of the noted man,
who, finger in his printed cheek, could not reply.

All three we drank together, mentioning love,
delights, friends, quick passion, and the fine pale sky.
So rapid cognac glittered in our heads,
while I to each gave sumptuous years; to one
her house with windows full of the green sea light;
and foretold one to have love wherever she goes.

And late, after the headlong passage of first desire,
now two alone, we lay awake in murmuring ease,
and spoke again of happiness, and of the élan of flight,
and as outdoors the high branch yielding to invisible air,
so she to her wish to learn the touch of that wind,
hold motor, and ride on the immeasurable gestures of space.

Night dwindling, from how many tranquil hands, white
morning extends the beautiful directions of the world;
luminous chasms, city of vertical south, north,
upward, dark march of windows, inlaid each by that star
softening with precious light in streams of dawn
toward the close court, the black leap, and the suicide's open eye.

Like a fall forward into time too fast, is death,
springing in each the coil of irreversible years:
the lymph and architecture of the self,
unique delirium, lust, and dreams of lightning,
the body remembered in luscious movement or at ease,
names lost forever, and childhood of wonderful snow.

Knees broken backward, refugees from life,
leaving behind the houses they have lived in,
the sweat on the walls, the toilet, the hateful embrace,
the colored mottoes and the step of the insane son;
or failure driving like point of dynamite into the heart
lifelong, till they escape across the impossible sill.

O space that lifts the monoplane strong did suck them down,
this act upon this stone; and shadows on it of living people,
noon, and dark twilight, and night with argon peaks,

matchless city, terrible, and I cried aloft
what monster, O what monstrous foot
here trod, leaving in blood the measure of its corruption?

Rages in this packed town, in this wilderness of hands,
beast over mankind, ruling with cruel mark;
on the delicate mind, on the beautiful mouth like syphilis,
sometime on everyone, on myself horrible I have seen it:
the perversion by money, wasting, mad, and universal,
measure of humanity, and its heavy assassin.

Here the strict labor of the many must support
the monotony of the useless; and luxury is got
with smiles, false kindness, marriage, or embezzlement;
he who can feign desire, praise poison, or hang by his teeth,
lives well, accumulates the powerful bond,
receives inhuman honor,—but the kind man is strangled.

Vaulting metropolis, under whose diagrams of eloquent light
wrestle decay and energy, both blind,—
I went in your purest hours, and met with friends,
some with familiar calm, or gay, or drunk in the bright rooms,
but I heard the terrifying pulse of other selves:
on the face of each I touched unknown the invisible tear.

In the membranes of the skull there lie in millionfold
powers and memories, and I find them forth
often: the deep smile, and the simple day at the zoo,
the voices over the bay, the avowal, and the window with leaves,
the joint of the thigh of the beloved person,
and the wish to live calmly on the highest level.

Yet who is it crawls on the subway's iron floor to sing
where all must give or listen, since the door is shut?

O in the proud mirrors of the brain, the ugly clerk
I see is myself! and the murderer trapped on the fire-escape;
and the desperate salesman; the thief; and the sick girl bought and
        awakened
to open herself again to the stranger's thrust.

I see a boy's hand move as pale as glass,
and women sleeping with infinite eyes, and all, all

I see are innocent; not walls, nor men
brutal, remote, stunned, querulous, weak, or cold
do crimes so massive, but the hideous fact
stands guilty: the usurpation of man over man.

Thus in the grating rack and torsion of society,
the inmost being cracks; gulfs there with groaning cliffs
disfigure hope; and secret fires grow; and chasms
unknown hold paralyzed the maelstroms of love; despair
with frigid pinnacles, hatred, silent catastrophes;
crevasses of self the self dares not discover,—

Between the inner and the outer face,
between the cold palm and the incestuous mind,
between the thought, the pleasure, and the indifference,
between the bright talk and the solitude,
between the oratory and the massacre,
between the music and the soundless scream.

James Neugass

TO THE TRADE

*The function of the intellectual has always been . . . to embellish
the boredom of the middle class.* —Maxim Gorky.

Gentlemen, we have spoken about these things before,
Yet in a thousand years there will still be sunsets,
Again there will arise questions of autumnal scenes,
Tenderness, the fearful landscapes of the mind, grace,
And all the fine swoonings of our historic aptitude:

But in the meantime, boys, we have a little job to do.
We have powder to pour, fuses to set, sparks to strike;
We shall be the book-keepers of international agony,
We shall be the sharpshooters, the bouncers at the door,
But—you can't pack a wallop, poets, on roller-skates.

Children, loose in the wardrobes of our literary dead,
Appendixes, deep in the bellies of the middle-class;
Freaks, black-sheep, ephebes, sourbellies and academes,
Thumbers of arabesque on the lyre of the pure senses—
All bullseyes for the dungs of literary office-help:

Yet ours is the finest blade of all; a slender lancet
With which to lay open the glaucous brains of statesmen,
An ax with which to clear the underbrush of these years,
A ploughshare to prepare acres of fallow, crusted minds;
Our best verses cut more deeply than other mens' volumes.

Gentlemen, poets, workers—we have a little job to do.
Afterwards, we will turn our eyes to Time and Space,
Consider the nautilus, drink again at the Lethean stream,
Again enmeter the grand passions of agony and manners,
Seine 24-carat eternal verities with our platinum nets.

WILL AND TESTAMENT

I was there. I saw it. That afternoon,
The last day of the General Strike,
I stood there in the crowd packed deep
Before the colonnades of the City Hall,
That fine, cold winter afternoon,
When the sun glittered down from a flaming sky
Past the marble eaves, to the snow on the sidewalk:
I was there when that last, final silence came.

The voices of the speakers died away,
The cheers and the murmuring abruptly stopped,
Uniformed guards came out on the imperial stone porches—
I saw them throw the first gas-bomb.
I saw it heaved back.

In that moment, the weight of all the work fell away:
The incessant meetings, failures, differences,
The hours at the typewriter and the mimeograph-crank—
The same words spoken again and again.
At staring, confused, ununderstanding faces;
The passing out of leaflets, the hours in jail,
The doubts, deviations, uncertainties:
These all raced past my eyes
And vanished, when I heard a thin crackling of shots,
Felt the great answering lunge of our mass.

To the end their radio spewed slander and filth,
Called for atrocities, then stopped.
The sure voices of the leaders took over the air,
Bells and sirens sounded out in the harbor,
Night and day and night.

I was there when we held the financiers upside down,
And shook out of their pockets
The rusty keys of mines, mills and factories.
The warehouses emptied out, the great empty
Mansions and apartment-houses filled.
We oiled, primed and started disused acres
Of engines, pumps and presses, lathes and looms.

Comrades, I saw it. I was there. Well, some afternoon

When factory whistles are blowing,
When the streets ring with the tread of classless crowds,
When powerhouses are letting off steam.
And the wind is making a hell of a racket all over town,
Drop my ashes in Miss Liberty's hand,
Let the wind blow them out to sea,
Out over the green, the one—and red—flagged seas.

THALASSA, THALASSA

"—twenty-five Greek freighters in the harbor of Buenos
Aires . . . on strike . . . and in spite of the actions of the
police and the reformist agencies, and with the assistance
of revolutionary trade unions on shore . . . won all de-
mands."
—Runa press dispatch.

Mariners, seabirds, sailing-ships of the lustrous early annals,
And the prow-scarred waves, and the seas, wine-dark to jewel-bright,
Known of all suns and moons and winds and weathers and waves.
Bravers of dragon'd watery abysses beyond the Pillars of Hercules,
Record-breakers in the Tyrrhenian, the Adriatic, the Dodecanese,
Cargoes of spices, gods, feathers and strange barbaric trophies:
They, these star-steerers and salt-bearded darlings of our scholars,
First sheeted home squaresails, in the shadows of templed headlands,
                    O mariners, seabirds, Greeks!

Perhaps and maybe: that was a long time ago. Ask the professors.
Here, in the anchorage at Buenos Aires, are twenty-five sooty
Greek freighters, riding high and black and empty, out on strike,
The crews of twenty-five argosies named for gods and owners' wives,
Out solid; no scabs and no rats but those below and the officers:
Against what, mariners of Greece?—fifteen dollars a month, bad meat,
Wormy bread, lice-stuffed mattresses, twelve-hour watches . . . Life?
—White rum, and naiads, at ten drachmas a throw, and doctor-bills,
                    O malcontents, roughnecks, reds!

And in the old days, yearned after by poets and schoolmasters
—Well, maybe it wasn't all amber and beryl, or "ivory and apes":
What were the Boeotian words for "crimp," "fink" and "doghouse"?
Sold over the counter, and shipped out to sea to fetch home gems,
Velvets, wines, whores for the temples and slaves for the vineyards:
Butchered by state enemies, on the decks of floating meatmarkets,

At the command of state pederasts, the philosophers and priests
—Well, maybe it wasn't all milk and honey, all culture and art.
                              O drudges, blindmen, Greeks!

"Romance, travel, adventure." So what? saleswords for slavery.
In Buenos Aires, they went out on strike and they went out solid,
Two went down under a third mate's Colt. The sharks got another.
They went out solid, they didn't scab, they stayed out and they won;
For the first time since the first oaken keel slid down the ways,
In our treasured ancient Greece, Greek seamen lifted their arms
Together and for themselves, pitched overboard their lying history,
Struck once and won the first small part of what shall be theirs,
                    O mariners, Greeks, free seamen of the world!

CONVOY

Snow went into the steaming radiators
    we pushed a sick camion into the drifts
        ate snow off our backs, then moved on

We pushed our Diamond-T's through sheep
    that choked a village street, made
        tow-ropes of bomb-torn telegraph lines

Sullen iron gray rollers of shrapnel
    hissed and fell on the beach-like road
        frozen mud filled the bomb-holes, we
        moved on

Planes stopped us: chewing-gum, soap
    string and barbed wire went into the engines
        chofers wiped glue out of their eyes and
        drove off

Fast as ants we stripped the carcass
    of a fallen car of tires bolts wire
        and parts until only frame-bones were
        left:

Fought off the back of roaring camions
   war wove through the mountains of Teruel
      fast as quicksilver red as flame white as
         death

Leaving a trail of cigarette butts
   brandy bottles and the stink of hot oil
      and frozen sweat in the deep tire tracks

With the echo of our songs rocketing
   like rifle-shots inside the ice walls
      of the Sierra Gudár, we moved up and
         on.

BEFORE BATTLE:
[THE LINCOLNS AT VILLANUEVA DE LA CANADA]

Long after the sun has gone down,
   long into the clockless hours of the
      night, the new Battalion waits at the roadside.

Knowing that the end of all waiting
   is to come the men sit quietly and talk
      light the darkness of their minds with cigarettes;

This was summer this was Spain and night
   late at night out in the countryside where
      only the howl of dogs marks the presence of men.

They have left all behind them but guns
   to defend their lives guns with which
      to take lives rifles to answer other rifles;

Here at the frontier of death five hundred
   men wait for the sound of trucks and listen
      for the droning of planes never never theirs.

Road and darkness are all they know
   the vein which will pump them like haemoglobin
      into the open festering moving wound of the Front.

No fire is lit but songs are sung,
   each man's heart is wrapped in the will
      he makes for himself "owning nothing but my rifle."

"Rich in bankruptcy, to the world
   I leave my heart to the Republic my gun
      to men's slow eyes my unvanishing footsteps":

No clock strikes when many trucks
   roll without lights out of the darkness:
      no order is given but the men come to their feet

In a clashing of iron load themselves
   solid into the steel boxes of the trucks
      many engines start and the convoy moves off.

Each minute is a passing kilometer
   how far is it to the Front how long?
      when will the sun rise when but not where

On the horizon the lights of a town appear
   they curse the village fools who make targets
      of the town and the road for night-flying bombers

When they come near they see that these
   are not street light but many white stars
      hanging low on the hills in this southern sky:

All night long trucks carry them
   through the darkness they do not know where
      they are going but nevertheless understand;

With the passing of each kilometer
   the enormous certainty grows although
      they hear no cannon, they sense that the hour is near.

Still in darkness the trucks stop:
   they have stopped before but this time they know:
      no orders are given but the men drop to the ground

It is summer and the night air heavy
   with the scent of grape leaves; the warm earth
      returns to the sun the heat it has taken up all day

If there are flowers in the villages
   each petal gives the night air its smell
      which blows cool on the lines of marching men

The smells of cooking and of woodsmoke
   hold the far memory of distant dreams:
      the eyes of a cat seem like green gun-flashes:

Burdened with iron, travelling light
   and carrying much metal they become tired
      the singing and the talk fade and are gone

Each man walks alone with his thoughts
   every ear listens for what it must soon hear
      the men know that they are new, untried troops

The last crossroad lies far behind
   the last backward step has been taken
      the final decision made the last doubt thrown away:

Like a bridal procession and a
   funeral parade they march to the altar,
      the grave, the center of the worldwide stage

Too tired to speak or sing
   quick to tire but long in strength
      now too tired to curse, the men advance:

An order comes: they stop, fall:
   the place is high rough treeless
      false daylight has begun to lift

Cold as the echo of a magnesium flare:
   color, purple yellow and poison-green
      floats into the kindling fires of day

Down below in the valley is a village
   "Villanueva de la Canada" the men whisper
      this town is Theirs but must be, will be Ours:

A sleeping town clean of war,
   every tree roof wall and window plant
      exactly patterned, perfect, sweet and still

The men understand that by sunset
　　this town has to go, go up in blood-red
　　　　sheets of flame and black fountains of dust:

And the sun comes up violently
　　sending its rays like bars of music
　　　　from great brass instruments and there is no sound:

Behind us our cannon fire three times
　　three cannon clap like iron fists on a pine door
　　　　advance! it is daylight! forward! day has broken!

Advance! leaving night and death behind
　　we advance into light and life! advance!
　　　　‘leaving the old world behind us we march into the
　　　　　　new!

No one hears the shot but our first man has fallen.

GIVE US THIS DAY

mejor morir a pie que vivir en rodillas.
—Pasionaria

Deep in the olive groves at sunset
　　longer than the memory of police chiefs
　　　　grow the shadows of headstone olive trees
Deadmen's shoes march on other feet
　　long after laces and soles are gone:
　　　　rifle straps fell away and string broke
Worn by the sweat of many a comrade's back:
　　fondly shells still slide into the chamber
　　　　the breechlocks of the anti-tank batteries
Have turned to museums of finger prints
　　but their beloved muzzles will throw
　　　　explosives so long as there is night.

how are the lines holding? where are the lines?
bring up cannon before sunrise, ammo, water

How could Spain have been rich?

nowhere were fat Swiss landscapes
  or comfortable park-like rural scenes
No mellow pastures or dreaming spires
  the streaked shoulders of the hills
   always a proving-ground for sunsets
For mobile brigades of battle clouds,
  hands of the wind fast scene-shifters
   preparing stagelike landscapes always for tragedy:
Thorn bushes burned toward evening
  like liquid flame: what wealth was there
   but in the skies and the hard empty hands?

Where was the glamor of historians?
  were they here? what did they see?
   who was rich? where was the wealth
Long deserts with oases of olive trees
  mirages of wheatfields and vines
   exhausted salt plains of Castile
Monotonous one-well towns of Aragon
  mud walls rising from mud ridge-strung
   like cascades of standing reddish dust

kitchens should be underground, dig schools deep
take the children to the deepest end of the refugio, dig.

The church towers were pretty
  the walls of monastery gardens strong
   churchwalls were strong as fortresses
The hermitage where the Bishop
  summered was as pretty as a calendar also
   his cedars were firewood for Alcoisa
Monotonously the people cooked
  in one dish and ate from one plate
   there were stoves only in the convents
Monotonously we used the half-built
  Republican schoolhouses for hospitals
   these were the only white walls in Aragon
Where was the glamor of that
  luminescent past of gilt and gold
   silver brass and flea-ridden satins?
Of banners pennants flags as red as blood
  and yellow as gold? none but belfry saints
   had seen the past: they looked down on us

With stone eyes full of grandeur
    as we marched out of the rising sunlight
        leaving our dead but taking their guns

because of the sky there was no rearguard
no rear every nursery and fireplace a trench

They were thirsty for Madrid
    ravenous for the spinal fluid of Madrid
        howitzers chewed away at the Gran Via
What they wanted They first destroyed
    they wanted Hijar and they dropped all
        but landing gear and tailskid on Hijar
They wanted Guernica Durango
    Lerida Barbastro Caspe Alcaniz and all
        the towns villages and hamlets in Spain
But that would have taken too long
    so They destroyed only what They wanted most
        with planes for every roof and all that moved
They always told us what They
    wanted: the telling came in the crackle
        of lead whips on the hams of the earth
Whistling iron lead copper zinc
    came out of the rock hills rose from
        the desert plain arched over the valley
We wanted their infantry our gunsights
    were hungry for Their infantry but could find
        nothing but earth rock and the walls of tanks
Earthquakes belled into the solid air
    the day had legion eyes and all were guns
        hungry gunsights searched the empty horizon

brace every ceiling fortify the cellars open all doors
lie motionless in the ditches do not move never run

The country was bleeding to death
    every day from many small wounds
        every day the imported meat grinders
Chewed a fingertip an ear a town,
    old wounds flowed across the villages
        but our vitals could never be reached
Perfect in echelon Their silver planes
    came over like bloody Gods that

owned the bloody bleeding sky blue skies
Swarming into the hide of the hills
civilians scratched and clawed themselves
into the earth like jiggers and skin lice
Breathing deep and loud and perfect
trimotors came on slow as sunset
birds wrangled in the dry poplars
Morosely a dog nosed bandages
along the soiled frozen river bank
grassblades and a sulphur jonquil shook
In the crevice where we lay
earth fell on us and the air pounded
unhurt we ran toward the screaming
Remote against the icy afternoon
our combat planes battled downward
guns and engines dove and climbed
Waterfalls of mixed smoke and fire
poured like rain into the dry earth:
then the air was sweet and clean

they will come again today again tomorrow
out of the infected sunlight and the sick moon.

We asked for little: give us this day
our bread gasoline and gunpowder
there was less bread and we did not eat
But the camions were ever ravenous
guns would not kill without shells
our rifles ate us out of cartridges
There was no rest: we did not sleep
but the camions would not run forever
gunbarrels grew too hot then too cold
There was little water: we did not drink
but the Maxims were unceasingly thirsty
without bread water sleep we did not fail
The hungry rifles grew too cold
the tanks of the camions were empty
big hearts and empty hands were not enough

where are the grenades and stick-bombs?
is the road clear?   where is the front?

Pyres lit the roads at night

bonfire pyramids of long unburied dead
fists and feet black as cattle hooves
All night long machine-gun pellets
of snow drilled against the windshield
too tired to curse, three chofers

Amiably fought to sleep
on a single stained still wet mattress
before morning many beds were empty
When the sun rose perfumed
by bread and gelinite, black armies
of shovel men sprang from the snowdrifts
Snow went into the steaming radiators
we rolled a sick camion off the road
ate snow off our backs: then moved on
We pushed our Diamnod T-s through sheep
that choked the village street, made
towropes of bomb-torn telegraph lines
Sullen iron gray rollers of shrapnel
hissed and broke on the beach-like road
frozen mud plugged the bomb holes; we moved on
Planes stopped us: string chewing gum
barbed wire and soap went into the engines
chofers wiped glue from their eyes and drove off
Fast as ants we stripped the carcass
of a slaughtered car of tires bolts wire
and parts until only frame-bones were left
Fought off the back of roaring camions
war wove through the mountains of Teruel
fast as quicksilver red as flame gray as death
Leaving a trail of cigarette butts
empty brandy bottles and the smell
of hot oil in the deep tire tracks
With the echo of our songs rocketing
like rifle shots inside the ice walls
of the Sierra Gudár: we moved on and up

don't take a wrong road oil your rifle
save the water keep your head down

'The war's getting rough' Al said
and those were his last words
we stripped the tourniquet from his leg

'You can't fool Charlie Regan'
    not for forty years and three wars
        a 75 fooled him and these were his last words
What can be done for a belly case?
    a lung case a head case a liver
        'we can do much but they die anyway'
'The avions sprayed us all day
    with fire bullets I lay still
        I did not move but I got it'
Ether other caffeine anestex:
    no hope left but a slap on the jaw
        first sew him up with decent red silk
An old wound in one arm a fresh one
    in the other, Wild Bill laughed while
        we put down his stretcher and rested
'I guess the war's about over for me'
    a rifle grenade caught him and it was
        Bill took two stretcher bearers with him
'How are the lines? am I bleeding?
    who wants my shoes? where are the lines?'
        these were their last words, 'salud! viva . . . viva . . .'
Those summer girls with dreamy
    eyes white and clean as sleep
        who slowly walk their big red mouths
Down the quiet streets of a city
    heartbreaking summer songs by the lake
        where were they? had we forgotten?

throw olive limbs on the cars camouflage
the hospitals camouflage the earth, dig.

We snaked the wounded four
    miles out of the Segura mountains
        on men when there were no mules
We pushed them through shellfire all
    day long through God's hideous sunlight
        we got the wounded out on tanks in trucks
Caissons carts and ambulances
    we rolled them down plane-infested roads
        slapped on tourniquets gauze and adhesives
We took the names and wrote last letters
    pumped the wounded full of morphine
        saline anti-tetanus and gas-gangrene

Fortunately the hospital had been hit
 by nothing heavier than a ten-kilo egg
  we soldered drilled sterilizer tins
Plastered wire splints to the stove pipe
 lit candles kerosene and olive oil lamps
  taped the openings in our wounded tents
We burned gasoline alcohol and wood
 over our wounded we filled them with
  good glucose blood adrenaline and morphine:
And then the bastards had to die on us
 and we had to bury them near and fast
  and at night: with neither lanterns nor songs

planes listen for those who speak of a new world
for culture peace progress freedom: dig!

Sleep had the smell of flowers
 in a funeral parlor there were flowers
  but no sleep: we longed for the perfume of
Woodsmoke, cooking and of home
 there were the tropical spring airs
  and nothing clean but children's eyes
We smoked dry olive leaves and straw
 go-lousies anti-tanks and pillow-slips
  we ate raw pork fat with wild onions
Pulled olives off the moonlit trees
 feasted the smearing of Moorish cavalry
  with beefsteak cut from their machine-gunned mounts
We slept in the olive groves of Quinto
 the plains of Aragon are scored with
  the foxholes our bayonets and mess tins dug
We curled into the frozen mud at Celadas
 stood sleeping against walls at Monte Rosario
  slept waist-deep in Escorial's irrigation ditches
Sucked moist mud in barrancas near Brunete
 came blinking out of the cellars of Teruel
  marched singing into sun-baked anthills at Valverde
But it was always a question of the lines:
 where were the trenches? were the men advancing?
  had we hauled the artillery closer each night?

yellow and red were Their banners: blood and gold
their program: blood and more blood silver and gold

Plucked clean as a tooth from the bomb-rotten
    village street then dumped on the road the Captain's
        laundry was lost the laundress her father mother:
Sunset bleeds woodsmoke down the fuming streets
    fire warms engines and coffee, in a smashing
        of icicles we move off, too sleepy to curse:
Headlights raised partridges which flew
    blind ahead of us up the road to the front
        hungry, we carried guns fit only to kill men:
We blew up the trapped ambulances
    We lowered the bandaged nurse
        to the cleanest part of the ditch:
There never was such an afternoon
    such keen Alpine evening air no such silence
        but for the single rifle shot over the hills:
They want war Their stomachs can eat
    only war the droning of planes sooths Them
        the sound of planes is morphine for Their sleep:
Armed with pawnshop rifles and a knowledge
    of why we had come, with memories that
        went back through centuries the men advanced
Still in the clothes in which
    we had left our jobs, singing the
        same song in many languages we advance:

are the trenches deep enough and dry and crooked?
have the bombing parties returned? where are the scouts?

In all the winterdry mountain deserts
    of Aragon there was no color but khaki:
        not yet green but pink water-red rosegray
Quiet as sunset clouds pink as sunset snow
    the cherry orchard was the best cover
        for artillery in all of lower Aragon
Under the cherry trees the throats
    of the Pasionaria battery coughed
        soundless as an earthquake, leaving
a hush-hush of suction in the solid air
    petals drifted loose but many were left
        the strongest would make the fattest fruit
Pasionaria's guns fired again
    cough of fire express-train vacuum rushed
        through the shattered blossom camouflage

Then planes came and power dove
    leveled off and opened up on the guns
        the gunners the cases of arms and the trees
Canvas slid from our anti-aircraft
    sunflash on the tumbling cartridges
        engine-roar hornet whistle of metal death
Wood hissed and the fresh earth rose
    number 3-gun sideslipped to her knees
        2-gun and I arched their throats fired
Their planes dove flattened and let fly
    spring cherry sap ran and fresher blood
        burned petals floated in the acid air
All afternoon the guns of the Pasionaria
    battery fired all afternoon relays of planes
        dove unloaded wheeled soared and returned
Until blossoms were gone guns gone
    planes and orchard and gunners gone
        there would be no cherries no trees
No Spain no earth: in all the
    mountain deserts of Aragon there was
        no color but khaki and dust and blood.

bring up the archies! prime the tank-traps!
long live dynamite! death to war!

Like sea worms in the timbers of a ship
    four cavalrymen curled into a wall of clay
        but there were no beams in the shallow ceiling
'Only a direct hit'—there was a direct hit
    we shoveled four asphyxiated cavalrymen
        rushed them to the hospital courtyard
Before they were cold we had
    taken the blood out of them before
        the blood was cold we had run it
Into the arms of our wounded
    the blood of the four cavalrymen lives
        it will always live and always fight
Red as the flags on the trucks
    that roll over mountaintops hot as the vapor
        that burns inside the charging cylinder heads
The I. B.'s were the most ragged
    filthy hungry red eyed bastards
        that ever went under the name of troops

But they could fight and they fought
    they cursed their officers, groused ans squawked
        but they held their lines and the lines held
Every man was his own general but they
    could obey; The Internationals never broke
        never was 'some day comrade' said with such longing
Some day: no soldier has ever oiled
    or used or hated his rifle so well
        no troops ever loved peace like them

they wanted nothing for themselves not for themselves
every grove is a sanctuary each hilltop a shrine

Forget the bronze tablets and
    hand-illumined scrolls leave out
        medals citation bars and stripes
Some day their history will
    be carved ineradicably across
        the earth by tractor-drawn plows
Mercifully let a last kind bomb
    save the informal cemetery
        of the International Brigades
From him who could not take our trenches
    let the fist never come unclenched the
        calloused right forefingers never grow soft
Unknown soldiers? they were all
    unknown: international as sunrise
        misty etchings of their olive grove tombs
Will never hang reverently draped
    in lace and immortelles in chapel-like
        parlors of Back Bay and Park Avenue
Whitehall Arlington and the Etoile
    will not pay bronze and marble to them
        every milestone is their cenotaph
Do not look for their metal names
    shaded by village memorial trees
        the horizon is their triumphal arch

write 'paid up and in good standing'
save the helmets save the shoes

When in the evening secret service men
    lock vaults of cross-indexed fingerprints

and the morgues of passport photographs
Where the faces of the Brigades
fade and bleach but do not die
longer than the memory of police chiefs
Grow the shadows of footstone olive trees
deep in battlefield orchards at sunset
thrushes the men had cursed for airplanes
Sleepily find places for the night
secure among boughs grafted by peace
to the seared and war-torn trunks
Only that the lines shall hold!
nothing else matters there is no
hardship no anguish no other pain
Dig the trenches deep and crooked
send shells and tanks and planes
fuel and the best guns to the Front
Let civilians feed wells of supply
guard crossroads keep the highways healthy
pulsing hot as the blood in our foreheads
Let the lines hold hard then advance
let those camions wind over mountaintops
let the color of the flags never fade
Hold them high as they flow above the
roaring camions: let the memory of the songs
the volunteers sang never die from our throats.

Kenneth Patchen

JOE HILL LISTENS TO THE PRAYING

Look at the steady rifles, Joe.
It's all over now—"Murder, first degree,"
The jury said. It's too late now
To go back. Listen Joe, the chaplain is reading:

Lord Jesus Christ who didst
So mercifully promise heaven
To the thief that humbly confessed
His injustice

              throw back your head

Joe; remember that song of yours
We used to sing in jails all over
These United States—tell it to him:
"I'll introduce to you
A man that is a credit to our Red, White
and Blue,
His head is made of lumber and solid as
a rock;
He is a Christian Father and his name is
Mr. Block."

                  Remember, Joe—
"You take the cake,
You make me ache,
Tie a rock on your block and jump
in the lake,
Kindly do that for Liberty's sake."

Behold me, I beseech Thee, with
The same eyes of mercy that

                  on the other

Hand we're driftin' into Jungles
From Kansas to the coast, wrapped
    round brake beams on a thousand
    freights; San Joaquin and Omaha
    brush under the wheels—"God made the summer
    for the hobo and the bummer"—we've been
    everywhere, seen everything.
Winning the West for the good citizens;
Driving golden spikes into the U. P.;
Harvest hands, lumbermen drifting—
    now Iowa, now Oregon—
God, how clean the sky; the lovely wine
Of coffee in a can. This land
    is our lover. How greenly beautiful
Her hair; her great pure breasts
    that are
The Rockies on a day of mist and rain.

We love this land of corn and cotton,
    Virginia and Ohio, sleeping on
With our love, with our love—
O burst of Alabama loveliness, sleeping on
In the strength of our love; O Mississippi flowing
Through our nights, a giant mother.

Pardon, and in the end
              How green is her hair,
    how pure are her breasts; the little farms
    nuzzling into her flanks
    drawing forth life, big rich life
Under the deep chant of her skies
And rivers—but we, we're driftin'
Into trouble from Kansas to the coast, clapped
    into the stink and rot of country jails
    and clubbed by dicks and cops
Because we didn't give a damn—
                  remember Joe
How little we cared, how we sang
    the nights away in their filthy jails;
                  and how, when
We got wind of a guy called Marx
    we sang less, just talked
And talked. "Blanket-stiffs" we were

But we could talk, they couldn't jail us
For that—but they did—
                              remember Joe
Of my life be strengthened
                    One Big Union:
    our convention in Chi; the Red Cards,
    leaflets; sleeping in the parks,
    the Boul Mich; "wobblies" now, cheering
    the guys that spoke our lingo, singing
    down the others. "Hear that train blow,
Boys, hear that train blow."

Now confessing my crimes, I may obtain

Millions of stars, Joe—millions of miles.

                    Remember Vincent St. John
In the Goldfield strike; the timid little squirt
    with the funny voice, getting onto the platform
    and slinging words at us that rolled
  • down our chins and into our hearts,
    like boulders hell-bent down a mountain side.
And Orchard, angel of peace
    —with a stick of dynamite in either hand.
    Pettibone and Moyer: "The strike
Is your weapon, to hell with politics."
                    Big Bill—remember him—
At Boise—great red eye rolling like a lame bull
    through the furniture and men
    of the courtroom—"This bastard,
His Honor."

    Hobo Convention:
(Millions of stars, Joe—millions of miles.)
"Hallelujah, I'm a bum,
Hallelujah, I'm a bum." His Honor,
    the sonofabitch!
One Big Strike, Lawrence, Mass—
    23,000 strong, from every neck
    of every woods in America, 23,000,
Joe, remember. "We don't need
    a leader. We'll fix things up
    among ourselves."

"Blackie" Ford and "Double-nose" Suhr in
Wheatland—"I. W. W.'s don't destroy
    property"—and they got life. "I've counted
The stars, boys, counted a million of these prison bars."

    San Diego, soap boxes,
Hundreds of them! And always
    their jail shutting out the sky,
    the clean rhythm of the wheels
    on a fast freight; disinfectant getting
    into the lung-pits, spitting blood
But singing— Christ, how we sang,
               remember the singing
Joe, One Big Union,
        One Big
            hope to be
With thee

What do they matter, Joe, these rifles.
They can't reach the towns, the skies, the songs,
    that now are part of more
    than any of us—we were
The homeless, the drifters, but, our songs
    had hair and blood on them.
There are no soap boxes in the sky.
We won't eat pie, now, or ever
    when we die,
        but Joe
We had something they didn't have:
    our love for these States
    was real and deep;
          to be with Thee
In heaven, Amen.
        (How steady are
    the rifles.) We had slept
    naked on this earth on the coldest nights
    listening to the words of a guy named Marx.
Let them burn us, hang us, shoot us,

                  Joe Hill,
For at the last we had what it takes
    to make songs with.

"LET US HAVE MADNESS OPENLY"

Let us have madness openly, O men
Of my generation. Let us follow
The footsteps of this slaughtered age:
See it trail across Time's dim land
Into the closed house of eternity
With the noise that dying has,
With the face that dead things wear—

> nor ever say

We wanted more; we looked to find
An open door, an utter deed of love,
Transforming day's evil darkness;

> but

We found extended hell and fog
Upon the earth, and within the head
A rotting bog of lean huge graves.

A LETTER ON THE USE OF
MACHINE GUNS AT WEDDINGS

Like the soldier, like the sailor, like the bib and tuck and bailer,
like the corner where we loiter, like the congressman and lawyer,
like the cop on the hill, like the lead in weary Will,
like the kittens in the water, like the names on Hearst's blotter,
like the guys and dames who laugh and chatter,
like the boys and girls who don't matter,
like the preacher and the Pope, like the punks who dish the dope,
like the hungry singing Home on the Range,
like Father Coughlin acting like Red Grange,
like the grumble of the tuba, like the sugar war in Cuba,
like the bill-collectors, like the Law-respecters,
like the pimps and prostitutes, like Mickey Mouse and Puss-in-Boots,
like the churches and the jails, like Astor's hounds and quails,
she's like you like her, now don't you try to spike her,
she's the nuts, she's a mile of Camel butts,
she's a honey in the money, she's my pearl,
what am I offered for being alive and willing to marry the girl?

though her insides rumble and her joints are out of whack,
let's give her a whirl, why grumble or try to draw back?
though her hair is false and her teeth are yellow,
let's get chummy, let's all get a break. For what's a fellow
got at stake, for what's a guy to do
who hasn't the guts to deal with sluts, guys like me and you.

23RD STREET RUNS INTO HEAVEN

You stand near the window as lights wink
On along the street. Somewhere a trolley, taking
Shop-girls and clerks home, clatters through
This before-supper Sabbath. An alley cat cries
To find the garbage cans sealed; newsboys
Begin their murder-into-pennies round.

We are shut in, secure for a little, safe until
Tomorrow. You slip your dress off, roll down
Your stockings, careful against runs. Naked now,
With soft light on soft flesh, you pause
For a moment; turn and face me—
Smile in a way that only women know
Who have lain long with their lover
And are made more virginal.

Our supper is plain but we are very wonderful.

STREET CORNER COLLEGE

Next year the grave grass will cover us.
We stand now, and laugh;
Watching the girls go by;
Betting on slow horses; drinking cheap gin.
We have nothing to do; nowhere to go; nobody.

Last year was a year ago; nothing more.
We weren't younger then; nor older now.

We manage to have the look that young men have;
We feel nothing behind our faces, one way or other.

We shall probably not be quite dead when we die.
We were never anything all the way; not even soldiers.

We are the insulted, brother, the desolate boys.
Sleepwalkers in a dark and terrible land,
Where solitude is a dirty knife at our throats.
Cold stars watch us, chum
Cold stars and the whores

A LETTER TO A POLICEMAN IN KANSAS CITY

A lot of men and armies stand to take
no chances with the prisoner Goddamn
them standing there near the bars watch their fingers
flex their eyes proud their legs firm their earth this
time next year last year a hundred years from now
they think it's all ours belongs to us we've got
you where we want for nothing

                         any painter
can't paint any carpenter can't build any
doctor can't cure any man can't say how deep
it goes inside to watch to stand dumb
in the streets of their cities and know
that your head's crummy your feet drip blood
that your belly rots your life is shot
                              your days
are spent in two-bit flops because of them
because they get away with murder away
with everything we are or ever were come
to think of it

        Goddamn them standing on
the cover of our world their eavy boots grinding
into our faces their ropes about our necks their guns
shut your mouth you bastard where do you live
what are you doing here look out

look out we don't know anything about that but
I'll tell you where we live and what we're doing here
tomorrow maybe I'll tell you then I'll tell you
when your guard is down when the thing breaks
I'll tell you all you want to know come to
think of it
        I'm not too starved to want food
not too homeless to want a home not too dumb
to answer questions come to think of it
                    it'll take a hell
of a lot more than you've got to stop what's
going on deep inside us when it starts out
when it starts wheels going worlds growing
and any man can live on earth when we're through with it.

William Pillin

TWO POEMS

ODE

O battallions! O disaster!
Banners! Hammers!
Iron hands!

(. . . this is decay . . . mud . . .
mummies sucking blood
of live men . . . stifling . . .
look! . . . they grovel on fat bellies
licking dust. . . . . .)

Granite boulders!
Tumbling!
Falling down!

O destruction! Higher! Higher!
Heave the shoulders!
Down! Down! Down!

POEM

Moving thru the drifting mist
of a blurred afternoon
I saw men sitting on benches.

The snow fell on black branches
of the naked bodies of trees
sprouting out of tired ground.

The eyes of men were haunted
with pale ghosts of hunger.
Their hands were in their pockets.

The snow fell on them
softly.

THE AVIATORS

Looking through the clean lens of sunlight
this wonderful struggle of hills and sky

is a flashing signal of rhapsodic fragments
in the storm of wings released and flying.

The flock of aerial birds cleaving the blue air
the mechanical arrows with a twang of cut air

over the bright constellations of hotels and cinemas
and cables strung in the air like steel nerves

somersaulting the slightly visible bridges
over the groaning and snoring tugboats.

Silver zeppelins carrying warmakers, the daredevil
stunt makers ballooning a mushroom canvas.

Most of all the air designs swifting cloudward
(someday to carry bombs and disaster).

Miles of clear blue hillspace photographed
a platinum streak roaring through altitudes

the slight framework of new steel
the blue duraluminum and the chromo-molybden.

And the windy fugue thundering the control strings
nor for sport but for murder.

A CHAPTER FROM GEOGRAPHY

Swift wild birds on wind and water:
their wings glide over this land
to this city where mists and smoke

and clouds of white vapor, chemic,
rise to the iron sky and dissolve:
the lake washes it clean in autumn:

a hard land to live in where
north and west the seasons blow
dust-clouds, sky-fire, steam and air:

and the corn is shrivelled
on the stalk, the earth powder
bites in the lungs of horses;

but here they came long ago
with their flocks and wagons
and settled

on the stern wastes, steeled
by the frosts, fighting to make
a people and a city;

where now—climate unchanged—
grown old they shiver, afraid
of this geography that makes

pagans of the young whose blood
takes to the struggle. If only
the wind and the rains were

not so uncertain, the elements ordered:
but this way. . . . one cannot . . .

their teeth rattle!

WE WERE OF THEM

Where are we going? Does the wind know?

Plagued by starvelings and sprawling
machinescapes of this trivial street
we took an overland express dreaming
of mountain air. It was inevitable.
We desired a crystal definition
to integrate our vision: bare snow
of vivid regions; innocent sky
shattered by an orange explosion.
Agility was the hope of our limbs.
We rifled blank days with danger
to revitalize our sense of being.
On this drab street only hunger thrives.
Steelglittering designs of death
rattle a gunsong.
                Do you remember?
Clubs tore our heads; driven, we retreated.
We molested none but the toughs had it.
The mounted brutes charged us and buried
the fighting blaze in our eyes.
We retreated shouting. Boys and men;
I know them all from the road, remembering
stolen switchlamps where freightcars stop.
Tough boys, hard pressed, singing hot jazz.

GRAND PARK, CHICAGO

It was morning when we approached
the great city, trembling with cold
and hungry.
              Pale splay of hyaline film, thin smoke
winding, a blue whisper in breathless void.
Lake Michigan winked with sparkling needles
edged with slim sails.
               We ate like buzzards
stale crumbs and onions, wilted cutlets flung
reluctantly from ptomaine alley joints.

A burst of whitewinged pigeons climbed
the dizzy stalactites of lakefront spires.

Grim derelicts on guilded borders of
Chicago's streamlined champion pomp
serenly doze unmindful of galvanic drone
of speeding motors, airplanes and boats.

Bending with double glance a nervous novice
picks cigarette stubs off the asphalt miles.

THE PRAIRIE

We wanted to feel at home somewhere;
desert, city, ocean, mountain, prairie.
In the dead of the night we arrived .
and slept till the farm beasts woke us.
We sniffed curls of gray smoke
and washed in the cold depths of a river.
The prairie muttered thunder; the sky
vaulted blue lightnings and spattered
sheaves of yellow corn with drops and hail
till the frost came and tightened the lake.
We thought we found a place to rest;
to bring vibrant elements of our aliveness
into this brittle vastness of dust and wheat.
But the people were stupid though kindly
and in the distance bloomed
electric flowers of a city, throwing
holiday lights on a nightscreen.
We wrung our shirts and left at noon
while brown silences slanted
against our cheeks and breezes
mingled with our hair.

AFTER THE 'RIOT'

Still life and movement, thunder and repose
is a law of nature or else is balance lost.

We must disperse now to gather vital strength
and make a flame of chilled folk
whose fire is in our veins.
Now it is colder, the streets are grey,
the open grasslands pungent with puffed smoke.
Everything is clearer in a naked way.
We will trust the stone mouth and the brutal fist
only at an end of a glinting gun's length
now that things are simpler—and the boy is dead.

Autumn, the pale season, blows the leaves away,
blows dark wings away to a whiter sun

and the northwest wind sweeps off the scum
from that tremendous puddle, Lake Michigan.
A pure burst of free air across this land;
the roofs are motionless like boulders heaved
on the faded lakesands by a blasting quake.

Statis, rotation, thunder and repose;
such is law of action, an axiom of life.

Nothing much has happened but the brain
is wounded by a brilliant light of dawn.
Knowledge makes muscles tense to leap.
Time's fierce alarm signals dawn's demands.
Another day begins and we have learned
to be gods in thunder and sages in repose
and crack like swords of lightning
when the drum of action calls.

BREAD

Where sways the bronze of heavy wheat,
where wingless skies look down on yellow,
I walked through rain and burning sun,
through dust and storm; heard folk songs

in summer fields when sheaves of wheat are stacked:
of ardent harvests and breadless days,
nightmares and laughter, tears and fantasies.

And I have seen grain flung to sun and blessed,
wind-winnowed kernels fall, chaff spray the air;
and cracked in grist and baked to brown
with all the elements of wind and sun
to nourish us.
    And there were hills of bread!

O city, city of ironic brain!
the howling jackals at Exchange
have filled the ciphers and the gate is closed:
    and now the grain
is cracked by clinking metal,
milled in paper notes, fed by cashiers.
    . . . and the wild bodies,
the strong bodies in Europe and Asia
suddenly self-conscious, tragic:
the ink of newspapers with RISING PRICES;
of sun and rain? of winds? of strong arms?
    . . . in the black forests,
river villages, alleyways of dark cities,
bodies bloated, mouths obscenely open
    and sturdy limbs
stiffened into sculptures of despair.

I was in the land of running flame.
I saw the planting and the harvest.
I swung the scythe, sun's rhythm on it.
I heard the laughter and the song.

I have not been to the vicinities of hunger.
I have not seen the hunger blackened lips
    nor the worried workmen standing in line.
They say at the meetings of strikers
    the talk is of bread. . . .

    . . . but I have seen the bread!

TWO LIVES

Between the sewing machine and the kitchen
the intervals are brief. She uses them to paint
spirals and verticals of proletarian slums;
smoke and stone, patched roofs, a littered porch.

And after a day of numbers and minutes, he comes.
He thunders headlines. News items on his lips
turn into slogans; he animates the room
with a methodic fervor and she nods
quietly, her mind on paints and rent.
"Energy is bread and water and sun; all this
the multitudes must make their own." Or else
he ponders: "The single, round word, 'masses'
dynamic like a drum, a gun, a signal."

A blueblond radiolove across the street
disturbs the air with bruised sexcravings.
"O, damn! Let's go. The meeting is for 8
but we can promenade that lighted zone of wealth,
Boul. Michigan, take in a show perhaps."
(There in the shadows they may find the myth
of swift modernity which fires the limbs to speed.)

This is the street. It's dark, mysterious.
A yellow spider gathers in the sky, blue stains
fall from the neon sign, the gutters stink
with broken bottles from the street saloon.
Motors shatter the evening.
Tumult, blue flame of loop.

The evening comes to flower in rebel thought
and leaflets hurried from a mimeograph,
an empty loft hung with red flags and signs.
Then home again. She looks
to see if poverty requires another daub
He recollects with pleasure his remark: "Our lives
we live so actually that we see death
where we are not."

        The miners, lockouts fade;
the surge of history, its international roar
dissolves into the night.

REQUIEM FOR THE '30's

Conquerors of this paltry decade, strut
a brief parade before the blunted stare
of tantrum boys and silver mouthed sluts:

movement of ghostlike masses entranced
by idiots burning brand; recall
how dull the pages are with Destiny!

Cynical vultures trail its carrion march
and angry clouds announce a singing sky
to cleanse foul traces of its pride.

Make a clay model of this wasted age:
its ailing will not strike elegiac chords.
Ten sneers at honor, ten blows at dignity.

A traitor banner flaunts on Byron's tomb.
Lindsay a suicide, Carnevali mad.
Corruption gilds the State's conniving knaves.

Youth grimacing at noble busts of Age:
glutted with trifling arts, debasing sports,
applauding Death's venereal dance to earth.

O costumed archangels, paranoiac seers;
erasing Christ, time's tolerant sweet smile:
thinking to blot the vitrant leaves of Marx

with mocking pittance and stage miracles:
building a pedestal of shining guillotines
as if a blade discriminates its necks.

This is your day. You could not have another.
This putrid age of mire and blood requires
a climax only you can demonstrate.

It needs a wound to shake plegmatic flesh
with antiseptic of a fiercer bite
than little sword cuts of today's offence.

This is your epoch ending like a glimpse:
the torrent sweeps the putrescent debris

and underneath reveals a crystal rock.

So lift your vision, syncopated chiefs,
to view the flapping vultures, hear
the thundering laughter of emerging dawn

cracking the crumbling clay of your defence.

Ettore Rella

CAESAR AND THE BLIND MEN

The blind men on fourteenth street are real:
Who hears them tapping tapping?
Their tapping canes are drops of water on stone—
When a penny sings in the desert
How shall they tell the poison from the pure?

Wall Street at midnight: through the deep shadow
Brutus, Ford and Morgan flee: on the Treasury steps
Caesar jerks a ligament and lies still—
The swirl of paper on the empty street
Settles in an obscure dirty corner.

But this is a busy street where the people are a tabloid
A year old. Look, the pictures have faded
In the seeping rain: which is the gangster, which is
The famous whore, where is the pain the laughter? Soft my friend
Their heads are full of dust, and memory only
Stands above the mouldering metropolitan rafters.
Their anonymity is wrenched today
To new distortion. Listen, this is the hour
The rain has stopped the sun has set the wind has fallen
The newsboy cries through the evening, 'Caesar's dead!'
The gutter trickles past the clock
The elevated thunders down the sky.

SUNDAY MORNING

(for D. M.)

Salvation army band
down the tunnel of the street
faintly and far and further
the exalted drum shakes awake
the cluttered canal:
the hasty resurrection of a lily
explodes brightly and men are afraid
of the sudden splendour.
                              They say
'let us by no means lift any dust'
(for there was a time, another time)
'let us by all means keep the house quiet:
'that's my uncle and this is my aunt:
'far away and long ago
'they died and were quietly covered with snow.'

But the secret is out and the parlour is filled
(I told you not to open the door):
what they drank and where they swilled
takes time to tell who knew them well:
they rip the velvet and piss on the straw:
how can time tell you what we saw?:
the fire revealed the infinite variety
that scales the amplitude of human virtue:
upward from a morass of groans
rose harmonious drops of love
emitting 'hallelujah, hallelujah':
old tapisserie stinks, the mirror is broken.

Now I however shall dare
the dark place of Sunday:
no pseudomartyr, I: being able to say
your breasts are very proximate, also very mild stars—
and I shall recapture somewhat the order
the music the light
of the evangelized imagination
(according as the confusion will allow)
because you have assuaged
my tumult with your hair

the storm of your hair upon my storm
where it floats pungently seaweed.

Yes I shall enter again the furtive place:
I suppose the forever phrase is selva oscura:
time's intertwined branches, no music of leaves
and so goddamned many sentieri—
and I shall play better
the problem of color and sound and mysterious affection
knowing should I look backward
should I feel suddenly lost
should I turn suddenly dark
would be your body
by the light of a lamp
high up and safe
and I would climb by your voice to your mouth.

Therefore I salute you
halflost I salute you:
I thank you for the solid house
on the edge of the endless space
where an unknown bird with enormous wings
moves the whole air and silently sings.

HIEROGLYPHS

I didnt choose these things
these souvenirs of a gay night
soaked with rain, sunken from ecstacy
skeletons cast on a shore devoted to business

7 A.M.
the man in the stained uniform of many days
shall come now that the splendour is broken, now that it lies
with no command, no asseveration—
the browbeaten parasites
the dogs the birds the mice
shall come now that the awful dominion is flown

these scavengers of society are up to par

work quietly, swiftly, have a right to their wages—
when they have had their fill and the street is clean
they push their implements around the corner

exeunt comes. interval of silence.
the sun shines down on the bones, the wind blows,
a ghost comes out of the ground,—soliloquy—

having cast off material implications
having achieved a vacuous frost
having screwed my eyes on the ditch where the tinsel
glittered, shall I stand here forever, shall I
precipitate the peace? this is the answer—
music comes out of the window behind me
twines into my ears refreshing leaves
spells into sound the treacherous fantasy
and I am able to turn and walk away
am able to buy a newspaper
greet my friends

but the waspish interrogation
recurs in the middle of breakfast—
who put them together
who put the births and deaths
in parallel columns
baptism by unction, cool
outposts of this midway fever?

a joyous countrywide response
from the tight phalanx instantly
rises on perfume of rhetoric—
be strong heart and you shall win
an income and family adulation
community respect and an automobile
judge for friend and jury duty
creased trousers and a hat in season
eleemosynary money and edification—
what else what else?—be strong heart

but the flesh goes to pieces
and the street goes strange
and a voice springs up
above the trucks

above the trains
above the children
above the bellow and the blood now still and dry
where humanity's epitomes
in every time in every place
have fallen
Agamemnon Saint Paul Star Faithful—
crying above and beyond the sea—
who put these things together?

these hieroglyphic sights and sounds
are obscure as a babylonian frieze.

THE BONE AND THE BABY

I

Do you see that gigantic bone
rotating coldly in the warm flesh
which never slips from the bone
but embraces it, clutches it?:
when shall the flesh be free from the revolving bone?

You ask: how did you get this way?—
the cells of my flesh
were broken apart, then put together again
like strips of film, each cell a square
containing an arrested image of time:
the couple caught short in Pompei
keep forever their frightful embrace in the
        next room
watching our orgasm, sweet, with a petrified leer—
my god I wish you could see the men the women the cities:
the picture was shown at reduced prices with
        special music
and my friends congratulated me not knowing that
I was dead
that the smooth gestures on the screen
were tiny, jerking bones in front of a lantern.

They claim me, those faces, clear and less clear

each one set in an emotion
demanding and getting a modern grin:
snares set for me, catching me:
I cant get up—
that's why I laugh at my brother who thinks there is
room for revolution.

II

I'll make room:
rape at the revolutionary time makes room for a baby
a violent baby to embarrass the brokers
clean and shiny, strong and new:
a star to be seen.

The world is old and beneath the ground:
a faint voice through a dark hole telling us what
          to do.
I see the old castle
where wooden statues of the holy family by Veronese
keep their contrived ecstasy and sightless eyes
suspended in the air above the tourist from Boston—
I see the president of the chamber of commerce
the patron of the militia
laid out in the aroma of his last cigar:
catafalque donated by the state and open to
          the public.

III

The hurt nerve of the people, aching for happiness
exposed to the weather like a moist white string
extends from the bone to the baby:
stretches across the proletarian bodies
shot down by machine guns in front of the factory
bleeding in the snow—
inhabits a boxcar on a sidetrack at night:
jesus christ it's cold, are we out of tobacco?
put out your light, you damn fool, what about the
          dicks?—
accumulates pain until it
dangles in the evening air

questions the odor of steak and potatoes
cries out: is this life? this narrow room every night
      after work?
    cant we afford to go to the movies?
and the nerve recoils
back on its pain and away from its desire
and says: it would feel good to sleep
SHUT OFF THAT GODDAMN RADIO AND LET ME GO TO
      SLEEP

but a voice
follows the nerve into the nightmare, calls it back—
a man in the square below, talking to a crowd:
I WANT TO TELL YOU SOMETHING ABOUT RUSSIA
and the shocked nerve struggles away from the nightmare
sends an impulse down through the street
over the skin of an orange
past the noise of machinery and the homeless feet
forward to the navel of the baby
where it sputters at the contact and takes
a flashlight picture of LENIN TRIUMPHANT
then sends the new voltage back along the nerve
to all the prostrate bodies
jerks them up out of the abandoned sewer on the
      edge of the city where they sleep
leads them FIGHT DONT STARVE in a swarm
toward the private park in the best part of town.

The noise of their approach
BARBARIANS FROM THE NORTH
quivers along the scented flesh
of the bourgeois fresh from his sunday bath—
the men and the women
exiled by the man in the park to his subconscious
      mind
    (to the apartment house near the gas tank)
ascend with violence up from the bottom
up through the rooms they were told not to enter:
they crash through the faded family portraits
they run up the polished stair where
there's supposed to be a statue in every niche
(but all the statues of the Colosseum have disappeared:

finished by Titus, 80 A.D., now grassgrown and
    a home for crows)—
at last on the top of his mind they stand, very tall,
    pressing upward in his skull.

SPRING RAIN

I

between winter and spring
out of season
between death and life
snowflakes fall on the muddy bank
but I shall not hear nor see the green explosion
of the branch thrust out into the valley
shaken by thunder, filled with a warm rain
for I shall be falling apart on the bed of the river
shall be shifting jerkily piecemeal towards the sea
past an outmoded flivver
sunken beyond competition
imbedded in the sand
past a litter of kittens in a gunnysack
anchored by a stone on a string

and thus never again shall the suicide be seen on the Main Drag
he loved the Lucky Strike lady and she betrayed him
she turned out in Cheyenne as an all around girl
sank lower and lower
prices fell and the banks were closed
she looked at her face in a mirror
the face that launched fullpage advertisements, nationwide
    hookups through the boom days
looked at it and wept
she took to dope when her trade declined
her enormous effigy above the square is disfeatured and faded
the suicide will return home circuitously
that cloud on the horizon is his body coming up from the sea
it will probably rain all night don't you think?
his thoughtless body will be whirled around forever in the circle
    of the year
unconscious of the Masses on the Main Drag
who are a straight line moving out of this circle

II

the last light slants through the coming storm
slants back on the town beneath the black clouds—
dust is blown against a wall
where faded posters still announce
buried events

three people meet on the Main Drag
hello
my father was a good union man
I intend to join the Communist party
I'm going to see the old shoemaker
who gave a copy of John Reed's book to the state university
hello
that bastard thinks he's smart
he told me to read the Daily Worker instead of the Denver Post
maybe he's right
I'm going down to the whorehouse to get out of the rain
hello hello
remember me—the blind syphilitic
standing in the doorway while the shower passes
a certificate was hanging on the wall saying
this girl is o. k.
signed by the doctor

III

people will say this is an allegory
but I was there
off the Main Drag
down by the river
where screwing and likker and smoke
conduct the nerves of the individual
away from the Masses to a small room
where the blinds are drawn and the door is locked

I'm inside the house
forgetful of the feet on the Main Drag
forgetful of the fathers of the feet—
the bones in the cemetery
who once danced together on top of the ground
axis to the whirl of delirious flesh
now muffled away in separate boxes, no air and no light

this house is surrounded by a dead world
by collapsing shacks once used for defecation by the prosperous
          merchants—
their initials, carved in their time of triumph
denote through the cobwebs and the darkness
the malodorous sarcophagi of their happy days

the betrayed body of the suicide
(he loved America)
drips from the shingles with a sad sound—
a thin stream reflecting from the alley the streetlight on the
          corner

did you hear those people go past the house?
hurrying someplace through the darkness and the rain—
is the bottle empty? are the smokes gone?
what else can we do to arrest the time?
pile all the fancy pillows against the door
keep out the sound of the feet, keep out the time

our gluttonous nerves writhe upward with ecstacy
our embraced bodies shoot us together through the stained
          wallpaper
and we arrive in a static area, barren and divine

I wanna go home
lemme go home to Marx and Engels willya?
the rain is coming through on the wallpaper
why dontya have the roof fixed?

the arrested flesh of a foetus
AN ABSOLUTE INDIVIDUAL
(it won't have time to become a member of society)
shall be carefully wrapped in your torn chemise and thrown in
          the river

MONKEYS FROM PARADISE

At the end of the street,—see?:
the gesture of the hero petrified in an arch over traffic—
          dim portico stuffed with dead men—

almost everyone is dead—
up here is only the topmost moment of the
      everdying life—
sunlight on the sidewalk and a breeze in the air—

and a gull from the sea—
          wingbeat after wingbeat
clocking the plunge of this hour.

Do you feel like listening to the man in the park?—
his amplified words
filter downward at various speeds through each
     peculiar complexity
then up again to the surface and a flash in the sun—
the people applaud,
they stand on their toes, they shade their eyes—
that foam must be where the water breaks
     on the shore of the world he says is emerging—
is it real or is it maybe?
is it rocks or is it beach?—is it beach?
IT'S BEACH,
white, gradual, soft and warm—

    anybody see my kid?—pulled loose from my hand,
         ducked through the crowd—
    ragged, footloose kid
    somewhere hopefully snubnosed against
    a plateglass cage full of monkeys from paradise.

He's through talking,—let's go—
the sky has come down to
this tremulous, man-made zodiac of neon:
     night-high wheels of satellite signs
      turning on the axis of the bullet-proof car of
           the immortal big-shot
          giving one more day the slip—

odor of evening and a wind dying inland from the sea,
night all-enfolding and the soft slap of seawater—
the teeth washed, Thriller Romance cast aside like an
       empty hypodermic—
the overworked spirit
withdrawn from this room to a safe place,

to a sure place
where the loss is balanced,
where the devils of yesterday go down before
                    the angels of tomorrow—
in the dreamfilled night
this faultless rehearsal for the showdown,
this immaculate gestation of the front page.

THE SCAB

—Two Choruses from a Play

when a millionaire gyps a millionaire
the loser has a long way to fall
down through all the levels of luxury:
kaleidoscope of three-color ads—
before assails him the knowledge that
man is a savage in the forest where
death leaps through the trees, that
the machines in his factory were gadgets merely
to keep death at a greater distance, that
now his soft hands must dig his grave—
when a worker gyps a worker, there's
no place to fall:
relegated to the bottom of the shaft
he peers through the darkness at the patch of sky
where the beautiful ads like clouds float by
and he knows damn well who's at the door:
precise as a western union clock—
his landlord, death

II

now that Zanelli, the sick man, is gone
you two left alone are assailed by doubt like a disease—
somewhere in the far-flung impersonal world
which you took for granted yesterday
a sabotage switch was thrown:
the trains are stalled, the lights are out:
mechanical arm truncated in mid-air:
semaphore like a broken wing

above the twisted rail where now at dawn
across the mangled bodies you two alone
face one another for your life in a dead world—
each of you crying hard for
his precious world, his sure world
where no treachery lurks
where a woman like wax has so often taken the impression
of how you feel that your loneliness breaks down
and pours singing into her body when she comes close—
where yesterday was rhythm of work
today each of you quickly out of hurt like a snail
pulls in to the shore of his sure investments
and speculates how dangerous the sea
between him and his friend who suddenly
is become a stranger

COSMETIC SURVIVAL

I

Legacy:
the estate, the tools
the mouth, the word
the face:
synthetic—

quick—if you hurry you can still see it:
skidding around the horizon in front of the train
stepping up speed to a blurred arc outside the window
gliding to a clarified stop back there amidst the
apparently dead accumulation.

The billboard smiles around the bend:
what state are we going through now, conductor?—
short, optimistic, boom-day stretch of
concrete sidewalk in front of
frustrated nucleus of a new town
beside the railroad—
woman wheeling perambulator stops—

"this is the valley of death:
archaeological hoax marked by
overnight legend:
cosmetic survival wreathed in
suburban neon—"

Turn away from the mirror:
dial silence, fold the newspaper,
crease the net result of your untold sacrifice
across the back of a chair—
in the glare of sleep
the submerged corpse of
what you feel and what you want
will catapult upward:
shoulders dripping out of the wave.

II

Where is the flesh that really feels?:
the people, lonely, unknown have died:
the corpse, unsought, undiscovered
gapes upward from sightless putrescence
against the sky where
whatever time it is
booms across like a bird and then
quiet once more through the thick trees where
the shapes of this time rot out of this time to
the level dusk of the moss.

In a grimy loft
the manufacture of masks by
starved girls with hands like claws:
creation of the face—

thumbtacked crucifixion of
magazine cover perfection
haloed by faint 25 watt landlord economy
laughs hysterical above
the plaint of a water-closet for six families
above hunger
above the high rouge of the dance where the feet
shuffle the white carnation and fern reminders
of the body fallen away from the mask

revealing for a moment before disruption
the last, supreme twist in
the sealed history of the real face.

III

They buried O'Toole in the Elks' plot—
a boy in a uniform trumpeted taps:
brassy knuckles of sound
knocking their way to silence
up the steep stair of the rimrock
windcarved around the mountain cemetery—
a splash of rain on his fresh soutane
geared up the drone of Father Schmidt who
will lead the escape from the open places, leaving
        the corpse to
the gravedigger and
to the sallow grin of the toothless bitch who
        wanted to see if
O'Toole received more flowers than Petrini.

The pall-bearing brethren of the lodge
replace their hats, drive back to town in a
        haze of havana
stop at the Hub Saloon where
after six rounds
their solar plexuses, fouled in a match with fear,
go soft again, though not quite happy—

the slip of the hand from the trapeze
the fall of each man inside himself to
a taste of the ultimate disaster,—
this had been concealed before by the mask-like
        faces and the white gloves—
now there's a jittery get-together:
nervous hands again on the high reaches
for the group take-off—
the signal is given
        (spun on the phlegm speckled with the blood of
        winner take all):
        it's me, your old friend: remember? bygones
        be bygones—
        we'll make it up with an even risk and fifty-fifty.

Up from the leafless year
the stiff, slow wings of the starving crows
rose internecine and black against
the sunset flare of the burning stacks of autumn—

ravine where the push was arrested:
pools of spilt likker on the lacquered bar
reflect the press of hysteria towards
communication—
here the voice choked and the wolf howled—
agonized expiration of the shapes on the plain
freezes to museum stasis beneath the soft fall of
the twilit snow—
the word the meaning the communication
slither away while the bead on the beer
winks out to a stale plunder across which blows
the rank odor of retrieveless days.

Edwin Rolfe

TO MY CONTEMPORARIES

1.

Jazz notes and Brahms intermittently
fleck the dusk-silence. Through the silhouettes
of sombre trees a lustrous blue
colors the heavens. The note still lingers
of the last thrush; its whistling rings
as if just uttered in the quiet air.
Now there is peace, and sounds are only
heard from afar: the distant train
winding its way along the river shore
bound for the city of tumult; the faint
night-blurred music of a gramophone
from a distant farmhouse; the occasional
noise of the insects
                and in this lighted room
shadows of moths on the walls, beating against the bulbs.

Now more than ever seems it rich to live,
to pluck the ripened fruit, to plant the seeds
whose growth and blossoming our heirs shall know
in years to come upon a richer earth . . .

But we have lived in furore all our lives.
This quiet stuns us like a fist's impact
against the jaw; and nothing as idyllic
as rural peace can now replace
the accustomed clamor of our daily lives—
the hurried visits, the spasmodic talks,
the too-few interludes that we have known,
the midnight meetings in smoke-filled rooms
and noise of numberless voices arguing.

And so we sit in separate rooms, you
intimidated by the silence, vaguely
feeling all's not well, too tired to read,
too restless to lie still, too stirred
to trace this strangeness to its source.

                                        And I
before this page write stray, fugitive thoughts:
things of half-meaning, impressions cut
far less than whole by this silence and its tension.
Here I am not surrendered to my poem
nor master of its words and images;
too great's the doubt in me to synthesize
fragmentary feelings, thought-lines that balk,
grow twisted, fade before they reach their ends.
I sit here only because the typewriter
is my oldest friend in this strange wilderness.
Sitting here thus I feel I've made
some last-straw contact with a friendlier world,
and clutch at it, refuse to let it go
lest I too sink to meaninglessness.

I invoke friends and fellow-Communists,
poets, sharers of my life and thought,
ponder the meaning of our words and deeds,
put questions that are answerless.

2.

You, Funaroff—where's the victory?
We've been composing poems,
each in our separate rooms, for many years.
The scraping of your pen, furious on paper,
quickens the blood of the world, and mine.
A stone in the days of my strength
could crash the window of your tenement
all the distance from Eleventh to Fourteenth.

But where's the victory? I read
in the Daily Worker the other day:
the Chinese peasants seizing arms and bread,
in Mexico they fashion dolls of clay,
chimneys spout red leaflets in Berlin,

Italian flyers bomb the land with calls
of *Avanti popolo!* and in
England a poet quits ancestral halls
to call for the knife, *the major operation*.

The Indians are dying on their reservations,
black men are lynched, the jobless legions creep
from day to hungry day, driven from railway stations.
We have no place to sleep.

But in the subway on a winter morning,
travelling from the Bronx to Union Square,
The *Times* folded at the want-ad page,
we blink from slumber at each station-stop.
The girl across the aisle—her eyes are blue—
reading the *Mirror*. Open your eyes, it's you
she's smiling at. Don't close your eyes again.
Don't surrender to the ache in your limbs,
the heaviness in your head. Look at her!
I look. I see the oval face,
but when the dusty light-bars strike her,
the cheekbones and the hollows; and her eyes
removed from the paper, are blue and wise.
She smiles again.
                        I could arise, I say,
mumbling to myself. I could arise
and go to where she sits and say
nothing that anyone could hear
but take her arm and face the door
and walk away with her,
guiding her to the platform in the rear
and look at her, into her eyes, deep
into her thoughts, and feel that the crowd
had disappeared and that no one was near
except the girl. I could say everything
without a word that any rider'd understand
and she would understand!

Look, Funaroff. Look up from the book!
You're a poet and companion. You can understand
the memories of faces seen on long-ago subway rides,
the persons whom you've known and tried to kill, but can't.
They grow the while you compromise with newer faces,

less clean-cut, blurred and blunted.
                                 You recall
our fathers' admonition: Covet not, my son,
but take what's yours by right.

It is hard to let go, it is pain to surrender
the fugitive fragments of an earlier self.
But the break must be made, the artery severed
and sewed again, the useless nerve numbed.

3.

The country quiet baffles me again.
This silence is deceptive, the flowers a fraud,
the streams polluted. To live here is a lie.
Escape from chaos is impossible;
the world's too muddled, the skies thunder
with guns, projectiles dealing death
but also, remember, the terrible cleansing storm!

To live in villages today a man must also
create a village-suburb in the brain:
partition the skull, decree which part
shall live, observe, feel joy and pain,
and which vast area grow dulled,
the senses, all awareness, killed.

You, Funaroff, and Hayes, and the others:
enter with me the farthest regions
of space and time, the body moving
across huge continents, the brain surveying
the contours of the land, destroying
the cancerous trees and men, restoring
the spark to bodies overwhelmed
by drudgery and dross and dust.
Blueprint the hills and rivers, mark
the meadows and the factories.
Harness the hordes of middlemen,
bankers and bosses, fiddle players
to generals, kings and presidents;
sweep them together and tie their hands
with their servile strings and ticker tape,
and lead the parasite pulp with you

to moldy manors and somnolent suburbs,
into the dead lands, beyond the outposts
of workingmen marching. Then lock the doors
and destroy the keys. Leave them to die.

Return with me to cities where the wind
finds chasms between skyscrapers, where men
reveal their thoughts in action, where mills
and factories are continual testament
to the war that only villages can hide.

Rejoin with greater vigor, rejoice
in new days, new companionships.
Revive the rural landscape, the girl
smiling across the subway aisle,
the oppressive silence, the news that flashes
from China to New York
                                   and synthesize
these memories within the single self
attendant on the mass of men
who march with us today, who blaze the way
from village to city, from city to the world
our minds foresee, our poems celebrate.

SOMEBODY AND SOMEBODY
ELSE AND YOU

Brother, consider as you go your way,
hemmed in by houses or flanked by fields,
conjunctions of roads through midland plains
or grain, watching dried cornstalks sway
dead and cracking in the wind's running:
who spews pennies on the streets of cities?
who jams the faucet, holds rain from crops?
who carves the sagging lines in roofs of barns
          and who reverses this?

They who have reaped your harvest
offer you the stalks. They
have teeth and fangs but their breasts

are dry, sucked empty. They have seen
millions of you stretching skeletal
hands toward them. They have been
deaf to everything you've had to say.

But you go your way, brother. They will go theirs.
By the time you meet you will have gathered
mass enough to challenge their right of way.

Maybe there won't be any doughnuts and coffee,
maybe you'll go a long time before you find
a house to shelter you, a bed to sleep in nights
and somebody to lie with, closely, and feel
here at last you've a moment for breathing
easily, peacefully, without hurry.

         But when have you had a house
         for nightrest, and a place
         to sleep in without rats
         gnawing in your head, and
         somebody with everything
         vital and whole and real?

You can read it in the papers every day
about somebody and somebody else found dead
in a furnished room (and think of all the bother
for the poor landlady, cleaning the mess away)
and nobody knows why they did it or who
they are or where the hell did they come from anyway
and no relations are there to claim the bodies
because their relations are far far away
in Chicago maybe, or Brooklyn, say.

The coroner will chant his Death-by-Suicide dirge
and nobody'll know
that somebody and somebody else have hit the eternal hay.

And maybe in the very same sheet you'll read
how somebody and somebody else are dead,
a couple of Mexicans this time. Headlines:
STARVING MEXICAN PEONS EAT GRASS, DIE.
You probably won't see it (it's in 12-point lightface.
Babe Ruth and Garbo rate 48-point bold)

but read it if you find it among the want ads.
Doughnuts to grass it will leave you cold.

Elsewhere in a city, Milwaukee maybe,
somebody'll say, "Isn't it terrible Mamie?"
staining the newsprint with everready tears
"and just think of it Mamie dear they died
without even an uncle around to bury them."

But you, brother, think as you go your way
reading this in papers under your flophouse mattress,
you know who pours the pennies and the lead, you know
who rots the watered crop, you know
who makes the walls of barns to sag
inward on emptiness
                            who waves a flag
and blows hot air through a star-spangled trumpet

while crops in fields and faces in streets
go slowly empty and yellow.

ROOM WITH REVOLUTIONISTS

For J. F.

Look at this man in the room before you:
he is young, his skin is dark, his hair
curly and black, his eyes are strangely blue,
he comes from a warmer land under the sun.
He hears a North American speak calmly
of a beautiful and faithless mistress
and is amazed. This man's a revolutionist,
painter of huge areas, editor
of fiery and terrifying words, leader
of the poor who plant, the poor who burrow
under the earth in field and mine.
His life's an always upward-delving battle in
an old torn sweater, the pockets always empty.

And this his companion across the room:
younger than he: the smooth deep forehead

sheathing a subtle and redoubtable brain;
his hair dark, eyes upward-slanting at the corners,
lips clean-etched and full. This man,
nurtured in a northern city,
is a poet, master of strong sensuous words,
artist in his own right. His oratory
before many listeners is like the sudden
startling completeness of summer rain:
warm, clear and clean, soaking into
the very heart of you, the sun just beyond.

This man is my brother, Communist, friend,
counsellor of my youth and manhood. He has crossed
the seething continent a hundred times,
leaving behind him his words
and the sound of them and their meaning.

The heavy drowsy wine of a tropic land
and the sharp bouquet of the northland intermingle
here in this room: these two are held
umbilical to a greater source and destiny,
welded each to each more firmly
than each to his native land.
                              Their vision
parallels their warmth, transcends all frontiers.

Look at them here at ease
relaxed in this pleasant room:
you will not see them again
together for many years.
Tomorrow each will go
his separate way on the maps of the globe
across great distances, talking, painting,
composing poems, organizing,
welding together South- and North-men,
destroying boundaries.

DEFINITION

Knowing this man, who calls himself comrade,
mean, underhanded, lacking all attributes
real men desire, that replenish all worlds
men strive for; knowing that charlatan, fool too,
masquerading always in our colors, must also
be addressed as comrade—knowing these
and others to be false, deficient in knowledge
and love for fellow men that motivates our kind,

nevertheless I answer the salutation proudly,
equally sure that no one can defile it,
feeling deeper than the word the love it bears,
the world it builds. And no man, lying,
talking behind back, betraying trustful friend,
is worth enough to soil this word or mar this world.

NOT MEN ALONE

What, you have never seen a lifeless thing flower,
revive, a new adrenaline in its veins?
Come, I shall show you: not men alone
nor women, but cities also are reborn;
not without labor, not before the hour
when flesh feels lacerated, mangled, torn.

Not only men are resurrected. I have seen
dull cities bloom, grow meaningful
overnight. Wherever class war comes
awareness is its courier, a newer life,
new depths in shallow, parallel streets
which may revert to commonplace, but never
relinquish scenes that have occurred on them.

Toledo's such a city. I remember
its dullness, how I always skirted
its edges on long trips west. Returning east,
I chose roads miles to the north or south
to escape its barrenness; the mind went dead,
the muscles flagged, in passing it.

Then the strike flared: the workers met
and merged at factories. The unions called
Down tools! and the militiamen
sped to the scene of combat. When the smoke
rose with the wind, a hundred men were maimed
but thousands more, the first time in their lives
were conscious of their needs, their role, their destiny.

I passed through Toledo yesterday.
The usual quiet prevailed, but from the eyes
of men and houses a newer spirit flamed.
The deadness I had felt before remained
but it was make-up only, mere disguise
for men aroused, a city awakened,
awaiting the propitious, inevitable day.

THE SIXTH WINTER

There still is coal in many houses,
I know, watching the chimney-smoke
the bitter wind drives south. There is
much gayety, banquets told of in *The Times*,
parties thrown by Lady So-and-So
at her Florida estate, where prattle
the shallow debutantes, the debonair and groomed
and empty young men who lounge around the pool,
their correctness reflected in the correctly-heated water.

Receptions, too, are a daily occurrence:
at the Waldorf, at the Plaza, at the City Hall,
for the lady novelist, for the visiting politician,
for the captain of industry and the general
        who beams good will, friendly understanding,
            closer ties between these two great nations,
his sword dangling at his side.

These things I read in the papers and
between the lines I reconstruct the scenes:
the tinkling of silver on translucent porcelain,
warm, buttered morsels of spiced food, poised
on forks, conveyed

to stomachs less delicate; the champagne
bubbling in fragile thin-stemmed crystal,
popping against sated lips, lips moist,
lips drooling, lips accustomed
to the curve of the silver spoon,
the afternoon teacup's edge,
the titled wineglass.

                    And from some unseen somewhere,
music; and soft, subdued, indirectly—lights;
and invisibly but always—warmth;
and cushions; and in the safe-deposit vault
the bankbooks, the jewels, the securities,
the cash, the gilt-edged bonds.

          And the other day
          my blood-brother Bill
          died frozen in Central Park
          asleep with *The Times*
          wrapped around his legs.

This is the sixth winter.
This is the season of death
when lungs contract and the breath of homeless men
freezes on restaurant window-panes, seeking
the sight of rare food
before the head is lowered into the upturned collar
and the shoulders hunched and the shuffling feet
move away slowly, slowly disappear
into a darkened street.

This is the season when rents go up.
Men die, and their dying is casual.
I walk along a street, returning
at midnight from my unit. Meet a man
leaning against an illumined wall
and ask him for a light.
                    His open eyes
stay fixed on mine. And cold rain falling
trickles down his nose, his chin.
"Buddy," I begin . . . and look more closely
and flee in horror from the corpse's grin.

The eyes pursue you even in sleep and
when you awake they stare at you from the ceiling;
you see the dead face peering from your shoes;
the eggs at Thompson's are the dead man's eyes.
Work dims them for eight hours. But then—
the machines silent—they appear again.
Along the docks, in the terminals, in the subway,
        on the street,
in restaurants—the eyes
are focused from the river,
among the floating garbage
that other men fish for,
their hands around poles
almost in prayer;
wanting to live,
wanting to live!
                who also soon
will stand propped by death against a stone-cold wall.

But there are other streets and other men.
I have seen them at work, I have heard their voices
cutting the winter air, the words
like knives through ice;
standing on boxes at street-corners, talking on the square,
halting the scorning men, gathering crowds
to listen to remember what they mean.

"The rifling of the city's treasury," one says,
"must end. We must have funds
to feed the foodless, rescue the rotting
men without roofs asleep along the rivershore
in summer; in winter lying frozen in doorways
in the snow in public parks at night . . .
Funds for children, for milk to replace
the dry, withered breast—beauty killed,
sought no longer in passion by lover's hands,
in hunger by hungry lips.
                WE DEMAND!"

And while he speaks, we listen in the square.
We are prepared for his words, we are stronger than to cry.
we are burdened with hunger but our eyes are dry.
We can see the blue-clad gunmen where

they stand, their hands on machine guns, mounted
on roofs surrounding the meeting place: police
like steel-blue vultures perched; and we brace
ourselves. They, not we,
are the hunted now and the haunted
by spectres not of want, but fear
festering in the brain.

In the committee room
committee men measure
the city's treasure,
determine for whom
this million; for what
that sop. They sign
the dotted line,
determine ways and means to rid
the city of vermin. Calculate
new budgets, minimum sums to sate
the hungry mouths, the populations
starved by the official rations
of previous administrations.
Will buy. Will sell. Large dividend
promised to hunger-contractor who will rid
the city of anger.

                    At last a bid!
Sold to the gentleman with the silk hat!
He is a former governor, a member of all
the uniformed fraternal orders. He agrees,
he sees the situation as we see it—
mayor, members of the board, the committee
of civic leaders and financiers.

For the stipulated millions he will feed
(he signs the papers) all the unemployed.

        Whose hand is this which lifts the receiver,
        dials the number? Whose the hand
        tapping out signal? And whose voice
        calls car and armored cycle to the scene?
        We shiver on the square.
        The north wind blows,
        driving the snow

raging over roofs.

The wind like a sword
cuts to the bone.
We are ten thousands,
bottled on all sides.
But we are not alone:
In a hundred other cities
men gathered on stormy squares
shout also
          WE DEMAND!

Knowing our words are more than words,
knowing in our heart their truth,
feeling in our limbs the need to transform
word to action, oration to living deed
                    knowing these
stirrings to be true, the seed imprisoned
straining to be free, to grow
to flower in freedom
                    we do not mind
the guns at our massed bodies aimed, nor fear
the terror awaiting us at night
on empty streets, cold dark lanes,
who have nothing to lose but our chains.
Night thickens and the cops withdraw.
They—we—return to our homes,
I to mine.
          The dark streets again,
muffled with piled snow,
leading to black hallways: stairs
that creaking caution: Careful now, careful!
Stairs that bear the body's weight only
if you are careful!
                    just as carefully
as tenderly as governments keep men
precariously alive who groan for death.

Up five long flights (we who have homes)
with two companions, invisible but tugging
downward, dead weights on the skeleton:
Hunger the one, the Landlord the other,
his one hand clutched before my eyes;
his other like a leech at my lapel.

How many others climb the stairs to hell?
and fall upon the bed not to sleep
but lie awake to keep
the memory fresh until tomorrow
of ten thousand faces
                              legs, arms, brains,
enough to maintain
life for millions,
move mountains, create
where nothing was before;
ten thousand men
lying also on beds
those who are fortunate

trying not to sleep but to remember,
not to dream but make plans,
never to forget
tomorrow, always to remember
tomorrow, to set
the clock's alarm at the appointed hour before
we sink to restless slumber.

ENTRY

Running from the shadow-coach,
silent on the darkling plain,
we whispered: be careful.
Recalled the always-dimmed headlights, the full halt,
the silence, the unspoken word.
All yesterdays blurred
while scouts advanced a mile,
returned, reported: All's well.
And in the deep dusk we relaxed, whispered,
thinking: now, now the beginning;
hastily passed the loaves of bread around,
tinned sardines, *Gauloises*, chocolate, cheese,
stuffed them in pockets; filled a few canteens
with wine; drew the stiff curtains down
and, choking, smoked—all fifty of us—
a final cigarette.

Then, two at a time, leaped the wide ditch,
ran cross-meadow, carefully climbed
the flank of a sharp ridge,
knowing already
what the word *enemy* means.

We counted heads in a hidden gully: all here.
The driver said *Salud* and disappeared,
whisper-humming the *Marseillaise*. Our guide
greeted us: *Salud!* Gave us instructions in Catalan
which somebody translated into French, others
to English, German, Finnish, Italian.
None but a few understood the original words.
But all understood.

Slowly the long single file advanced
silent through sleeping country, leaping ditches,
treading the worn earth, avoiding pits and twigs
ready to snap, betray us.
But we set the dogs to barking:
wherever we went, there was the sharp alarm
of the watchdogs yelping, howling, barking,
bursting the drowsy silence, giving alarm
to cowled sleepers of the countryside.
We could see them, almost: uneasy, turning
heavily, punchdrunk with sleep, raising
the hundred-ton head of night from the magnet
        pillow,
trying to listen—and failing,
falling again, eyes easily closed while
the sound of the dogs merged with their heavy
        dreams,
fused with the peaceful dark and, in the sky,
seen through the peacetime window, the lone visible
        star.

Then, in the huge darkness, out of forbidding sky,
the Pyrenees loomed, frightful, gigantic,
wonderfully to welcome us.

And the word ran down the line like a snake's
body, coiling, undulating:
Stop now. Rest.

We halted, gathered in a small, warm gully
again. *Feet higher*, the whispers said,
Gets the blood out of them, eases them for climbing.

Going toward what we hated, feeling no hatred,
only the *now, now* pounding
before it's too late in the brain,
we paused, nibbled at bread, cheese, chocolate,
cupped our cigarettes' glow in careful palms,
stooped to drink at a spring, then stretched
bodies full on the thick grass,
resting waiting listening
searching the uncharted skies
where border patrols flashed rainbow beams
of light into the darkness; straining
eyes for distance, seeing much,
foreseeing more; wondering:

> Will we make it? Will we make it?
> No question of daring. The deed, begun, was done.
> Now only the mountains faced us, the moon rising,
> and only a shallow river in its dry summer bed.

Moving, the man ahead always in sight, thinking:
   this Spain we go to, this is no land of
   postcard ruins, though we have seen them. This is
   not what remains of half-remembered lectures:
   bull fights, the matador suave in silk,
   his mastodon enemy, buffalo-shouldered,
   facing him. No land of *flamenco*
   or Rabbi Israel's son courting the phobic maid
   under a moonlit balcony near Zaragossa.
   No land of oranges, or olive groves,
   or vines heavy with grapes in geometric vineyards,
   nor steel that sings and bends like a slim girl
            dancing,
      nor *gitanos* and *guitarristas*. No,
   none of these tourist dreams alone is Spain.

Spain is yesterday's Russia, tomorrow's China,
yes, and the thirteen seaboard states.
Spain is all lands and all times when clash
the hopes and the wills of the men in them;

the kindliest, seeking only life,
and the cruellest, in love with death.

We were right: how right we never discovered
there in the midnight fields of slumbering France.

CITY OF ANGUISH

for Milton Wolff

At midnight they roused us. In the distance we
          heard
verberations of thunder. "To the cellar," they ordered.
"It's safest under the stairway." Pointing,
a veteran led us. The children, whimpering,
followed the silent women who would never
sing again strolling in the *Paseo* on Sunday evenings.
In the candle-light their faces were granite.

"Artillery," muttered Enrico, cursing.
Together we turned at the lowest stair.
"Come on," he said. "It's better on the rooftop.
More fireworks, better view." Slowly we ascended
past the stalled lift, felt through the roof door,
squinted in moonless darkness.

We counted the flashes, divided the horizon,
90 degrees for Enrico, 90 for me.
"Four?" "No, five!" We spotted the big guns when
the sounds came crashing, split-seconds after light.
Felt the slight earthquake tremor when shells fell
square on the Gran Via; heard high above our heads
the masculine shriek of the shell descending—
the single sharp rifle-crack, the inevitable dogs
barking, angry, roused from midsummer sleep.

The lulls grew fewer: soon talking subsided
as the cannonade quickened. Each flash in darkness
created horizon, outlined huge buildings.
Off a few blocks to the north, the *Telefónica*

reared its massive shoulders, its great symbol profile
in dignity, like the statue of Moses pointing,
agèd but ageless, to the Promised Land.

2.

Deafening now, the sky is aflame with
unnatural lightning. The ear—
like the scout's on patrol—gauges each explosion.
The mind—neither ear nor eye is aware of it—
calculates destruction, paints the dark pictures
of beams fallen, ribs crushed between them; beds
blown with their innocent sleepers to agonized
death.
            And the great gaping craters in streets
yawn, hypnotic to the terrified madman,
sane a mere hour ago.
                        The headless body
stands strangely, totters for a second, falls.
The girl speeds screaming through wreckage; her
            hair is
wilder than torture.
                        The solitary foot,
deep-arched, is perfect on the cobbles, naked,
strong, ridged with strong veins, upright, complete . . .

The city weeps. The city shudders, weeping.
The city weeps: for the moment is silent—
the pause in the idiot's symphony, prolonged
beyond the awaited crashing of cymbals, but
the hands are in mid-air, the instruments gleaming:
the swastika'd baton falls! and the clatter of
thunder begins again.
                        Enrico beckons me.
Fires there. Where? Toward the *Casa del Campo*.
And closer. There. The *Puerta del Sol* exudes
submarine glow in the darkness, alive with
strange twisting shapes, skyfish of stars,
fireworks of death, mangled lives, silent lips.
In thousands of beds now the muscles of men are
aroused, flexed for springing, quivering, tense,
that moments ago were relaxed, asleep.

3.

It is too late for sleep now.
Few hours are left before dawn. We wait for
the sun's coming . . . And it rises, sulphurous
through smoke. It is too late for sleep.

The city weeps. The city wakens, weeping.

And the Madrileños rise from wreckage, emerge
from shattered doorways . . .
                    But always the wanderer,
the old woman searching, digging among debris.
In the morning light her crazed face is granite.
And the beggar sings among the ruins:

   All night, all night
   flared in my city the bright
   cruel explosion of bombs.
   All night, all night,
   there, where the soil and stone
   spilled like brains from the sandbag's head,
   the bodiless head lay staring;
   while the anti-aircraft barked,
   barked at the droning plane,
   and the dogs of war, awakened,
   howled at the hidden moon.
   And a star fell, omen of ill,
   and a man fell, lifeless,
   and my wife fell, childless,
   and, friendless, my friend.
   And I stumbled away from them, crying
   from eyeless lids, blinded.
   Trees became torches
   lighting the avenues
   where lovers huddled in terror
   who would be lovers no longer.

   All night, all night
   flared in my city the bright
   cruel explosion of hope—
   all night
   all night . . .

4.

Come for a joyride in Madrid: the August morning
is cleared of smoke and cloud now; the journalists
dip their hard bread in the *Florida* coffee,
no longer distasteful after sour waking.
Listen to Ryan, fresh from the lines, talking
  (Behind you the memory of bombs beats
  the blood in the brain's vessels—the dream broken,
  sleep pounded to bits by the unending roar of
  shells in air, the silvery bombs descending,
  rabid spit of machine guns and the carnival flare
  of fire in the sky):
                "Why is it, why?
when I'm here in the trenches, half-sunk in mud,
blanket drenched, hungry, I dream of Dublin,
of home, of the girls? But give me a safe spot,
clean linen, bed and all, sleep becomes nightmare
of shrapnel hurtling, bombs falling, the screaming
     of bullets,
their thud on the brain's parapet. Why? Why?"

Exit the hotel. The morning constitutional.
Stroll down the avenues. Did Alfonso's car
detour past barricades? Did broken mains splatter
    him?
Here's the bellyless building; four walls, no guts.
But the biggest disaster's the wrecking of power:
thirty-six hours and no power: electric
sources are severed. The printer is frantic:
how print the leaflet, the poster, or set
the type for the bulletin?
             After his food
a soldier needs cigarettes, something to read,
something to think about: words to pull
the war-weary brain back to life from forgetfulness:
spirited words, the gestures of Dolores,
majestic Pasionaria speaking—
mother to men, mother of revolutions,
winner of battles, comforter of defenders;
her figure magnificent as any monument
constructed for heroes; her voice a symphony,
consoling, urging, declaiming in prophecy,

her forehead the wide plateaus of her country,
her eyes constant witness of her words' truth.

5.

Needless to catalogue heroes. No man
weighted with rifle, digging with nails in earth,
quickens at the name. Hero's a word for
peacetime. Battle
knows only three realities: enemy, rifle, life.

No man knows war or its meaning who has not
stumbled from tree to tree, desperate for cover,
or dug his face deep in earth, felt the ground
          pulse with
the ear-breaking fall of death. No man knows war
who never has crouched in his foxhole, hearing
the bullets an inch from his head, nor the zoom of
planes like a Ferris wheel strafing the trenches . . .

War is your comrade struck dead beside you,
his shared cigarette still alive in your lips.

FIRST LOVE

Again I am summoned to the eternal field
green with the blood still fresh at the roots of flowers,
green through the dust-rimmed memory of faces
that moved among the trees there for the last time
before the final shock, the glazed eye, the hasty mound.

But why are my thoughts in another country?
Why do I always return to the sunken road through corroded hills,
with the Moorish castle's shadow casting ruins over my shoulder
and the black-smocked girl approaching, her hands laden with
          grapes?

I am eager to enter it, eager to end it.
Perhaps this one will be the last one.
And men afterward will study our arms in museums

and nod their heads, and frown, and name the inadequate dates
and stumble with infant tongues over the strange place-names.

But my heart is forever captive of that other war
that taught me first the meaning of peace and of comradeship

and always I think of my friend who amid the apparition of bombs
saw on the lyric lake the single perfect swan.

Muriel Rukeyser

THEORY OF FLIGHT

You dynamiting the structure of our loves
embrace your lovers solving antithesis,
open your flesh, people, to opposites
conclude the bold configuration, finish
the counterpoint—sky, include earth now,
flying, a long vole of descent
renders us land again.
Flight is intolerable contradiction.
We bear the bursting seeds of our return
we will not retreat; never be moved.
Stretch us onward   include in us the past
sow in us history, make us remember triumph.
    O golden fructifying, O the sonorous calls
    to arms and embattled mottoes in our war
    brain versus brain for absolutes, ring harsh!
    Miners rest from blackness—reapers, lay by the sheaves
    forgive us our tears   we go to victory
    in a commune of regenerated lives.
    The birds of flight return, crucified shapes
    old deaths restoring vigor through the sky
    mergent with earth, no more horizons now
    no more unvisioned capes, no death; we fly.

Answer together the birds' flying
reconcile rest to rest
motion to motion's poise
    the guns are dying the past is born again
    into these future minds the incarnate past
    gleaming upon the present
                        fliers, grave men,
    lovers—do not stop to remember these,

think of them as you travel, the tall kind prophets,
the flamboyant leapers toward death,
the little painful children
                              how the veins were slit
into the Roman basins to fill Europe with blood
how our world has run over bloody with love and blood
and the misuses of love and blood and veins.
Now we arrive to meet ourselves at last
we cry beginnings
the criers in the midnight streets call dawn
respond   respond
you workers   poets   men of science and love

Now we can look at our subtle jointures, study our hands,
the tools are assembled, the maps unrolled, propellors spun,
do we say *all is in readiness—*
the times approach, here is the signal shock—?

—Master in the plane shouts "Contact"—
master on the ground: "Contact!"
        he looks up—"Now?" whispering—"Now."
        "Yes," she says. "Do."
        Say yes, people.
        Say yes.
        YES

THE LYNCHINGS OF JESUS

I.   PASSAGE TO GODHEAD

Passage to godhead, fitfully glared upon
by bloody shinings over Calvary
this latest effort to revolution stabbed
against a bitter crucificial tree,
mild thighs split by the spearwound, opening
in fierce gestation of immortality.

Icarus' phoenix-flight fulfils itself,
desire's symbol swings full circle here,
eternal defeat by power, eternal death
of the soul and body in murder or despair

to be followed by eternal return, until
the thoughtful rebel may triumph everywhere.

Many murdered in war, crucified, starved,
loving their lives they are massacred and burned,
hating their lives as they have found them, but
killed while they look to enjoy what they have earned,
dismissed with peremptory words and hasty graves,
little calm tributes of the unconcerned.

Bruno, Copernicus, Shelley, Karl Marx :   you
makers of victory for us :   how long?
We love our lives, and the crucifixions come,
benevolent bugles smother rebellion's song,
blowing protection for the acquiescent,
and we need many strengths to continue strong.

Tendons bind us to earth, Antaeus-ridden
by desperate weakness disallied from ground,
bone of our bone; and the sky's plains above us
seduce us into powers still unfound,
and freedom's eagles scream above our faces,
misleading, sly, perverse, and unprofound.

Passage to godhead, shine illuminated
by other colors than blood and fire and pride.
Given wings, we looked downward on earth, seen
uniform from distance; and descended, tied
to the much-loved near places, moved to find
what numbers of lynched Jesuses have not been deified.

II. THE COMMITTEE-ROOM

Let us be introduced to our superiors, the voting men.
They are tired ; they are hungry ; from deciding all day
around the committee-table.
       Is it foggy outside?   It must be very foggy
       The room is white with it
The years slope into a series of nights, rocking sea-like,
shouting a black rush, enveloping time and kingdom
and the flab faces
       Those people engendered my blood swarming
       over the altar to clasp the scrolls and Menorah

the black lips, bruised cheeks, eye-reproaches   :
    as the floor burns, singing Shema
Our little writers go about, hurrying the towns along,
running from mine to luncheon, they can't afford
to let one note escape their holy jottings:
today the mother died, festering   :   he shot himself   :   the bullet
        entered the roof of the mouth, piercing the brain-pan
    How the spears went down in a flurry of blood;
    how they died howling
                                how the triumph marched
    all day and all night past the beleaguered town
    blowing trumpets at the fallen towers;
    how they pulled their shoulders over the hill, crying
    for the whole regiment to hear   The Sea   The Sea
Our young men opening the eyes and mouths together,
facing the new world with their open mouths
                                        gibbering war
                                        gibbering conquest
Ha.   Will you lead us to discovery?

What did you do in school today, my darling?
        Tamburlaine rode over Genghis had a sword
        holding riot over Henry V Emperor of and
        the city of Elizabeth the tall sails
        crowding England into the world and Charles
        his head falling many times onto a dais
        how they have been monarchs and
        Calvin Coolidge who wouldn't say
                                however, America

All day we have been seated around a table
                                all these many days
One day we voted on whether he was Hamlet
or whether he was himself and yesterday
I cast the deciding vote to renounce our mouths.
Today we sentinel the avenue solemnly warning
the passers (who look the other way, and cough) that we
speak with the mouths of demons, perhaps the people's,
but not our own.
            Tomorrow
the vote's to be cast on the eyes, and sex, and brain.
Perhaps we will vote to disavow all three.

We are powerful now   :   we vote
                        death to Sacco a man's name
                        and Vanzetti a blood-brother; death
                        to Tom Mooney, or a wall, no matter;
                        poverty to Piers Plowman, shrieking anger
                        to Shelley, a cough and Fanny to Keats;
                        thus to Blake in a garden; thus to Whitman;
                        Thus to D. H. Lawrence.
                                        And to all you women,
                        dead and unspoken-for, what sentences,
                        to you dead children, little in the ground
                        :   all you sweet generous rebels, what sentences

This is the case of one Hilliard, a native of Texas,
in the year of our Lord 1897, a freeman.
Report . . . Hilliard's power of endurance seems to be
the most wonderful thing on record   His lower limbs
burned off a while before he became unconscious;
and his body looked to be turned to the hollow.
Was it decreed (oh coyly coyly) by an avenging God
as well as an avenging people that he suffer so?
                                        We have
16 large views under magnifying glass.
8 views of the trial and the burning.
For place of exhibit watch the street bills.
                Don't fail to see this.

Lie down dear, the day was long, the evening is smooth.
The day was long, and you were voting all day
                hammering down these heads
                tamping the mould about these diamond eyes
                filling the mouths with wax
                                        lie down my dear
the bed is soft lie down to kindest dreams

                all night they carried leaves
                bore songs and garlands up the gradual hill
                the noise of singing kept the child awake
                    but they were dead
                    all Shakespeare's heroes   the saints   the Jews   the rebels
                    but the noise stirred their graves' grass
                    and the feet all falling in those places
                    going up the hill with sheaves and tools
                    and all the weapons of ascent together.

III. THE TRIAL

The South is green with coming spring ;   revival
flourishes in the fields of Alabama.   Spongy with rain,
plantations breathe April   :   carwheels suck mud in the roads,
the town expands warm in the afternoons.   At night the black boy
teeters no-handed on a bicycle, whistling The St. Louis Blues,
blood beating, and hot South.   A red brick courthouse
is vicious with men inviting death.   Array your judges; call your
                                        jurors; come,
here is your justice, come out of the crazy jail.
Grass is green now in Alabama; Birmingham dusks are quiet
relaxed and soft in the park, stern at the yards:
a hundred boxcars shunted off to sidings, and the hoboes
gathering grains of sleep in forbidden corners.
In all the yards   :   Atlanta, Chattanooga,
Memphis, and New Orleans, the cars, and no jobs.

Every night the mail-planes burrow the sky,
carrying postcards to laughing girls in Texas,
passionate letters to the Charleston virgins,
words through the South   :   and no reprieve,
no pardon, no release.

A blinded statue attends before the courthouse,
bronze and black men lie on the grass, waiting,
the khaki dapper National Guard leans on its bayonets.
But the air is populous beyond our vision:
all the people's anger finds its vortex here
as the mythic lips of justice open, and speak.

Hammers and sickles are carried in a wave of strength, fire-tipped,
swinging passionately ninefold to a shore.
Answer the back-thrown Negro face of the lynched, the flat forehead
                                        knotted,
the eyes showing a wild iris, the mouth a welter of blood,
answer the broken shoulders and these twisted arms.
John Brown, Nat Turner, Tóussaint stand in this courtroom,
Dred Scott wrestles for freedom there in the dark corner,
all our celebrated shambles are repeated here   :   now again
Sacco and Vanzetti walk to a chair, to the straps and rivets
and the switch spitting death and Massachusetts' will.
Wreaths are brought out of history

here are the well-nourished flowers of France, grown strong on
    blood,
Caesar twisting his thin throat toward conquest, turning north from
               the Roman laurels,
the Istrian galleys slide again to sea.
How they waded through bloody Godfrey's Jerusalem   !
How the fires broke through Europe, and the rich
and the tall jails battened on revolution   !
The fastidious Louis', cousins to the sun, stamping
those ribboned heels on Calas, on the people;
the lynched five thousand of America.
Tom Mooney from San Quentin, Herndon   :   here
is an army for audience
              all resolved
to a gobbet of tobacco, spat, and the empanelled hundred,
a jury of vengeance, the cheap pressed lips, the narrow eyes like
          hardware;
the judge, his eye-sockets and cheeks dark and immutably secret,
the twisting mouth of the prosecuting attorney.

Nine dark boys spread their breasts against Alabama,
schooled in the cells, fathered by want.
    Mother   :   one writes   :   they treat us bad.   If they send us
    back to Kilby jail, I think I shall kill myself.
    I think I must hang myself by my overalls.

Alabama and the South are soft with spring;
in the North, the seasons change, sweet April, December and the air
loaded with snow.   There is time for meetings
during the years, they remaining in prison.
                In the Square
a crowd listens, carrying banners.
Overhead, boring through the speaker's voice, a plane
circles with a snoring of motors revolving in the sky,
drowning the single voice.   It does not touch
the crowd's silence.   It circles.   The name stands   :
Scottsboro

          . . . . .

Earth, include sky   ;   air, be stable to our
feet, which have need of stone and iron stance;
all opposites, affirm your contradictions,
lead, all you prophets, our mechanic dance.

Arches over the earth, conform, be still,
calm Roman in the evening cool of grace,
dramatic Gothic, be finally rounded now
pared equal to the clean savannahs of space,

grind levels to one plane, unfold the stones
that shaped you pointed, return to ground, return,
bird be no more a brand upon the sky
no more a torch to which earth's bodies burn

fire attracting fire in magnetism
too subtle for dissection and proponence,
torturing fire, crucifying posture
with which dead Jesus quenches his opponents.

Shall we then straddle Jesus in a plane
the rigid crucified revived at last
the pale lips flattened in a wind a rain

of merging conquered blast and counterblast.
Shout to us   :   See   !
the wind   !
Shout to us   :
FLY

CITY OF MONUMENTS

Washington 1934

Be proud   you people   of these graves
      these chiseled words   this precedent
From these blind ruins shines our monument.

Dead navies of the brain will sail
      stone celebrate its final choice
      when the air shakes, a single voice
a strong voice able to prevail   :

Entrust no hope to stone although the stone
shelter the root   :   see too-great burdens placed
with nothing certain but the risk

set on the infirm column of
the high memorial obelisk

erect in accusation sprung against
a barren sky taut over Anacostia   :
give over, Gettysburg   !   a word will shake your glory   :
blood of the starved fell thin upon this plain,
this battle is not buried with its slain.

    Gravestone and battlefield retire
    the whole green South is shadowed dark,
    the slick white domes are cast in night.
    But uneclipsed above the park

    the veteran of the Civil War
    sees havoc in the tended graves
    the midnight bugles blown to free
    still unemancipated slaves.

Blinded by chromium or transfiguration
we watch, as through a microscope, decay   :
  down the broad streets the limousines
advance in passions of display.

Air glints with diamonds, and these clavicles
emerge through orchids by whose trailing spoor
the sensitive cannot mistake
the implicit anguish of the poor.

The throats incline, the marble men rejoice
careless of torrents of despair.

Split by a tendril of revolt
stone cedes to blossom everywhere.

BOY WITH HIS HAIR CUT SHORT

  Sunday shuts down on this twentieth-century evening.
  The El passes. Twilight and bulb define
  the brown room, the overstuffed plum sofa,

the boy, and the girl's thin hands above his head.
A neighbor radio sings stocks, news, serenade.

He sits at the table, head down, the young clear neck
          exposed,
watching the drugstore sign from the tail of his eye;
tattoo, neon, until the eye blears, while his
solicitous tall sister, simple in blue, bending
behind him, cuts his hair with her cheap shears.

The arrow's electric red always reaches its mark,
successful neon! He coughs, impressed by that precision.
His child's forehead, forever protected by his cap,
is bleached against the lamplight as he turns head
and steadies to let the snippets drop.

Erasing the failure of weeks with level fingers,
she sleeks the fine hair, combing: "You'll look fine tomorrow!
You'll surely find something, they can't keep turning you down;
the finest gentleman's not so trim as you!" Smiling, he raises
the adolescent forehead wrinkling ironic now.

He sees his decent suit laid out, new-pressed,
his carfare on the shelf. He lets his head fall, meeting
her earnest hopeless look, seeing the sharp blades splitting,
the darkened room, the impersonal sign, her motion,
the blue vein, bright on her temple, pitifully beating.

MORE OF A CORPSE THAN A WOMAN

Give them my regards when you go to the school reunion;
and at the marriage-supper, say that I'm thinking about them.
They'll remember my name; I went to the movies with that one,
feeling the weight of their death where she sat at my elbow;
          she never said a word,
          but all of them were heard.

All of them alike, expensive girls, the leaden friends:
one used to play the piano, one of them once wrote a sonnet,
one even seemed awakened enough to photograph wheatfields—

the dull girls with the educated minds and technical passions—
        pure love was their employment,
        they tried it for enjoyment.

Meet them at the boat: they've brought the souvenirs of boredom,
a seashell from the faltering monarchy;
the nose of a marble saint; and from the battlefield,
an empty shell divulged from a flower-bed.
        The lady's wealthy breath
        perfumes the air with death.

The leaden lady faces the fine, voluptuous woman,
faces a rising world bearing its gifts in its hands.
Kisses her casual dreams upon the lips she kisses,
risen, she moves away; takes others; moves away.
        Inadequate to love,
        supposes she's enough.

Give my regards to the well-protected woman,
I knew the ice-cream girl, we went to school together.
There's something to bury, people, when you begin to bury.
When your women are ready and rich in their wish for the world,
        destroy the leaden heart,
        we've a new race to start.

MEDITERRANEAN

On the evening of July 25, 1936, five days after the out-
break of the Spanish civil war, the Americans with the
anti-fascist Olympic games were evacuated from Barcelona
at the order of the Catalonian government. In a small
Spanish boat, the *Ciudad di Ibiza,* which the Belgians had
chartered, they and a group of five hundred, including
the Hungarian and Belgian teams as well as the American,
sailed overnight to Sète, the first port in France. The only
men who remained were those who had volunteered in
the loyalist forces: the core of the future International
Brigades.

I

At the end of July, exile. We watched the gangplank go
cutting the boat away, indicating: sea.

Barcelona, the sun, the fire-bright harbor, war.
Five days.

Here at the rail, foreign and refugee,
we saw the city, remembered that zero of attack,
chase in the groves, snares through the olive hills,
rebel defeat: leaders, two regiments,
broadcasts of victory, tango, surrender.
The truckride to the city, barricades,
bricks pried at corners, rifle-shot in street,
car-burning, bombs, blank warnings, fists up, guns
busy sniping, the torn walls, towers of smoke.
And order making, committees taking charge, foreigners
commanded out by boat.

I saw the city, sunwhite flew on glass,
trucewhite from window, the personal lighting found
eyes on the dock, sunset-lit faces of singers,
eyes, goodbye into exile. Saw where Columbus rides
black-pillared: discovery, turn back, explore
a new-found Spain, coast-province, city-harbor.
Saw our parades ended, the last marchers on board
listed by nation.

I saw first of those faces going home into war
the brave man, Otto Boch, the German exile, knowing
he quieted tourists during machine-gun battle,
he kept his life straight as a single issue—
left at that dock we left, his gazing Breughel face,
square forehead and eyes, strong square breast fading,
the narrow runner's hips diminishing dark.
I see this man, dock, war, a latent image.

The boat *Ciudad di Ibiza*, built for two hundred,
loaded with five hundred, manned by loyal sailors,
chartered by Belgians when consulates were helpless,
through a garden of gunboats, margin of the port,
entered: Mediterranean.

II

Frontier of Europe, the tideless sea, a field of power
touching desirable coasts, rocking in time conquests,

fertile, the moving water maintains its boundaries,
layer on layer, Troy-seven civilized worlds,
Egypt, Greece, Rome, jewel Jerusalem,
giant feudal Spain, giant England, this last war.

The boat pulled into evening, underglaze blue
flared instant fire, blackened towards Africa.
Over the city alternate light occurred;
                    and pale
in the pale sky emerging stars.
No city now, a besieged line of light
masking the darkness where the country lay,
but we knew guns
bright through mimosa
singe of powder
and reconnoitering plane
flying anonymous
scanning the Pyrenees
tall black above the Catalonian sea.

Boat of escape, dark on the water, hastening, safe,
holding non-combatants, the athlete, the child,
the printer, the boy from Antwerp, the black boxer,
lawyer and Communist.
    The games had not been held.

A week of games, theater and festival;
world anti-fascist week. Pistol starts race.
Machine-gun marks the war. Answered unarmed,
charged the Embarcadero, met those guns.
And charging through the province, joined that army.
Boys from the hills, the unmatched guns,
the clumsy armored cars.
Drilled in the bullring. Radio cries:
To Saragossa! And this boat.

Escape, dark on the water, an overloaded ship.
Crowded the deck. Spoke little. Down to dinner.
Quiet on sea: no guns.
The printer said, In Paris there is time,
but where's its place now; where is poetry?

This is the sea of war; the first frontier

blank on the maps, blank sea; Minoan boats
maybe achieved this shore;
mountains whose slope divides
one race, old insurrections, Narbo, now
moves at the colored beach
destroyer, wardog. "Do not burn the church,
compañeros, it is beautiful. Besides,
it brings tourists." They smashed only the image
madness and persecution.
Exterminating wish; they forced the door,
lifted the rifle, broke the garden window,
removed only the drawings: cross and wrath.
Whenever we think of these, the poem is,
that week, the beginning, exile
remembered in continual poetry.

Voyage and exile, a midnight cold return,
dark to our left mountains begin the sky.
There, pointed the Belgian, I heard a pulse of war,
sharp guns while I ate grapes in the Pyrenees.
Alone, walking to Spain, the five o'clock of war.
In those cliffs run the sashed and sandaled men,
capture the car, arrest the priest, kill captain,
fight our war.
The poem is the fact, memory falls
under and seething lifts and will not pass.

Here is home-country, who fights our war.
Street-meeting speaker to us:
                              ". . . came for games,
    you stay for victory; foreign? your job is:
    go tell your countries what you saw in Spain."
The dark unguarded army left all night.
M. de Paîche said, "We can learn from Spain."
The face on the dock that turned to find the war.

III

Seething, and falling black, a sea of stars,
black marked with virile silver. Peace all night,
over that land, planes
death-lists——a frantic bandage
the rubber tires burning——monuments,

sandbag, overturned wagon, barricade
girl's hand with gun———food failing, water failing
the epidemic threat
the date in a diary———a blank page opposite
no entry—
however, met
the visible enemy heroes: madness, infatuation
the cache in the crypt, the breadline shelled,
the yachtclub arsenal, the foreign check.
History racing from an assumed name, peace,
a time used to perfect weapons.

If we had not seen fighting
if we had not looked there
    the plane flew low
    the plaster ripped by shot
    the peasant's house
if we had stayed in our world
between the table and the desk
between the town and the suburb
slow disintegration
male and female
If we had lived in our cities
sixty years might not prove
    the power this week
    the overthrown past
    tourist and refugee
Emeric in the bow speaking his life
and the night on this ship
and the night over Spain
quick recognition
male and female

And the war in peace, the war in war, the peace,
the face on the dock
the faces in those hills.

IV

Near the end now, morning. Sleepers cover the decks,
cabins full, corridors full of sleep. But the light
vitreous, crosses water; analyzed darkness
crosshatched in silver, passes up the shore,

touching limestone massif, deserted tableland,
bends with the down-warp of the coastal plain.

The colored sun stands on the route to Spain,
builds on the waves a series of mirrors
and on the scorched land rises hot.
Coasts change their names as the boat goes to
France, Costa Brava softens to Côte Vermeil,
Spain's horizon ghost behind the shapeless sea.

Blue praising black, a wind above the waves
moves pursuing a jewel, this hieroglyph
boat passing under the sun to lose it on the
attractive sea, habitable and old.
A barber sun, razing three races; met
from the north with a neurotic eagerness.

They rush to the solar attraction; local daybreak finds
them on the red earth of the colored cliffs; the little islands
tempt worshipers, gulf-purple, pointed bay;
we crowd the deck,
welcome the islands with a sense of loss.

V

The wheel in the water, green, behind my head.
Turns with its light-spokes. Deep. And the drowning eyes
find under the water figures near
in their true picture, moving true,
the picture of that war enlarging clarified
as the boat perseveres away, always enlarging,
to become clear.

Boat of escape, your water-photograph.
I see this man, dock, war, a latent image.
And at my back speaking the black boxer,
telling his education: porter, fighter, no school,
no travel but this, the trade union sent a team.
I saw Europe break apart
and artifice or martyr's will
cannot anneal this war, nor make
the loud triumphant future start
shouting from its tragic heart.

Deep in the water the Spanish shadows turn,
assume their brightness past a cruel lens,
quick vision of loss. The pastoral lighting takes
the boat, deck, passengers, the pumice cliffs,
the winedark sweatshirt at my shoulder.
Cover away the fighting cities
but still your death-afflicted eyes
must hold the print of flowering guns,
bombs whose insanity craves size,
the lethal breath, the iron prize.

The clouds upon the water-barrier pass,
the boat may turn to land; these shapes endure,
rise up into our eyes, to bind
us back; an accident of time
set it upon us, exile burns it in.
Once the fanatic image shown,
enemy to enemy,
past and historic peace wear thin;
hypocrite sovereignties go down
before this war the age must win.

VI

The sea produced that town: Sète, which the boat turns to,
at peace. Its breakwater, casino, vermouth factory, beach.
They searched us for weapons. No currency went out.
The sign of war was the search for cameras,
pesetas and photographs go back to Spain,
the money for the army. Otto is fighting now, the lawyer said.
No highlight hero. Love's not a trick of light.

But.—The town lay outside, peace, France.
And in the harbor the Russian boat *Schachter*;
sharp paint-smell, the bruise-colored shadow swung
under its side. Signaling to our decks
sailors with fists up, greeting us, asking news,
making the harbor real.
                    Barcelona.
Slow-motion splash. Anchor. Small from the beach
the boy paddles to meet us, legs hidden in canoe,
curve of his blade that drips.
Now gangplank falls to dock.

                    Barcelona
everywhere, Spain everywhere, the cry of planes for Spain.
The picture at our eyes, past memory, poems,
to carry and spread and daily justify.
The single issue, the live man standing tall,
on the hill, the dock, the city, all the war.
Exile and refugee, we land, we take
nothing negotiable out of the new world;
we believe, we remember, we saw.
Mediterranean gave
image and peace, tideless for memory.

For that beginning
make of us each
a continent and inner sea
Atlantis buried outside
to be won.

Isidor Schneider

YOUNG REVOLUTIONIST

Death will come, but not age.
The young man Lenin died;
the young man Ruthenberg
was laid in a grave.
Someday to us all will come death
but not age, not the slow
breakdown and decay,
emotion shallowing
and the brain a puddle.

Look among us.
Soon some will die,
but none grow old.

Look at the athlete—
an old mind tottering
on young muscle;
look at the ascetic—
scolding his senile senses.

By these arts age
may be lured to look away
but not to break its stay.

We share the youth
of the young revolution;
its infinite horizon
trains the mind;
its infinite passion
keeps our senses fresh;
its infinite duties
keep our bodies hard.

COMRADE – MISTER

(We hear it still, hey mister,
Mister You, he separating, simpering
opiate word—oh, Mister, Mister here—)

But once this patient, democratic word
was spruce and haughty, marshall of orations, though now
in his own hand-me-downs, a servant word,
it grooms the way for others—a word
with which to clear one's throat.
                              Study it,
it has a sounding past, and can be read
biography of a revolution; it had
impassioned freedom for an ancestor
ambitious to make monarchs by the million
but bad at bargains, satisfied to soothe
with solemn sirring a million monarch slaves.

Americans in seventeen-seventy-six,
the French in eighty-nine, and others
reddening a century with rebellion
fought to be named mister.
                              MASTER,
                                        there!—
there was the crime men tried to legislate
a virtue! Presumptive masters all, they gave
right to be masters to the tyrant-hearts,
right to the cunning, to the morbid-nerved,
to the badged bullies, and to the capitalists
who hired and mastered all,
who took the right to wall the land
and roof the sky, toll all
the ways of life, the while our mister-mass
adjust their mister-word, their robe of sound, plod on
like soldiers let limp home in uniforms.

II

(We hear it more and more, Comrade
the unifying word, that greets us all
into the brotherhood of man!)

Now, the red revolution comes.
No march of masters
on a trampled world.

Oh, light of tread, on joyful feet, men meet
to build the sweet, the masterless, new world.
They know, they live, the unifying way;
they know, they speak, the unifying word.
Comrade!
      You.
        I.
            Comrade, we go.
Over the vast roused body of humanity
stroking it with our laboring hands to drain out fear
as from the quaking earth a swamp is drained;
and opening into hate the springs of love
as through dry mire and desert clots
new veins of water pulse and fructify.
Humanity that of our comradeship is born
will make of its divisions, now its joints;
through you, through me, through all, comrades—
Comrades, oh unifying name, oh name of peace.

PORTRAIT OF A FALSE REVOLUTIONIST

He has the watery desire
to quench our fire,
to wilt the firm,
to soak in us until
we sink to our lowest level.

He has the indoors art
to catch you in a chair
and drug the air;
all motion under balk
that he may talk.

He'll chant red song
like a cricket all day long,
if you let him hum

safe and warm
out of the storm.

"Oh, see the other side!"—
and if we ride
that pendulum's idle arc
his aim is won;
nothing will be done.

But most beware
when he calls you rare,
better than the others;
that is his knife
to stab your brothers.

IN A HOTEL LOBBY

These are the well-to-do, the managers of the nation.
Trains from the North and West and South,
ships from the East, planes through the sky
from capitals and emporiums have rushed them here.
Porters with ironic eyes and automatic, sirring lips
escort them here to sit, lined deep in plush.

Beside them stir their imperious women.
Their hair threatens like lions' manes;
their eyes rove like killing eagles;
their lips look cut from stone;
their hands take lightly like the hands
of Aztec priests who timed fresh human hearts
beating on their palms.

Strange beside their cruel beauty are the mutilated men.
Bushmen chiefs with knives and spikes and stains
have not more marred themselves, than have these chiefs
of the capitalist jungle, gouged and torn
with pointed worries and with hooking scorn.

Here anxiety has almost split a cheek; and here
suspicion digs trenches round the eyes;
here arrogance has filed the lips like blades;

and here indulgence pulled them out like tongues;
and greed has sliced and envy burned
and graft has squeezed and flattery turned.

And do they know their doom? Out of the jungle to be driven?
The jungle of Capital is being cleared;
in Russia first and soon to thrive the world.

In the morning, following their razor's traces
do they see the omens on their faces?

TO THE MUSEUMS

Come to the museums, workers; and under every landscape
paste this label: "Workers! Is the earth as beautiful where you live?
you on the poverty farms, boarded to hogs,
your sore fields scratched to the stone by the chickens?
You in the slums who can span between two fingers
all you can have of the free horizon; who must lean,
somehow, over a tenement's shoulder to see the sun?
This is your homestead, farmer. Worker, this is your summer place.
It has been kept beautiful by your labor. Enjoy its grace.

Come to the museums, workers; under each gleaming nude
paste this label: "This is the working woman, this is her worker's body,
undeformed,—by anxiety uneaten, undisordered by too many birhts,
the flesh unbloated by the puffing food
of eight cent diets; her smile is a discharge of health;
it spreads comfort upon us, calms us within a laughing peace.
Gracious she is in native dignity, at last untied
out of the cringe of poverty, straightened to full stature, pride
in the workers' world.

Come to the museums, workers, and under each madonna and child
paste this label: "Workers, in this fable, see, they damned our bodies;
here they cursed our sex. Worship for motherhood, reverence for life
they sought with a maternal virgin and a baby god!
And Joseph the carpenter is scorned and pushed aside.
Not of a worker's blood this child; too good for a worker such a bride.
Oh Comrades, our madonnas smile, invite their lovers' seed,
welcome the ripening, are brave to bring forth

children into the free, unharried, workers' world.

Come to the museums. On all the gates, the pillars, put up posters:
"Workers enter here. Claim what is stored here. It is yours.
Labor of artists; for the mind must be worked before it yields,
plowed, hoed, watered and weeded, till the ripened vision
is plucked by the acting hand; and for what use?
Not to be wiped on aching eyes; not to be draped
a shroud of dreams upon a stillborn day!
but plans to be enacted; visions to be made real
within the workers' world.

DOLLARS

Cut dollars in the shape of men;
in the shape of men they best declare themselves.
The treasurer's stamp, and runes, and seals,
let be their thread and buttons.

To let men know that when they buy and sell
men are the payment—men—stamp dollars in
the shape of men. Cut tens to the cramped hips
of shop girls, soldiers' board backs, and limp
of errand boys; outline the twenty-fives
on angle-shouldered clerks, and fifties on
mug necks of foremen and the creep
of ministers; cut hundreds plump to fit
brag bosoms of our young executives.
With thousands, oh, be very delicate;
the ruffle chins of bankers scallop clean
and neatly curve the ripe, pluck bodices
of movie queens, the suck of all men's eyes;
cut carefully the bevelled noses of
star actors famous for the faultless sneer.

But singles frame to the shape of naked men
nicked between ribs and stamped from blue white paper.

When dollars are made in the shape of men
how loud will be the journals with confession!
Gov'ment will shrink to name the public debt,

the uncome generations it has spent
to spread the flag a shadow on bright earth.

Banks may beware of posting on brass signs
how many men are on deposit there.

THE SUN, THE WORKER

I

I work, roars the sun.
I sweat flame,
I plow the earth.
Plow you after me;
from my countless rays
let glance your countless furrows.
Out of the ocean
I steam up water.
Wind bundles it into cloud,
hauls and delivers it
on the parched land.

Do you follow after.
Trap the spill with dams
and drain it into the places
missed by the splashing winds.

Work, oh man!
My laboring light is in you,
stored in the seventy-year cell,
your body; and that coiled,
fire-fondling filament, your brain,
whose wick I lit at your birth,
touching it off in your eyes.

II

And those who keep you from work,
saying, now your work profits me not,
leave my workshops, leave my tools,
no longer take my tokens to buy bread—

against them I bid you
kindle my best fire,
the red fire of revolution.
Take, each one his spark, my heroes.
By the hundreds heap yourselves as faggots,
till the flames roar,
echoing me.
The earth is the workers'.
As I am bright with work,
so make the earth bright.

THE REICHSTAG TRIAL

The hard eyes glittered ill, the hard voice said,
"This hall has smoked for sixty years.
It's time the fire appears."
And the sky went red.

The hard eyes searched, the hard voice ordered out
the pack. "The Communist hand go catch
and in it put the match
and 'arson!' shout."

And four men guiltless, and a fifth drugged dumb
in chanting chains confound the court.
Blood hunters hot for sport
grow cold, grow numb.

The four have comrades who the world alarm.
Fifth tells, his dim narcotic head
swollen with drugs and dread,
who poised his arm.

Dimitroff's courage, the world workers' wrath,
build high and wall the court around.
The lies from it rebound,
drop in their path.

Back in the kindling hand now leaps the fuse.
The hard eyes faint, the hard voice drools,

the curses its dull tools.
The accused accuse.

Oh judges, lawyers, officers, how glare
your faces in that fire you lit.
No threat, nor legal wit
can shade you there.

Nor bonfires in the path, nor murders stop
the Revolution's march. Strip bare
to beasts in your despair;
all pretense drop.

You thugs of Capital, your muscle sold
to a fleshless system, sour with death,
you'll poison in its breath
when it vomits gold.

The frenzied old mistakes its palsies, thinks them blows,
stands for this hour like a fighter still.
Oh soon the risen masses will
bring on its throes!

TO COMRADE LENIN

"The Tartar eyes . . .
cold . . . inscrutable . . . Asian mystery . . ."

The paid pens pour out their blots
to hide you from us.
                    The janitors of History
work to drag you through their halls . . . of Fame,
wreathed with cartridge clips, haloed in gun blasts,—
you the builder to be put with the destroyers,
Napoleon . . . Cromwell . . . Caesar . . . Genghis
    Khan . . .

They cannot take you from us, Comrade Lenin.
Forever to us you are the leading comrade!
                    Mystery man?—

Only to those whom darkness prospers, only to
the clouded minds who, till they foul them, cannot see
the clear; only to corrupters of ideas, who brew
the dyes of mystery that discolor color.

Comrade, how can you be a mystery to us,
whom, when we were drowning in illusion,
you led up the steep banks of reality.

II

Up the steep banks, on the safe land you led us.
safe land you led us.
In the campfires of the revolution we scorched out
to the last vapor the Capitalist illusions.
Free and strong, with uncompromised arms
we built with you, in Russia, the worker's state.
The land obeyed us, and toiled with us;
where the miners went the mountains kneeled;
in the factories we stepped solidly like men in their homes,
and the sounds of the machines are peaceful
like the purring of cats at firesides.

In America the task waits to be done.
Lead us, Comrade Lenin, we will follow.
Here the earth is against us, pitted with debt.
Men pray for drouths, and cheer when cattle drown,
and curse their crops, and leave the land bald.
In Washington officials willingly would go
guides to the cyclone, pilots to the flood.
From the mines the coal, the ores, shoot out,
the gas fumes up, the oil coats us, in the old war
against the workers; and we are mixed with the fuel
that feeds the fires of industry. Our factories
are eight hour, ten hour, twelve hour prisons.
The sound of the machines is a roar of hatred;
the smallest scolds and spits at us.
And when we are let home, we drag after us
chains of debt, of fear, of want . . .
                              Comrade Lenin,
we know the rotting system cracks.
We at the bottom feel first the crumbling mortar
on our heads. In our united strength, following you,

we'll heave the thing over; clear it away;
build where it stood the workers' state in America,
add it to the Soviet Union of the World.

Herman Spector

OUTCAST

I am the bastard in the ragged suit
who spits, with bitterness and malice to all.

needing the stimulus of crowds,
hatred engendered of coney-island faces,
pimps in a pressedwell parade,

I, looking into faces
(some say nothing; or with a leer—
see what the years have done to me,
and be confused,
unbroadway heel!)

at times the timid christ,
longing to speak . . .
women pass hurriedly, disdainfully by.
men, pigsnouted, puff
and puke at the stars . . .

recalling the verses of sensitive men
who have felt these things . . .
who have reacted, to all things on earth,
I am dissolved in unemotion.
won by a quiet content,
the philosophy of social man . . .
The high hat gods go down the aisles.
I am at one with life.

URBANITE DELAPIDATE

friend, you are wearied,
as from no knowledges of death,
nor with ennui . . .
but sitting, never more than whistling things,
your face is softly tragic now; you seem
to have a certain solemn majesty
amid the flare of steel, whitepaint,
and passengers asquirm.

whence comes this sudden evening sadness, peace?
what brings the frightful frown to be forgot?
the venomed lust, now hidden, and a sheet
of unread morning paper on your lap . . .
your nodding head.
ah, you are tired.
wearied, not of life
nor from wise knowledges of death . . .

but the damn misery of flesh
awaiting loveliness:
the stark and neverfelt caress
of softness like the night

not knowledges of death.
nor consciousness of things forgot,
but simply, longings: tortured lusts,
that makes this business vulture's head to swim . . .
and gives him such a majesty
in sleep.

NIGHT IN NEW YORK

the city is a chaos;
confusion of stone and steel,
the spawn of anarchic capitalism.

it is night;
the clock in the square points the hour:
nine.

pornographic offerings,
eruptions on the skin of streets
from the tainted blood of commerce,
are electricly alight and lewd.

signs flash bargain messages.
with twinkling of legs, a slim whore passes,
turns a corner, disappears.
several remarkably interesting ideas
walk up and down the streets . . .
and the trolleys clatter.
taxis slide softly.
the blare of evening hurried movements
welcomes me, a friend, a customer.

whaddeyeread?—
telegram! journal! mail!
newspapers; blazoning forth with each edition,
news of the most momentous import;
their blatancy a sterile farce
in the subtle night.
the "el" trains rumble,
with a menacing undertone of hate.

and the city laughs rattlingly.
trolleys . . . clatter, back and forth.
taxis slide softly.
slick, suave limousines sneer, tooting horns.
a cop blows his shrill whistle . . .

all day in the shop and my back hurts,
my feet are like lead.
my stomach grumbles . . .
i belch.

the city is a chaos;
confusion of stone and steel,
the spawn of anarchic capitalism.

TIMECLOCK

a big mack rolling and rumbling down the long street,
and lo, morning!
pavements glisten with cold assurance of concrete
achievement; cash-confidence exudes from roughspores of stone
(bigtime belching out of black funnels,)
and milliondollar plants white, virginal in the sudden sun,
tiers of windows rising sightless from moist sorrows of night:
radios fermenting blood with jazz.

john hawley awakes, an old weariness in young bones.
minutes are decisive units of salary,
looming large upon the hideous timeclock,
ticking regularly.
he looks out the window, past the twisting el
a mack-truck farts and wheezes;
people like vermin
flee into dark subways.
the scene is always the same:

each morning john hawley adorns his meekness
with a necktie flamboyant as a hollywood movie,
and emerges, whistling blithely, from a musty hallway,
the irridescent answer to a maiden's prayer.
each morning john hawley jaunts to the job
via streetcar in the summertime,
absentmindedly proffers his fare
(the motorman has a sweaty face),
turns to the sportsection of the paper with habitual
indifference . . .
aware of the sweet sharp tang of wrigley's gum:
THE FLAVOR LASTS.

morning sizzles like something toothsome in vats,
preparing miraculous fodder for the keen appetite,
and the refreshed mind sniffs . . .

but he tracks timidly in unctuous labyrinths,
uprooted, clamped to revolving mechanisms
until evening comes
                    an incubus,
stale with the stink of sweat, forgetful,
cold.

(a white collar clerk: an amorphous slug,
found in abundance in mire,
in fecund, obfuscate cities . . . disgusting to the touch.
thus the political dictionaries.)

laborers have souls that writhe
to the clattering crescendo of power-machines,
and little hunchbacked men dream and moan
where the wheels spin in rhythms upon the brain
like surf beating on the sloped shores,

but john hawley, a fileclerk, a catholic christian,
number 178, punching IN and OUT,
a pale young man wearing a kleenkut suit
and a straw hat in the summer
has been perforated, stamped:
AMERICAN-MADE.
drugged by the clock portentously measuring
stingy minutes of salary,
the mind deformed and poisoned by headlines
("a paper for people who think")
to become the cruel convenience of capitalists:
the slave echoing the master's wish.

but at evening
john hawley, dropped like a plummet
past thirty-odd floors
reaches the street, and (somewhat dizzy),
feels the blood flowing back into veins
sapped by gestures of obeisance and meaningless
frivols of toil,
and bulbs enunciate time's wealth
startling an idea of vengeance
THE FLAVOR LASTS
out of confusion and weariness . . .

now the city froths insane at night;
its panting, throbbing breath
fogs the solitary lamps;
a restless humming underneath,
music of its peculiar fever . . .

john hawley is an entity
stifled by bricks and steel and electric-
lights,

wandering aimless, alone, through the ghoulish
squares

freedom is a girl with tangled hair
whose breasts are worthy of caresses,
whose eyes, imperious with a larger lust,
vitriol the tissues of the virtuous;

out of the night, impassive,
saying there is no god,
no caesar,
no allembracing goodness;
nothing, nothing, only stone . . .
she is a pretty piece
throwing kisses from a necessary distance,
singing throaty, sentimental songs
in a jazzband voice.

john hawley glimpsed,
through movies of incessant reels
(all-talking-dancing-whoring),
the dwindled whiteness of her thighs—
a super-super-nymth,

and walked
far
seeking her bed
the sky was endless, glimmering
into dawn . . .
and he crept, vanquished, an old weariness overcoming his bones,
past the garish sconce in the musty hallway,   ·
painfully up the carpeted flights
to his room.

on the twisting el
trains scudded and droned;
he slept, respiring with the wind,
haggard as the gray, pitiless world
that called him citizen.

HARLEM RIVER

by the huge dead yards
where freight trains wait
and brood, warehouses' vacant eyes
stare out at a world made desolate;
but the tugs,*bloot* their egregious pride,
and the scummy waters twinkle with light.

they've suicided from this bridge—
ginks out of jobs, and the dames for love—
their peaked, pale faces rise in the dark
futile with yearning, tear-wet, stark:
i wonder what vast, dim dream of peace
they sought, in the susurrant waves' embrace.

night's breasts were soft, cajoling sleep . . .
her lewd eyes beckoned their weariness.
and now they are ground to the ultimate dust
that settles between red tenement bricks;
and now they are one with the particled past
siltering up weird, hopeless streets.

but high spires glow in the lonely gloom.
trains clatter and roar, and softly, laugh.
the pavements, endless in grim contempt
of hunger and lust, glitter like glass.
in the brief white glare of the smart arc-lamps
strange shadowshapes loom, and threaten, and pass.

SADLY THEY PERISH

(A DIRGE FOR THE OBJECTIVIST POETS.)

now in the perfumed dusk,
                              a pause
the phosphoroscent worms emerge
like vacant, jangling trolleycars. . . .
a purblind peace,
the gentry of the bourgeoisie
squirm into purple space.

5 years: the ivory towers crack,
the walls are eaten with decay.
the eliots, the ezra pounds
play jazztunes of profound regrets
in hideouts of expatriates . . .
"this is coming to you by remote control."
the sacred muse, an anxious cockroach, darts
here and there along the floor. . . .

"oh death, where is thy sting?"
a rain of shrapnel in the streets:
clubs, teargas, speeches, bayonets,
the castor oil, the rubber hose,
the raids, the lynchings, pogroms, wars . . .
but butterflies have gauzy wings;
blue buzzards roost on empire-state.

confused, confused,
the images awry
like sappy roosevelt grins in coney-island twisted mirrors;
some little fanfare for the weird esthetic guy
        then shrugs and sneers,
applause that gutters to a hiss . . .
prince hamlet scrapes a violin,
wears rubber heels:
absorb the shocks that tire you out . . .

fascism yawns,
        black pit of death.
objectivists stuff cotton into ears,
disdain the clear emphatic voices of revolt
yet seem to hear, though dimly to be sure,
the ancient rocking-chairs of ease
creak absent-minded praise . . .
and pansy poets bow, and sway,
launch battleships and yachts of plutes
with girlish giggles and champagne salutes;
or else (thank-god) remember yesterdays,
fingering the junk of medals on their breasts . . .

sadly they perish, each by each,
whispering madness, they disappear . . .
into the isolate doom of dreams,

into the cold gray vaults of dust.
and who will gather the darlings up,
arrange them in anthologies?
what mussolini-horse will drop
bouquets upon their mouldering graves?

5 years: the ivory towers crack!
cockroaches scuttle after crumbs . . .
the harried line of workers holds;
repulsed, returns to the attack!
in trenches, behind the barricades,
electric eyes pierce walls of fog . . .
in arid wastes of no-man's land
white grubs squirm into purple space.

SUICIDE BEFORE COFFEE
IN A FURNISHED ROOM

. . . each time it rains,
the landlord suffers neuralgic pains;
meek tenants rise as spiral wraiths
(it stops,)
descend as tinkling ice.
the aftermath: nostalgic, nice
placid, the world remains unchanged.

electric shuttled the scuttling winds,
banged blistered shutters in the rooming house,
swung the streetdoor on its screaming hinge
(soundeffects announcing turmoil, strife,)
revived faint thunder in recurring trains,
rasped wires slapping the windowpanes,
tapping cornices and cluttered pipes;
then fled in terror down the gurgling drains.

what blackguard battered his cringing brain?
he shrank from moist, catarrhal streets,
phlegm in the gutters, cracked concrete,
to fetid hallways, stairs that creaked,
vanished along the balustrade.

what purpose in this endless seeking?
always, his modest dreams betrayed.
listen: the landlord's new shoes squeaking;
end of the week, the rent unpaid.

evenings and evenings whizzed past corners;
he knew the trickle of secret bleeding,
throttled by wavering shapes of fear
peered at elysium, receding
filled with the gas, and drifted upward
smiling above pale hills of peace . . .
flakes of snow, a coldness tingling
fluttering free like rentreceipts

dawn; the papers shrill in warning:
government spending must decrease,
government spenders must desist . . .
     decrease, desist
substantial citizens insist,
   government;
   government;
   government,
         cease

WISEGUY TYPE

The smart little gent with the shoebutton eyes,
   with the folded nose, twice-over, so;
   with the diffident smile, and the spectacles
   like a hornéd owl, so wise, so wise,

Is a sharpshooter born in a cabaret, to a rattle
   of drums, and a spastic shudder, by a pinkish
   floozie with powdered thighs,
   and a monocled punk in a cutaway,
and a tinhorn song, and a clicking jig,
   and a swift, pat fade
     and a getaway . . .

Is a wise, wise baby who won't take sides,
   playing the middle against the ends;

shuffles the cards with a crack and a flutter,
   looks sharp in the dark for omens and friends,
Concedes wih a mutter, You may be right,
   It may be true but I can't decide;
   If the cards are stacked then what does it matter,
   If death is the answer, what's the use? . . .
I'm a lonesome wolf in a cold, hard winter,
And I'm standing pat: so it's up to Youse.

Genevieve Taggard

INTERIOR

A middle class fortress in which to hide!
Draw down the curtain as·if saying *No*,
While noon's ablaze, ablaze outside.
And outside people work and sweat
And the day clangs by and the hard day ends.
And after you doze brush out your hair
And walk like a marmoset to and fro
And look in the mirror at middle-age
And sit and regard yourself stare and stare
And hate your life and your tiresome friends
And last night's bridge where you went in debt;
While all around you gathers the rage
Of cheated people.
                    Will we hear your feet
In the rising noise of the streets? *Oh no!*

LIFE OF THE MIND, 1934

(The words in the books are not true
If they never act in you.)

Fret fools the days away
Best sellers for their food.
And bad philosophy.
Fret fools. But we,
We dare not read for long,
But snatch our thought, our song,
As soldiers do their meat.
Necessity to eat,
Necessity to act,

And act aright renews
The mind's link with the arm.
Imperative to choose,
Imperative to do,
This time's dynamic form.
Once we were students. Then
Grave faces hours pored
Over the activity stored,
The energy of great men.

That time must come again.
If not for us for those
We will to endow once more
With tested word-in-deed.
All poetry and the great prose
Born in a like uproar
Where someone had to bleed.

The battle of the mind,
Tranquillity, too, the kind
Quick teachers face, the jest,
Keen argument with a friend,
That sport and the sweet zest,
All fall, must fall, behind.
That time is at an end.

Now action like a sword.
Now to redeem the word.
Now blood for stubborn proof
No one may cut apart
Word from the living deed,
Or live this life aloof.
Fear is a flimsy creed.
"I believe with all my heart"
In the one way to believe.
"This thing is good—I give
My living to see it live."

Bleak thought and bastard art,
How easy to relinquish both!
So to be wise, so learned
If never more returned
To temporary peace!

So not to die of sloth,
Or live best-seller's ease.
But to stand upon our oath.

TO MY DAUGHTER, 1936

AFTER REFUSING TO TAKE OUT LIFE-INSURANCE

They come to me talking about your safety,
  your future. The heavy odds.
They paint a black picture. How shall our children
  survive?
As if with all mothers and fathers, and since the first
  day of your life
I had not worried in big ways and small. Knowing the
  perils. The frauds.
As if I needed an actuary with slide rule to give me
  a pang.

Insure? How insure against pain? Is there perhaps
  no class-struggle?
How is it with millions of children? With you as
  with them.
A different insurance, darling. One safety, one hope,
  my hope, my resolve:
Your face lifted with a million others, laughing,
  under red banners.

MILL TOWN

(DEDICATED TO PAUL DE KRUIF)

*. . . the child died, the investigator said, for lack of proper
food. After the funeral the mother went back to the mill.
She is expecting another child . . .*

            . . . then fold up without pause
The colored ginghams and the underclothes.

And from the stale
Depth of the dresser, smelling of medicine, take
The first year's garments. And by this act prepare
Your store of pain, your weariness, dull love,
To bear another child with doubled fists
And sucking face.
              Clearly it is best, mill-mother,
Not to rebel or ask clear silly questions,
Saying womb is sick of its work with death,
Your body drugged with work and the repeated bitter
Gall of your morning vomit. Never try
Asking if we should blame you. Live in fear. And put
Soap on the yellowed blankets. Rub them pure.

FOUR FRESCOES OF THE FUTURE

Multitude and no tumult: a maze on march,
Slow march, strong body and heart bowed down,
And head bowed down to the solitude of the dead,
Brutish grief down trodden under march of feet,
Death put down with the dead, and grief put down . . .

Then an end, an end to this. Say enough, return
Nourish, tend, to work, to shop, return
In the name of the living, in the name of our span.

Multitude and no tumult; sweet gusts of song
Floating, delirious hope, pure notes; so sing
Song, chiming and climbing chain. As no one sang
Alone, aloft in the old days. This chant our lore
Our love, our will, our bold blithe gale of sound. . . .

Then an end, an end to this; singing, return.
Nourish, tend, to work, to shop, return
In the name of the living, in the name of our span.

Multitude and no tumult; galleries intent—
Men in great congress, active in applause,
The agile argues, the logical man again
Utters, exhorts, expands and again expounds,
Pauses. Applause. O orator, reply!

Then an end, an end to this; disperse, return
Nourish, tend, to work, to shop, return
In the name of the living, in the name of our span.

Multitude and no tumult. Long frolick lines,
O gaiety of wind; child flung in foam to swim.
Races and feats, games, parachutes, flags,
Roar for the athlete trim and brown as bronze,
O festivals, O spectacles, enchant, enchant—encore!

Then an end, an end to this. Pick up, go home.
Nourish, tend, to work, to shop, return
In the name of the living. In the name of our span.

A MIDDLE-AGED, MIDDLE-CLASS WOMAN AT MIDNIGHT

In the middle of winter, middle of night
A woman took veronal in vain. How hard it is to sleep
If you once think of the cold, continent-wide
Iron bitter. Ten below. Here in bed I stiffen.
It was a mink-coat Christmas said the papers . . .
Heated taxis and orchids. Stealthy cold, old terror
Of the poor, and especially the children.
                                        Now try to sleep.
In Vermont near the marble-quarries . . . I must not think
Again, wide awake again. O medicine
Give blank against that fact, the strike, the cold.
How cold Vermont can be. It's nerves, I know,
But I keep thinking how a rat will gnaw
In an old house. Hunger that has no haste . . .
Porcupines eat salt out of wood in winter. Starve
So our children now. Brush back the hair from forehead,
See the set faces hungrier than rodents. In the Ford towns
They shrivel. Their fathers accept tear gas and blackjacks.
When they sleep, whimper. Bad sleep for us all.
Their mouths work, supposing food. Fine boys and girls.
Hunger, busy with this cold to make barbarian
These states, to haunt the houses of farmers, destroyers
Of crops by plan. And the city poor in cold-water flats
Fingering the gas-cocks—*can't even die easy*

If they turn the gas off. I'm sick I tell you. Veronal
Costs money, too. Costs more than I can pay.
And night's long nightmare costs me, costs me much.
I'll not endure this stink of poverty. Sheriffs, cops,
Boss of the town, union enemy, crooks and cousins,
I hope the people win.

TO AN AMERICAN WORKMAN
DYING OF STARVATION

Swell guy, you got to die.
                    Did you have fun?
I guess we know you worked.
                    I guess we saw you.
It got you just the same.
                    Say it with flowers.
So long. We got the breaks. But we'll be seeing you.
There's a little job we got to attend to up here first.

AUTUMN SONG FOR ANTI-FASCISTS

The leaves come down with little grieving,
Soft in the season of unleafing.
Secure in change, in temporary
Death the old sad heart is merry.
Delicate death and leaf-stem pliant. . . .
General death no nature fears,
Indifferent to tears.
Grief in the world strides like a giant.
Grief's mask, his bully forehead bare
Comes catapulting close, his stare
Frightens to death the old and ill.
Here the mould of green, the chill
Comforts the pulse, the black heart-ache,
So that we listen while the bland trees shake
And put aside all fear
In the innocent withering of the year.
The brave assault the bully, bleed

Red on grasses and dying weed,
And redden the trampled ground.
Soldier dead, sleep sound.
Leaves of pale yellow softly pile
Where we put you, single-file.

SILENCE IN MALLORCA

I

Our stony island, Spain's laconic child
Quiet. Nada. Cover the glowing spark.
Hush all the hótas and hush hush the wild

Arabian cries. Now in Europe's dark
Whisper weep secretly plot but never sing.
On cliffs against the sky moves the new mark

Shape of the plane, the loathed imperial thing
The hawk from Italy, the spy of black.
Ground where we labor darkens with its wing.

A few shot first. Then nothing. Then the attack.
Terror of the invader. Puff of shells,
And Juan our best man ambushed in the back.

Hide hide in the caves; listen in the dry wells. . . .
Clang—the obedient treachery of church bells.

II

They shot the mayor of Inca. They jailed
The poor the free the poor the free the brave.
Out of the puerto when the felucca sailed

Planes roared and swooped and shot them on the wave.
Our people serve the invader and his gun.
Our people, Spain. Slow tempo of the slave.

We are cut off. Africa's blazing sun
Knew these same hawks that now around us prey.

And Barcelona suffers. Is there no one

To save us but ourselves? From far away
After victorious battle. . . . Cry, we cry
Brothers, Comrades help us. Where are they?

Our island lying open to the sky.
Mallorca, the first to fall, the last to die.

III

O wild west wind. . . . Liberty's open roar,
Blow on this island, blow the ocean clean,
Drown our tormentors, blow equinox, blow war

Away from the world. Drive to us the unseen
Battalions, clouds of planes by workers flown,
Give us our land again, quiet and green,

Our children singing and our land, our own
Ways, our wives, our delegates. Blow here.
The indifferent sea washes the beach of stone,

And Mediterranean silence, primitive fear
Steps in the foot of Tomàs, the new slave.
Moves in the hovering hawk, spiraling near.

We bend, we work,—this island inferno and grave.
Come with the wind of your wings. And save.

John Wheelwright

THE WORD IS DEED

FOR KENNETH BURKE

John begins like *Genesis*:
In the Beginning was the Word;
Engels misread: *Was the Deed*.
But, before ever any Deed came
the sound of the last of the Deed, coming
came with the coming Word
(which answers everything with dancing).

In our Beginning our Word:
'Make a tool to make a tool'
distinguished Man from Brute.
(Men who dance know what was done.)
Good and Evil took root
in this, the cause of Destinies
whence every Revolution rose and stirred.

Jubal Cain and Tubal Cain
made the plow and jubilee
to protest, in ranks hostile to Seth
Seth's all-too-loyal mutiny.

Ways to work determinate
moulds for intelligence.
Discoveries follow thence
obscured by fallibilities'
compensating philosophies
doubted soon as heard.
(Who dance not know not what they do.)

But when, against Fate, error wards:
"Frustrate while ye mirror kind
Disaster, blind
Chance, enemies at once and guards . . ."
muscles of thought comply:
"Think, act in answer to desire;
from the will springs Promethean fire."

Deeds make us. May, therefore, when our Last
Judgment find our work be just:
all tools, from foot rules to flutes
praise us; and our deeds' praise find
the Second Coming of the Word.
(Dance, each whose nature is to dance;
dance all, for each would dare the tune.)

BREAD-WORD GIVER

FOR JOHN, UNBORN

John, founder of towns,—dweller in none;
Wheelwright, schismatic,—schismatic from schismatics;
friend of great men whom these great feared greatly;
Saint, whose name and business I bear with me;
rebel New England's rebel against dominion;
who made bread-giving words for bread makers;
whose blood floods me with purgatorial fire;
I, and my unliving son, adjure you:
keep us alive with your ghostly disputation
make our renunciation of dominion
mark not the escape, but the permanent of rebellion.

Speak! immigrant ancestor in blood; brain
ancestor of all immigrants I like. Speak,
who unsealed sealed wells with a flame and sword:
    'The springs that we dug clean must be kept flowing.
    If Philistines choke wells with dirt,—open
    'em up clear. And we have a flaming flare
    whose light is the flare that flames up in the people.

'The way we take (who will not fire and water
taken away) is this: prepare to fight. If we
fight not for fear in the night, we shall be surprised.
Wherever we live, who want present abundance
take care to show ourselves brave. If *we* do not try
they prevail. Come out,—get ready for war;
stalwart men, out and fight. Cursed
are all who'll come not against strong wrong.
First steel your swordarm and first sword.
But the second way to go? and deed to do?

'That is this: Take hold upon our foes and kill.
We are they whose power underneath a nation
breaks it in bits as shivered by iron bars.
What iron bars are these but working wills?
Toothed as spiked threshing flails we beat
hills into chaff. Wherefore, handle our second
swords with awe. They are two-edged. They cut their
                    wielders' hearts.'

TITANIC LITANY

FOR LEON TROTSKY

Prometheus!
Prototypal Christ, pre-crucified
pushing the invisible
advance upon our pushes upon chaos.
Discoverer and inventor, never let 'em say:
"Human nature cannot change."
Institutor of fire's Sacrament
and outward forms of conscious inner will;
Prometheus!
Forethought of freedom (freedom
for her and him; concrete, in that and this)
Titan, tortured by the tyrant vulture
whom Vulcan riveted as firmly as machines
can rivet laborers to capital;
Prometheus!

O, let it never be said that the human of nature cannot
change. Saul changed to Paul. All saints change
man's nature, as men change nature's change.
Show us in our own acts that we hear our supplication.
Never a Saint is revered who was not reviled
as a rebel. Every rebel, in so far prophet
breeds holy doubt and skeptic faith in deeds'
Melchizedekian Succession.
While boom the double guns of Act and Word,
mutating fire swims through the protestant
blood of Christ, erect above your shadowed rock
Prometheus!
Our supine Crucifixion.

IN POETS' DEFENCE

FOR VAN WYCK BROOKS

Rebel poets, who've given vicar aid
to murdered agitator and starved miner,
starve in your mind and murder in your thought
indignant will-to-help unfused with Revolution.
Nurture the calm of wrath. Though Labor fumble
a second Civil War, prevent a memory
like its first forged golden chain
to bind white peon and black serf apart.
      While labor power'd come too nearly free
in the open market of free trade for jobs,
choose from Concord conspirators their thoughts
which still remain Sedition; forget braggarts
after victory whose rage contrived defeat.
Not by old images of grief and joy,
nor mummied memory of the Civil War,
nor Mayflower Compact, nor by rebel oaths
which made the Thirteen States palladium
and shield and shibboleth, adjure ourselves.
      Now boom the double guns of Word and Deed
while liberal persons fall in love with ice men
and Wilson's ghost'll vampire Lenin's mummy.
Every memory of hope, every thought,
passions and nerves our stern philanthropy

with cheer, with eager patience for laborers' slow
smoldering of hate to crack down pedestals,
compact from bones and gold, of Quirinus and Mars.

SKULLS AS DRUMS

FOR MALCOLM COWLEY

When the *first* drumtaps sound and trumpets buzz
through doors and windows, then may no one stir.
May listeners keep their seats while orators
fear to speak to the point. In chalky schoolrooms
may schoolboys not look up; in bridal chambers
heart clocks'll keep "Tick-Tock" although the drums
beat to a different time; or the same time.

In the plowed field, or field of ripened grain,
may farmers look up,—and spit. However drums
pound or whirr, however shrill horns blow,
housewives'll make beds,—as usual.
Let men and women sleep with deafened ears.
    Only the timid fear not fear; only
a coward stops his tears. Father, remember;
remind the boy of 'bravery'! Mother,
entreat your heart! You who are fond of talking,
continue in conversation. You who are silent,
silently close your window; while heavy drums'll
rattle quicker to a wilder and wilder bugle.

When *more* drums beat and shriller bugles squeal;
armored hearses snarl around that tomb
where covered skeletons play with live corpses.
. . . Roll your great stone before the door.
(They will stifle breathing air
so foetal grey with funk.) Now, charge your wire
that'll bring a galvanic startle to their great
Jack-in-the-Box. Open the lid. Look in:
    Whoever stifles fear, he is the coward.
Gaze on the corpse, pre-mortified
—gas bloated—of Mars. And on the fearful
helm of Suicide, Inc., drum, drum, drum

drum louder to drum up more fear.
From fear *and* fear a sterner fear is born
whose name is Wrath,—a filament of light
in every man. O, snarling bugles!
Crack the great stone before the door.
Drill the fat corpses for a brave parade.
Send the brave skulls and bones under the yoke
with thump of muffled drum and trumpet blurr.

Richard Wright

I HAVE SEEN BLACK HANDS

I am black and I have seen black hands, millions and millions of
them—
Out of millions of bundles of wool and flannel tiny black fingers have
reached restlessly and hungrily for life.
Reached out for the black nipples at the black breasts of black
mothers,
And they've held red, green, blue, yellow, orange, white, and purple
toys in the childish grips of possession,
And chocolate drops, peppermint sticks, lollypops, wineballs, ice
cream cones, and sugared cookies in fingers sticky and
gummy,
And they've held balls and bats and gloves and marbles and
jack-knives and sling-shots and spinning tops in the thrill of
sport and play

And pennies and nickels and dimes and quarters and sometimes on
New Year's, Easter, Lincoln's Birthday, May Day, a brand new
green dollar bill,
They've held pens and rulers and maps and tablets and books in
palms spotted and smeared with ink,
And they've held dice and cards and half-pint flasks and cue sticks
and cigars and cigarettes in the pride of new maturity . . .

II

I am black and I have seen black hands, millions and millions of
them—
They were tired and awkward and calloused and grimy and covered
with hangnails,
And they were caught in the fast-moving belts of machines and
snagged and smashed and crushed,

307

And they jerked up and down at the throbbing machines massing
    taller and taller the heaps of gold in the banks of bosses,
And they piled higher and higher the steel, iron, the lumber, wheat,
    rye, the oats, corn, the cotton, the wool, the oil, the coal, the
    meat, the fruit, the glass, and the stone until there was too
    much to be used,
And they grabbed guns and slung them on their shoulders and
    marched and groped in trenches and fought and killed and
    conquered nations who were customers for the goods black
    hands had made.
And again black hands stacked goods higher and higher until there
    was too much to be used,
And then the black hands held trembling at the factory gates the
    dreaded lay-off slip,
And the black hands hung idle and swung empty and grew soft and
    got weak and bony from unemployment and starvation,
And they grew nervous and sweaty, and opened and shut in anguish
    and doubt and hesitation and irresolution . . .

III

I am black and I have seen black hands, millions and millions of
    them—
Reaching hesitantly out of days of slow death for the goods they had
    made, but the bosses warned that the goods were private and
    did not belong to them,
And the black hands struck desperately out in defence of life and
    there was blood, but the enraged bosses decreed that this too
    was wrong,
And the black hands felt the cold steel bars of the prison they had
    made, in despair tested their strength and found that they
    could neither bend nor break them,
And the black hands fought and scratched and held back but a
    thousand white hands took them and tied them,
And the black hands lifted palms in mute and futile supplication to
    the sodden faces of mobs wild in the revelries of sadism,
And the black hands strained and clawed and struggled in vain at the
    noose that tightened about the black throat,
And the black hands waved and beat fearfully at the tall flames that
    cooked and charred the black flesh . . .

IV

I am black and I have seen black hands
Raised in fists of revolt, side by side with the white fists of white
        workers,
And some day—and it is only this which sustains me—
Some day there shall be millions and millions of them,
On some red day in a burst of fists on a new horizon!

BETWEEN THE WORLD AND ME

And one morning while in the woods I stumbled suddenly upon the
        thing,
Stumbled upon it in a grassy clearing guarded by scaly oaks and elms.
And the sooty details of the scene rose, thrusting themselves between
        the world and me. . . .

There was a design of white bones slumbering forgottenly upon a
        cushion of ashes.
There was a charred stump of a sapling pointing a blunt finger
        accusingly at the sky.
There were torn tree limbs, tiny veins of burnt leaves, and a scorched
        coil of greasy hemp;
A vacant shoe, an empty tie, a ripped shirt, a lonely hat, and a pair of
        trousers stiff with black blood.
And upon the trampled grass were buttons, dead matches, butt-ends
        of cigars and cigarettes, peanut shells, a drained gin-flask, and
        a whore's lipstick;
Scattered traces of tar, restless arrays of feathers, and the lingering
        smell of gasoline.
And through the morning air the sun poured yellow surprise into the
        eye sockets of a stony skull. . . .
And while I stood my mind was frozen with a cold pity for the life
        that was gone.
The ground gripped my feet and my heart was circled by icy walls of
        fear—
The sun died in the sky; a night wind muttered in the grass and
        fumbled the leaves in the trees; the woods poured forth the
        hungry yelping of hounds; the darkness screamed with thirsty
        voices; and the witnesses rose and lived:

The dry bones stirred, rattled, lifted, melting themselves into my
      bones.
The grey ashes formed flesh firm and black, entering into my flesh.
The gin-flask passed from mouth to mouth; cigars and cigarettes
      glowed, the whore smeared the lipstick red upon her lips,
And a thousand faces swirled around me, clamoring that my life be
      burned. . . .

And then they had me, stripped me, battering my teeth into my
      throat till I swallowed my own blood.
My voice was drowned in the roar of their voices, and my black wet
      body slipped and rolled in their hands as they bound me to
      the sapling.
And my skin clung to the bubbling hot tar, falling from me in limp
      patches.
And the down and quills of the white feathers sank into my raw flesh,
      and I moaned in my agony.
Then my blood was cooled mercifully, cooled by a baptism of
      gasoline.
And in a blaze of red I leaped to the sky as pain rose like water,
      boiling my limbs.

Panting, begging I clutched childlike, clutched to the hot sides of
      death.
Now I am dry bones and my face a stony skull staring in yellow
      surprise at the sun. . . .

WE OF THE STREETS

Streets are full of the scent of us—odors of onions drifting from
      doorways, effluvium of baby new-born downstairs, seeping
      smells of warm soap-suds—the streets are lush with the
      ferment of our living.
Our sea is water swirling in gutters; our lightning is the blue flame of
      an acetylene torch; billboards blossom with the colors of a
      billion flowers; we hear thunder when the "L" roars; our strip
      of sky is a dirty shirt.
We have grown used to nervous landscapes, chimney-broken horizons,
      and the sun dying between tenements; we have grown to love
      streets, the ways of streets; our bodies are hard like worn
      pavement.

Our emblems are street emblems: stringy curtains blowing in
    windows; sticky-fingered babies tumbling on door-steps;
    deep-cellared laughs meant for everybody; slow groans heard
    in area-ways.
Our sunshine is a common hope; our common summer and common
    winter a common joy and a common sorrow; our fraternity is
    shoulder-rubbing crude with unspoken love; our password the
    wry smile that speaks a common fate.
Our love is nurtured by the soft flares of gas-lights; our hate is an icy
    wind screaming around corners.
And there is something in the streets that made us feel immortality
    when we rushed along ten thousand strong, hearing our chant
    fill the world, wanting to do what none of us would do alone,
    aching to shout the forbidden word, knowing that we of the
    streets are deathless. . . .

AH FEELS IT IN MAH BONES

Mister, things ain't never been all stirred up this way befo'!
It ain't never been that Ah couldn't place a stake.
Now everything's done changed, an' ain't nobody got no go,
An' all the folks talkin' 'bout something's goin' to break.
An' by Gawd Ah b'lieves it—
Ah feels it in mah bones!

Yes sir! Ah sho thought for awhile things was goin' to pick up.
Ah was plannin' on winnin' rolls of yellow dough
An' long-lopin' mah old proud sweet stuff like a greyhound pup!
But shucks, seems like them days just ain't comin' no mo'!
The whole world just done changed—
Ah feels it in mah bones!

Look, here! It's done got so bad Ah can't even beg a dime,
An' mah bread-basket's a-swearin' mah throat's been cut!
Ah's done got as naked as a jaybird in whistlin' time
Tryin' to make mah old rounds on a empty gut!
Ah'm's got to make a change—
Ah feels it in mah bones!

Naw, Sir! Ah ain't a-worryin' no mo' 'bout mah brownskin gal!
Done laid mah razor down an' told mah spotted boys good-bye!

(An' even mah good luck-piece don't seem to work so well.)
Ah'm's ready—mah sail's set for whatever wind's in the sky!
An' brother, there's something a-comin'—
Ah feels it in mah bones!

I AM A RED SLOGAN

I AM A RED SLOGAN,
A flaming torch flung to lead the minds of men!
I flaunt my messages from a million banners:
WORKERS OF THE WORLD, UNITE!
I AM A RED SLOGAN,
The axe that whacks to the heart of knotty problems:
STOP MUNITION SHIPMENTS!
FIGHT FASCISM!
DEATH TO LYNCHERS!
I bloom in tired brains in sleep:
BREAD!
LAND!
FREEDOM!
I AM A RED SLOGAN,
Brawny knuckles thrust in the face of profiteers:
EXPROPRIATE THE EXPROPRIATORS!
I AM A RED SLOGAN,
Lingering as a duty after my command is shouted:
DEFEND THE U. S. S. R.!
I haunt the doors of your mind until I am taken in:
SELF-DETERMINATION FOR MINORITY PEOPLES!
I am the one red star in the workers' black sky:
TURN IMPERIALIST WAR INTO CIVIL WAR!
I AM A RED SLOGAN,
The crest of the wave that sweeps to victory:
ALL POWER TO THE SOVIETS!

STRENGTH

The life of a lone comrade
when pitted alone in action
against the legions of tyranny
is a gentle breeze, ineffectually tearing
at granite crags. But when
united with millions and millions
of other lives, steeped in the sense
of an historic mission, the magnitude
of a task to be done, steeled
by the inevitable victory to be—
it becomes a raging hurricane vast and powerful,
wrenching and dredging by the roots the rottening husks of the trees
    of greed.

CHILD OF THE DEAD
AND FORGOTTEN GODS

O you innocent liberal!
O you naive darling!
O you poor lost child of the dead and forgotten gods!
What a prize find you are!

Do tell us what ilk or brand of sweetened milk you sip!
Do tell us how you can plead for mercy at the bargain-counters
    of justice!
Do show us the magic talisman you use in dispelling the
    blood and stench of history!
Do tell us of the enchanted oil you would spread upon the
    bitter and irreconciliable waters of the class struggle!

What did you say?
Louder! I can't hear you!
Louder, please! There's so much noise!
Speak louder, for the pounding of police clubs on the skulls
    of strikers
and the scream of the riot-siren to disperse the unemployed
And the noise and clamor of slaughter and rapine and greed
drowns out your soft talk of peace and brotherhood!

TRANSCONTINENTAL

(For Louis Aragon, in praise of *Red Front*)

Though trembling waves of roadside heat
We see the cool green of golf courses
Long red awnings catching sunshine
Slender rainbows curved above spirals of water
Swaying hammocks slung between trees—
Like in the movies . . .

America who built this dream

Above the ceaseless hiss of passing cars
We hear the tinkle of ice in tall glasses
Clacks of croquet balls scudding over cropped lawns
Silvery crescendos of laughter—
Like in the movies
On Saturday nights
When we used to get paychecks . . .

America who owns this wonderland

Lost
We hitch-hike down the hot highways
Looking for a ride home
Yanking tired thumbs at glazed faces
Behind the steering wheels of Packards Pierce Arrows
Lincolns La Salles Reos Chryslers—
Their lips are tight jaws set eyes straight ahead . . .

America America America why turn your face away

O for the minute
The joyous minute
The minute of the hour of that day
When the tumbling white ball of our anger
Rolling down the cold hill of our lives
Swelling like a moving mass of snow
Shall crash
Shall explode at the bottom of our patience Thundering
HALT
You shall not pass our begging thumbs
America is ours

This car is commandeered
America is ours
Take your ringed fingers from the steering wheel
Take your polished shoe off the gas
We'll drive and let you be the hitch-hiker
We'll show you how to pass 'em up
You say we're robbers
So what
We're bastards
So what
Sonsofbitches
All right chop us into little pieces we don't care
Let the wind tousle your hair like ours have been tousled
Doesn't the sun's hot hate feel sweet on your back
Crook your thumbs and smudge the thin air
What kind of a growl does your gut make when meal-time comes
At night your hips can learn how soft the pavements are
Oh let's do it the good old American way
Sportsmanship Buddy Sportsmanship
But dear America's a free country
Did you say Negroes
Oh I don't mean NEEEGROOOES
After all
Isn't there a limit to everything
You wouldn't want your *daughter*
And they say there's no GOD
And furthermore it's simply disgraceful how they're distriminating
          against the children of the rich in Soviet schools
PROLETARIAN CHILDREN
Good Lord
Why if we divided up everything today we'd be just where we are
          inside of a year
The strong and the weak The quick and the slow You understand
But Lady even quivering lips can say
PLEASE COMRADE MY FATHER WAS A CARPENTER I SWEAR
          SWEAR HE WAS
I WAS NEVER AGAINST THE COMMUNISTS REALLY
Fairplay Boys Fairplay
America America can every boy have the chance to rise from Wall
          Street to the Comintern
America America can every boy have the chance to rise from
          River—River-side Drive to the General Secretaryship of the
          Communist Party
100% Justice

And Mister don't forget
Our hand shall be on the steering wheel
Our feet shall be on the gas
And you shall hear the grate of our gears
UNITEDFRONT—SSSTRIKE
The motor throbs with eager anger
UNITEDFRONT—SSSTRIKE
We're lurching toward the highway
UNITEDFRONT—SSSTRIKE
The pavement drops into the past The future smites our face
America is ours
10 15 20 30
America America
WOORKERSWOORKERS
Hop on the runningboard Pile in
We're leaving We're leaving
Leaving the tired the timid the soft
Leaving pimps idlers loungers
Leaving empty dinner-pails wage-cuts stretch-outs
Leaving the tight-lipped mother and the bare meal-can
Leaving the shamed girl and her bastard child
Leaving leaving the past leaving
The wind filled with leaflets leaflets of freedom
Millions and millions of leaflets fluttering
Like the wings of a million birds
AmericaAmericaAmerica

Scaling New England's stubborn hills Spanning the Hudson
Waving at Manhattan Waving at New Jersey
Throwing a Good Bye kiss to Way Down East
Through mine-pirred Pennsylvania Through Maryland Our Maryland
Careening over the miles Spinning the steering wheel
Taking the curves with determination
AmericaAmerica
SOFT SHOULDER AHEAD
AmericaAmerica
KEEP TO THE MIDDLE OF THE ROAD
AmericaAmerica
The telegraph poles are a solid wall
WASHINGTON—90 MILES
AmericaAmerica
The farms are a storm of green
Past rivers past towns

50 60 70 80
AmericaAmerica
CITY LIMITS
Vaulting Washington's Monument
Leaping desks of Senators Ending all bourgeois elections
Hurdling desks of Congressmen Fascist flesh sticking to our tires
Skidding into the White House Leaving a trail of carbon monoxide
      for the President
Roaring into the East Room Going straight through Lincoln's portrait
      Letting the light of history through
AmericaAmerica
Swinging Southward Plunging the radiator into the lynch-mob Giving
      no warning
Slowing Slowing for the sharecroppers
Come on You Negroes Come on
There's room
Not in the back but front seat
We're heading for the highway of Self-Determination
UNITEDFRONT—SSSTRIKE
Dim your lights you Trotskyites
UNITEDFRONT—SSSTRIKE
Lenin's line is our stream line
UNITEDFRONT—SSSTRIKE
Through October's windshield we see the road Looping over green
      hills Dipping toward to-morrow

AmericaAmericaAmerica
Look back See the tiny threads of our tires leaving hammer and
sickle prints upon the pavement
See the tree-lined horizon turning slowly in our hearts
See the ripe fields Fields ripe as our love
See the eastern sky See the white clouds of our hope
See the blood-red afterglow in the west Our memory of October
See See See the pretty cottages the bungalows the sheltered homes
See the packing-box cities the jungles the huts
See See See the skyscrappers the clubs the pent-houses
See the bread-lines winding winding winding long as our road
AmericaAmericaAmerica

Tagging Kentucky Tagging Tennessee
Into Ohio Into the orchards of Michigan
Over the rising and falling dunes of Indiana
Across Illinois' glad fields of dancing corn

Slowing Comrades Slowing again
Slowing for the heart of proletarian America
CHICAGO—100 MILES
WOORKERSWOORKERS
Steel and rail and stock All you sons of Haymarket
Swing on We're going your way America is ours
UNITEDFRONT—SSSTRIKE
The pressure of our tires is blood pounding in our hearts
UNITEDFRONT—STRIKE
The steam of our courage blows from the radiator-cap
UNITEDFRONT—SSSTRIKE
The wind screams red songs in our ears
60 70 80 90
AmericaAmericaAmerica

Listen Listen to the moans of those whose lives were laughter
Listen to the howls of the dogs dispossessed
Listen to bureaucratic insects spattering against the windshield
Listen to curses rebounding from fear-proof glass
Listen to the gravel of hate tingling on our fenders
Listen to the raindrops mumbling of yesterday
Listen to the wind whistling of to-morrow
Listen to our tires humming humming humming hymns of victory
AmericaAmericaAmerica

Coasting Comrades Coasting
Coasting on momentum of Revolution
Look Look at that village Like a lonesome egg in the nest of the hills
Soon Soon you shall fly all over the hillsides Crowing the new dawn
Coasting Indulging in Lenin's dream
TUNE IN ON THE RADIO THE WORLD IS LAUGHING
Red Baseball
Great Day in the Morning

> *. . . the Leninites defeated the Redbirds 3 to 0.*
> *Batteries for the Leninites: Kenji Sumarira and*
> *Boris Petrovsky. For the Redbirds: Wing Sing and*
> *Eddie O'Brien. Homeruns: Hugo Schmidt and Jack*
> *Ogletree. Umpires: Pierre Carpentier and Oswald Wallings . . .*

The world is laughing the world is laughing
> *. . . Mike Gold's account of the Revolution sells*
> *26 millions copies . . .*

26 million copies . . .
The world is laughing The world is laughing
    . . . beginning May 1st the work day is limited to
    five hours . . .
The world is laughing The world is laughing
    . . . last of the landlords liquidated in Texas . . .
The world is laughing The world is laughing

Picking up speed to measure the Mississippi
AmericaAmericaAmerica
Plowing the richness of Iowa soil Into the Wheat Empire
Making Minnesota Taking the Dakotas Carrying Nebraska
On toward the Badlands the Rockies the deserts the Golden Gate
Slowing once again Comrades Slowing to right a wrong
Say You Red Men You Forgotten Men
Come out from your tepees
Show us Pocahuntus For we love her
Bring her from her hiding place Let the sun kiss her eyes
Drape her in a shawl of red wool Tuck her in beside us
    Our arms shall thaw the long cold of her shoulders
The lights flash red Comrades let's go
UNITEDFRONT—SSSTRIKE
The future opens like an ever-widening V
UNITEDFRONT—SSSTRIKE
We're rolling over titles of red logic
UNITEDFRONT—SSSTRIKE
We're speeding on wheels of revolution
AmericaAmerica
Mountain peaks are falling toward us
AmericaAmerica
Uphill and the earth rises and looms
AmericaAmerica
Downhill and the earth tilts and sways
AmericaAmerica
80 90 100
AmericaAmerica
Every factory is a forttress
Cities breed soviets
AmericaAmerica
Plains sprout collective farms
Ten thousand Units are meeting
AmericaAmerica
Resolutions passed unanimously

The Red Army is on the march
AmericaAmerica
Arise, ye prisoners . . .
AmericaAmerica
Speed Faster
Speed AmericaAmerica
Arise, ye wretched . . .
AmericaAmerica
Speed Faster
Ever Faster America America
For Justice America America *Thunders*
AmericaAmericaAmerica

The Authors

STANLEY BURNSHAW, born in New York in 1906, was from 1958–1968 a vice-president of the publishing firm of Holt, Rinehart and Winston; before that he had been president and editor-in-chief of the Dryden Press (1939–1958). He was a drama critic and one of the four fulltime editors of the *New Masses*, but he did not limit his writings to those matters that were of interest only to the Left. His many publications include a study and translation of *André Spire and His Poetry* (1933); a novel, *The Sunless Sea* (1948); a play, *The Bridge* (1945); two anthologies of modern foreign verse, *The Poem Itself* (1960) and *The Modern Hebrew Poem Itself* (1965); a collection of essays, *Varieties of Literary Experience* (1962); and several volumes of poetry, *The Iron Land* (1936), *Early and Late Testament* (1952), and *Caged in an Animal's Mind* (1963). In commenting on *The Iron Land*, from which many of the poems in this collection are taken, Harriet Monroe wrote that "there is a profound pity in the poem, but no spilling-over of romantic emotionalism. Its tone rises to the level of tragedy. . . ." Burnshaw's most recent works include *The Seamless Web* (1970), *In the Terrified Radiance* (1972), and *Mirages: Travel Notes in the Promised Land* (1977).

JOY DAVIDMAN is best known for her collection of poems, *Letter to a Comrade* (1938), which was published as part of the Yale Series of Younger Poets when Ms. Davidman was twenty-three years old. In his foreward to the collection, Stephen Vincent Benét wrote: "Here is what an intelligent, sensitive, and vivid mind thinks about itself and the things of the modern world. It will be obvious enough, to anyone who reads *Letter to a Comrade*, that the heroes of the Twenties are not Miss Davidman's heroes nor their demons her demons. . . . This is a generation that knew the Depression in its 'teens, the War not at all. It is just now beginning to be articulate. And you will find plenty of indignation here, but not a willingness to accept frustration." Ms. Davidman's other works include *Anya* (1940) and *Weeping Bay* (1950). She also edited *War Poems of the United Nations* (1943), which was sponsored by the League for American Writers.

KENNETH FEARING, one of America's finest satiric poets, was born in Chicago in 1902. His first collection of poems, *Angel Arms*, was published in 1929. In 1935 Dynamo Press published his slim volume entitled *Poems*, which prompted Robert Cantwell to comment that "more than any other writer Fearing sums up the attitude of his generation; and in time the publication of his new poems may be recognized for what it is—a cultural event of the first importance." After *Poems* came *Dead Reckoning* (1938), *Collected Poems* (1940), *Afternoon of a Pawnbroker* (1943), *Stranger at Coney Island* (1948), and *New and Selected Poems* (1956). Fearing was also the author of several novels, perhaps the best-known of which is *The Big Clock* (1946). He died in 1961.

JOSEPH FREEMAN was born in the Ukraine in 1897, and came to the United States in 1904. He joined the editorial staff of the *Liberator* in 1922, where he remained until its demise in 1924. In 1926 Freeman helped to establish the monthly *New Masses*, and in 1927 he became the publicity director for the American Civil Liberties Union. His first book, *Dollar Diplomacy: A Study in American Diplomacy*, written with Scott Nearing, was published in 1925. Freeman next collaborated with Joshua Kunitz and Louis Lozowick on *Voices of October: Art and Literature in Soviet Russia*, which was published in 1930. In 1935 he wrote the introduction to *Proletarian Literature in the United States*, and the following year published his best known work, *An American Testament: A Narrative of Rebels and Romantics*. Two novels were published in the 1940s: *Never Call Retreat* (1943) and *The Long Pursuit* (1947). Freeman also completed two volumes of sonnets during this period but they were never published. In the mid-fifties he wrote: "I published a good deal of poetry in the 1920's and 1930's. Though little of my verse has appeared in print in the past decade and a half, I have kept on writing it. I like to read poetry because it tells more about the world than any other form of communication, and I like to write it because it is the medium in which I speak most freely. I now feel that my experience in rhetoric, sociology, politics and journalism was something through which I passed on my way to my present view of the world. This is primarily ethical, occasionally mystical with a complete acceptance of science. . . ." Freeman died in August, 1965.

SOL FUNAROFF, who frequently used the pseudonym Charles Henry Newman, was born in 1911. He served on the editorial staff of *New Theatre*, and was the editor of *Dynamo* and the Dynamo Poets Series. He edited an anthology of Federal poets for the *New Republic* and a Federal writers' issue for the *New Masses*. He was one of the four poets represented in *We Gather Strength* (1933), and had his poems collected in two volumes: *Exile From a Future Time*, a limited edition gathered by his friends in 1943 (the year after his death) and the earlier and more impressive, *The Spider and the Clock* (1938). The latter volume contained the following note on "What the Thunder Said: A Fire Sermon," Funaroff's most ambitious poem: "[It] is a poem of the Russian Revolution and is based upon Marxian philosophical concepts. As symbol and as history this event challenges the fundamentally political and religious attitudes of negation, frustration, the martyrdom of the individual and the decay of the materialistic world which find their most significant poetic expression in T. S. Eliot's *The Waste Land*. The setting, which serves as a framework for the poem, is a street meeting at sunset. A speaker addresses a crowd of workers while a thunderstorm threatens. I have attempted to transmute this speech into poetic form and to transform the metropolitan scene with its vista of skyscrapers, bridges, airplanes, buildings in construction, etc., into a cinematic language which, as in montage, correlates and fuses the objects and symbols that visualize the changing themes of the speaker. In this manner, through cross-references and the swift development and transition of images, I have attempted to form a dialectic image pattern which would enable me to present simultaneously sensuous, historical, and philosophical relationships within the poem."

ROBERT GESSNER was born in 1907. He was a prolific writer whose works include a book-length poem, *Upsurge* (1933); two novels, *Broken Arrow* (1933) and *Treason* (1944); *Massacre: A Survey of Today's American Indian* (1931); *Some of My Best Friends Are Jews* (1936); and *The Moving Image: A Guide to Cinematic Literacy*

(1968). At the time of his death in 1968, Gessner was professor of cinema at New York University.

MICHAEL GOLD, generally regarded to be the "Dean of the proletarian writers in the U.S.A.," was born Itshok Isaac Granich in New York on April 12, 1893. He was an assistant editor of *The Masses*, one of the founders of *Liberator* (which he edited from 1920–1922), and he helped to establish the *New Masses*. His major works include *120 Million* (1929), *Jews Without Money* (1930), *Change the World!* (1937), and *The Hollow Men* (1941). He was also one of the editors of *Proletarian Literature in the United States* (1935), and collaborated with Michael Blankfort on a play about John Brown entitled *Battle Hymn* (1936). In the April–May 1935 issue of *Partisan Review*, Edwin Rolfe paid tribute to Gold's influence on the young social poets of the 1930s by noting that "we owe much of our zeal and fire and conviction to Michael Gold's early poetry." Gold died in 1967.

HORACE GREGORY, winner of the Bollingen Prize (1964) and recipient of the Academy of American Poets award for Distinguished Poetic Achievement, was born in Milwaukee, Wisconsin in 1898. His first book of poems, *Chelsea Rooming House,* was published in 1930. It was, Gregory said, "merely the beginning of my effort to combine the idiom of contemporary life with my early (and entirely) literary influences." His other volumes of poetry include *No Retreat* (1933), *Chorus for Survival* (1935), *Medusa in Gramercy Park* (1961), *Collected Poems* (1964), and *Another Look* (1976). In addition, Gregory has written studies of D. H. Lawrence, Amy Lowell, Dorothy Richardson, and James McNeill Whistler; has translated Ovid and Catullus; edited *News Letters in America* (with Eleanor Clark, 1937) and *The Portable Sherwood Anderson* (1949); and, with his wife Marya Zaturenska, has written a *History of American Poetry 1900–1940* (1946). In 1971 he brought out "a cycle of memoirs," *The House on Jefferson Street,* and two years later published a volume of collected essays, *Spirit of Time and Place.* "No matter what others may think of my work," Gregory has commented, "I should like to have said of me what was said of Baudelaire, a far greater poet than I: 'He belonged to no school. . . . He copied no one, but he used everyone that suited him, making what he had taken his own and something new.'"

ALFRED HAYES was born in London in 1911 and grew up in New York. He was a member of the editorial board of *Partisan Review*, where many of his social poems written during the 1930s first appeared. In 1943 he joined the army and drew upon his war experiences for the novels, *All Thy Conquest* (1946) and *The Girl on the Via Flaminia* (1949). *Shadow of Heaven*, a novel about a labor organizer, was published in 1947; and, in 1960, three novellas were collected under the title, *The Temptation of Don Volpi*. Hayes has also published several volumes of poetry, including *The Big Time* (1944), *Welcome to the Castle* (1950), and *End of Me* (1968).

JOSEPH KALAR was born in Eveleth, Minnesota, in 1906. In his youth he was a lumber worker and a papermill mechanic, and during the 1930s he was active in trade-union work and political efforts on the part of the Farm Labor Party of Minnesota. His short story, "Funeral," which originally appeared in the November–December, 1934, issue of *The Anvil*, was included in the Roll of Honor of *The Best Short Stories, 1934*. Kalar was one of the poets represented in *We Gather Strength* (1933), where he was described as "a mystic, invoking the strong mysterious wind, or lost in wonder because snow is falling on the planet. He is a mystic, and he works in a papermill, sweating and starving. This is the contradiction, and this is the secret of his Communism." His works have been translated into German, French, Russian, and Chinese. He died in 1972.

H. H. LEWIS has spent most of his life on his father's farm in Cape Girardeau, Missouri. He was dubbed the "Bard of the Ozarks" by Jack Conroy, who published Lewis's autobiographical sketch, "Down the Skidway," in the first issue of *The Anvil* (May 1933). Although disgruntled with the American Communist Party, Lewis believed fervently in the Soviet Union. His collections of poems include *Thinking of Russia* (1932), *Salvation* (1934), and *Road to Utterly: Poems Written By a Missouri Farmhand and Dedicated to Soviet Russia* (1935). James Rorty, reviewing the first volume in the July, 1932, issue of *The Rebel Poet* wrote: "Here is a good, honest, quarter's worth of revolutionary doggerel, clear uncut working class hatred, sound, healthy barn-yard and freight-yard obscenity and yes, some poetry, too. . . . It reveals the hard core of personality, the unmistakable fact of talent; one of the best of the younger revolutionary poets." Biographical information about Lewis is to be found in Harold L. Dellinger's "Pegasus and the Plow," *Foolkiller*, 3 (Fall 1976), 6–7.

NORMAN MACLEOD was born in Oregon in 1906. He has held many literary positions including founder-director of The New York Poetry Center, editor of *Front* (1930–1931), American editor of *Morada* (1930–1932), editorial director of *The Maryland Quarterly* (1942–1944), editor of *The Briarcliff Quarterly* (1944–1947), and, since 1968, editor of *Pembroke Magazine*. He is the author of two novels—*You Get What You Ask For* (1939) and *The Bitter Roots* (1941)—and several volumes of poetry. *Horizon of Death*, his first collection of poems, was published in 1934 and was "Dedicated to a Bitter Age." It was followed by *Thanksgiving Before November* (1936), *We Thank You All The Time* (1941), *A Man in Midpassage* (1947), and *Pure as Nowhere* (1952). In 1975, a volume of *Selected Poems* was issued, and two years later *The Distance: New and Selected Poems (1928–1977)* was published. In 1948 Alfred Kreymborg wrote in *The Saturday Review of Literature*: "The poetry of Norman Macleod is not for readers who yearn for an evening's escape from the turmoils of this age, but for tough-minded beings who seek some measure of truth in what they read. His work is in line with poets of the middle and younger generations who were torn from the roots of innocence and forced into personal and worldly dilemmas conditioned not by themselves but by men in high places whose leadership has degenerated and cast an uncertain shadow over mankind. In the midst of social, economic, and political conflicts, Macleod tries to maintain an individual view, only to find himself driven by internal conflicts reflecting the desperation of the children of Adam generally."

BEN MADDOW, born in New Jersey in 1910, was a member of the original editorial board of *Partisan Review*, and during the 1930s frequently published under the name of David Wolff. Presently a film writer and director, his films include *The Asphalt Jungle*, *The Savage Eye*, *The Unforgiven*, and *The Secret of Santa Vittoria*. He has published one novel, *44 Gravel Street* (1952), a study of *Edward Weston: Fifty Years* (1973), and several short stories. The most recent story, "You, Johann Sebastian Bach," was reprinted in the *O. Henry Prize Stories for 1969* and in *The American Literary Anthology #2* (1969). His play, *In a Cold Hotel*, was included in *New Theatre in America* (1965). In 1940, "The

City," which first appeared in *Poetry*, won the Harriet Monroe Prize.

JAMES NEUGASS was born in 1905. He served as an ambulance driver with the International Brigade during the Spanish Civil War and was wounded near Hijai, Aragon. When he returned to the United States he wrote his best known work, "Give Us This Day," about which Archibald MacLeish commented: "I don't believe I have read anything which gave more convincingly or authentically the sense of courage.... It is [a] scrupulous and honest work such as all of us must envy—or would envy of there were left any room for such pettiness in the shadow of so great a subject." Neugass died in 1949, shortly before the publication of his novel, *Rain of Ashes*.

KENNETH PATCHEN, "perhaps the one genuine American surrealist," was born in Niles, Ohio, in 1911; he died in 1972 in California where a spinal disease had kept him bedridden since 1960. A prolific writer, his works include *Before the Brave* (1936), *First Will and Testament* (1939), *Journal of Albion Moon* (1941), *Cloth of the Tempest* (1943), *Memoirs of a Shy Pornographer* (1945), *Sleepers Awake* (1946), *Hurrah for Anything* (1957), *Because It Is* (1959), and *Collected Poems* (1969). Upon the publication of *First Will and Testament,* from which many poems in this collection are reprinted, John Peale Bishop wrote: "Beyond any book of poems I have encountered, *First Will and Testament* gives a real sense of what it is to be a young man in America in a time when, for more of the young than we like to think, living and dying have lost all meaning." A forty-five page "Homage to Kenneth Patchen" was included in the Winter, 1968–1969 issue of *The Outsider*.

WILLIAM PILLIN, who frequently used the first name Vladimir, has been a prolific contributor of poetry to "little magazines" for more than thirty years. His poems have appeared in such journals as *Western Poetry, Left Front, Direction, Planes, Voices, Epos, Kayak*, and *Circle*. His collections of poetry include *Dance Without Shoes* (1956), *Pavanne for a Fading Memory* (1963), and *Everything Falling* (1971).

ETTORE RELLA was born in Telluride, Colorado, in 1907. During the 1930s his poems appeared in *This Quarter, Fifth Story Window, Contempo, Dynamo*, and *Partisan Review and Anvil*. While he was serving in the Pacific during World War II, some friends privately printed a collection of his poems, *Here and Now*; and in 1966 a second collection, *Spring Song on an Old Theme*, was published by Trident Press. In addition to his poems, Rella has written a number of plays in verse; the first, *Please Communicate*, was produced by the San Francisco Theatre Union in 1939, and a later play, *Sign of Winter*, was produced Off-Broadway in 1958. "Monkeys from Paradise" and "Cosmetic Survival" are printed here for the first time; "The Bone and the Baby" originally was published in a somewhat different form in the March–April, 1934, issue of *Dynamo*.

EDWIN ROLFE, born in Philadelphia in 1909, was singled out in the July, 1936, issue of *Poetry* as being "the best among those inflammatory young men and women." He was twenty-four when his poems were published in *We Gather Strength*, and only twenty-seven when his first collection of poems, *To My Contemporaries*, appeared in 1936. In the summer of 1937 he went to Spain, where he served in the Lincoln Battalion; upon his return to the United States he wrote a history of the battalion, *The Lincoln Battalion*, which was published by Random House in 1939. In 1951 a second collection of poems, *First Love and Other Poems*, was published; and in 1955, a year after his death, a final volume, *Permit Me Refuge*, was issued by *The California Quarterly*. Rolfe's poems have appeared in numerous anthologies, including *A New Anthology of Modern Poetry*, *War Poems of the United Nations*, *New Poems*, *The New Pocket Anthology of American Verse*, *Treasury of Jewish Poetry*, and *This Generation*.

MURIEL RUKEYSER was born in New York in 1913. Her first book, *Theory of Flight*, was the 1935-volume in the Yale Series of Younger Poets, and it was included in *The Nation's* "Annual List of Outstanding Books," where it was described as "a first volume by a young revolutionary poet who combines resourcefulness of technique with a high degree of intellectual honesty and bold inventive power." A second volume of poems, *U.S. 1*, was published in 1938 and was followed by *Beast in View* (1944), *The Green Wave* (1948), *Selected Poems* (1951), *Body of Awakening* (1958), and *Waterlily Fire* (1961). In addition, Rukeyser has published several books for children, a biography of Willard Gibbs (1942), and a study of the relationship between poetry and other disciplines entitled *The Life of Poetry* (1949). Of her work, Ms. Rukeyser has said: "The uproot of the 1914 war produced Imagism, answering chaos with the life of colors and flowers and islands and matching heads, in their bare existence. We have another wave of such years now, witnesses to whose chaos are facts such as Spain and Gauley Bridge and Scottsboro and the creativeness of certain lives and the gifts of certain poems and gestures. I live in New York and do my work there; all this cluster is proved in any single place. I wish to make my poems exist in the quick images that arrive crowding on us now (most familiarly from the screen), in the lives of Americans who are unpraised and vivid and indicative, in my own 'documents.' That last is an ill-favored word; for me it means a binding down to a neighborhood of meaning which I cannot ignore. What I can ignore, on the other hand, is the whole critical circus whose acrobatics are to the effect that poetry is dead. I do not think so." Muriel Rukeyser's recent work includes *The Speed of Darkness* (1968), *Breaking Open* (1973), and *Gates* (1977).

ISIDOR SCHNEIDER was born in the Ukraine in 1896 and arrived in the United States five years later. His numerous works include *Dr. Transit* (1925), *The Temptation of Anthony and Other Poems* (1928), *From the Kingdom of Necessity* (1935), *Comrade, Mister* (1936), and *The Judas Time* (1947). He was one of the editors of *Proletarian Literature in the United States*, and, in 1964, he edited *The World of Love*. Of his connection with the Left, Schneider has written: "All my experience of life, in later happier times as well as in my childhood, made me feel that social changes to eliminate want and insecurity were necessary before a defensible culture could develop in our mechanized world. After 1929 this was the almost unanimous sense of American writers, the exceptions being the few who for some strange reason found beauty in a landscape of human ruins, or found order in it, since order meant hierarchy with themselves in the upper ranks. The painful but instructive Depression years turned me into a 'left' writer and realist. I was now able to examine my own past without rigging up any mechanism of fantasy." Schneider died in August, 1977.

HERMAN SPECTOR, who died in 1959 at the age of sixty-four, was an editor of *Dynamo*, and contributed to *The Rebel Poet, Free Verse, New Masses, Bozart, The Left,* and *Partisan Review*. Ten of his poems were included in *We Gather Strength* (1933), where Michael Gold wrote of him: "I have always felt a peculiar kinship with Herman Spector. Bitter and lonely, the 'bastard in a ragged suit,' this poet of youthful revolt roams our familiar New York streets at midnight. He is the raw material of New York Communism. Confused, anarchic, sensitive, 'at times the timid Christ,' nauseated by the day's ugly and meaningless work, he prays for quick death to fall on this monstrous capitalist city. Then, 'a big Mack rolling and rumbling down the street and lo! morning.' It is with such deeply felt metropolitan images and symbols that this proletarian poet builds." A collection of his work was published in 1977 under the title *Bastard in the Ragged Suit.*

GENEVIEVE TAGGARD was born in Washington State in 1894 and raised in Hawaii. Her first volumes of poems were *For Eager Lovers* (1922) and *Hawaiian Hilltop* (1923). In 1930 she published her only prose work, *The Life and Mind of Emily Dickinson.* This was followed by several collections of poetry, including *Remembering Vaughan in New England* (1933), *Not Mine to Finish* (1934), *Calling Western Union* (1936), *Collected Poems* (1938), *The Long View* (1942), and *Slow Music* (1946). About her social poems Ms. Taggard wrote: "[They] translate the strong anti-fascist convictions of our times into living realities, with emphasis on the struggles of labor, the sufferings of the city and country poor, and the part of the humane middle-class person in the intelligent movement against reaction." She was a member of the English Department at Sarah Lawrence from 1935 until her death in 1948.

JOHN BROOKS WHEELWRIGHT was born in Massachusetts in 1897, a direct heir to what Austin Warren has called the "two major strains in the New England character: the Yankee trader and the Yankee saint (often a complex of scholar, priest, and poet)." Wheelwright was tenth in descent from the Reverend John Wheelwright, a catalytic figure in the Antinomian controversy, and his great-great-grandfather was Peter Chardon Brooks, a merchant prince and Boston's first multimillionaire. As a prep school student he rebelled against his family's church (Unitarian) by becoming an Anglo-Catholic, and in the 1930s he turned against his class by becoming a Socialist and then a Trotskyist. Wheelwright published three volumes of poetry during his lifetime: *Rock and Shell* (1933), *Mirror of Venus* (1938), and *Political Self-Portrait* (1940). At the time of his death in September, 1940, he was working on a fourth collection, to be called "Dusk to Dusk." The poems in that collection, as well as those in the three published volumes, were brought together by Alvin Rosenfeld in 1972 as *Collected Poems of John Wheelwright.*

RICHARD WRIGHT was born in Mississippi in 1908. He joined the Chicago chapter of the John Reed Club in 1934, and remained a member of the Communist party until 1944. (His break with the party is related in *The God That Failed* [1950].) During the 1930s he contributed to *Left Front, International Literature, New Masses,* and *Partisan Review*; he also became associate editor of *Challenge,* to which he frequently contributed. Wright eventually joined the editorial board of *New Masses,* won *Story* magazine's prize for "Uncle Tom's Children," and published *Native Son* (1940). In 1941 he wrote the text for *120 Million Black Voices,* then told of his childhood in *Black Boy* (1945), and in 1947 moved to Paris. There he wrote eight books, including *The Outsider* (1953), *Black Power* (1954), and *White Man, Listen!* (1957). He died in Paris in 1960. His posthumous autobiographical work, *American Hunger,* was published in 1977.

Bibliography

Aaron, Daniel. *Writers on the Left: Episodes in American Literary Communism*. New York, 1961.

Beach, Joseph Warren. *Obsessive Images: Symbolism in the Poetry of the 1930's and 1940's*. Minneapolis, 1960. (Includes comments on Fearing, Gregory, Hayes, Patchen, and Rukeyser.)

Burnshaw, Stanley. "Notes on Revolutionary Poetry," *New Masses*, 10 (February 20, 1934), 20–22.

———. "The Poetry Camps Divide," *New Masses*, 12 (July 31, 1934), 21–23.

Conroy, Jack. "H. H. Lewis: Plowboy Poet," *December*, 11 (1969), 203–206.

Drew, Elizabeth (with John Sweeney). *Directions in Modern Poetry*. New York, 1940. (See pages 95–112.)

Gilbert, James. *Writers and Partisans: A History of Literary Radicalism in America*. New York, 1968.

Glicksberg, Charles L. "Poetry and Democracy," *South Atlantic Quarterly*, 41 (July, 1942), 254–65.

Gregory, Horace, ed. *New Letters in America*. New York, 1937.

——— and Marya Zaturenska. *A History of American Poetry*. New York, 1946. (See pages 431–81.)

Gurko, Leo. *The Angry Decade*. New York, 1947. (Reprinted 1968; see pages 245–59.)

Guttmann, Allen. "The Brief Embattled Course of Proletarian Poetry," *Proletarian Writers of the Thirties*, ed. David Madden. Carbondale, Ill., 1968.

Hicks, Granville, *et. al.*, eds., *Proletarian Literature in the United States*. New York, 1935.

Josephson, Matthew, "Improper Bostonian: John Wheelwright and His Poetry," Southern Review, 7 (Spring 1971), 509–540.

Kahn, Sy. "Kenneth Fearing and the Twentieth Century Blues," *The Thirties: Fiction, Poetry, Drama*, ed. Warren French. DeLand, Fla., 1967.

Luccock, Halford E. *American Mirror: Social, Ethical and Religious Aspects of American Literature 1930–1940*. New York, 1940. (See pages 201–35.)

Monroe, Harriet. "Poetry of the Left," *Poetry*, 48 (July, 1936), 212–21.

North, Joseph, ed. *New Masses: An Anthology of the Rebel Thirties*. New York, 1969.

Novak, Estelle. "The *Dynamo* School of Poets," *Contemporary Literature*, 11 (Autumn, 1970), 526–39.

Rodway, Allan, ed. *Poetry of the 1930s*. London, 1967.

Rolfe, Edwin. "Poetry," *Partisan Review*, 2 (April–May, 1935), 32–42 and 43–51.

Rosenthal, M. L. "On the 'Dissidents' of the Thirties," *University of Kansas City Review*, 17 (Summer, 1951), 294–300.

————. "Muriel Rukeyser: The Longer Poems," *New Directions in Prose and Poetry #14*. New York, 1953.

Salzman, Jack, ed. (with Barry Wallenstein). *Years of Protest: A Collection of American Writings of the 1930s*. New York, 1967.

Schneider, Isidor. "Proletarian Poetry," *American Writers' Congress*, ed. Henry Hart. New York, 1935.

Skelton, Robin, ed. *Poetry of the Thirties*. Middlesex, England, 1964.

Warren, Robert Penn. "The Present State of Poetry in the United States," *The Kenyon Review*, 1 (August, 1939), 384–98.

Wilder, Amos. "Revolutionary and Proletarian Poetry: Kenneth Patchen," in *The Spiritual Aspects of the New Poetry*. New York, 1940.

Q2